BOATS

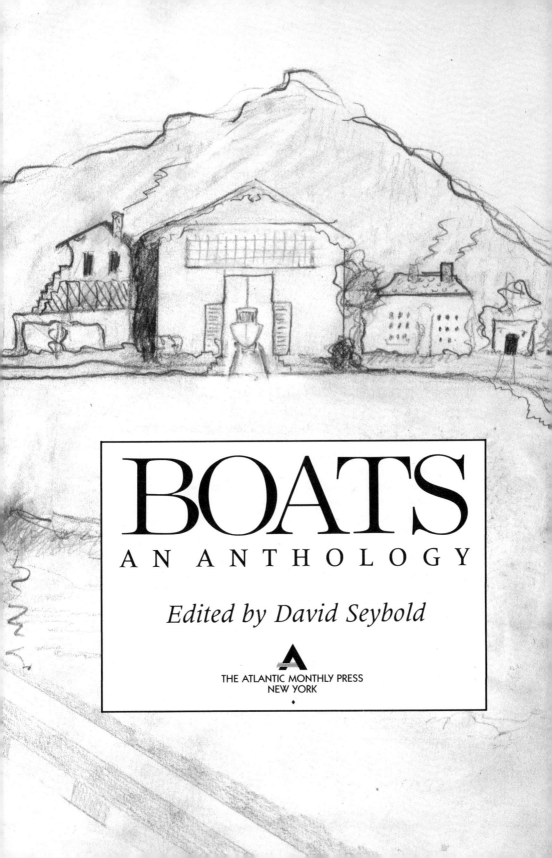

BOATS

AN ANTHOLOGY

Edited by David Seybold

THE ATLANTIC MONTHLY PRESS
NEW YORK

First Atlantic Monthly Press paperback edition published in 1997

Published simultaneously in Canada
Printed in the United States of America

Library of Congress Cataloging-in-Publication Data

Boats : an anthology / edited by David Seybold. — 1st Atlantic Monthly Press pbk. ed.
    p.   cm.
    "First published by Grove Weidenfeld in 1990"—T.p. verso.
    ISBN 0-87113-677-5
    1. Boats and boating—Literary collections.   2. American literature—20th century.
I. Seybold, David.
    [PS509.B63B6   1997]
    810.8'0356—dc21   97-1355

Designed by Irving Perkins Associates
Illustration on title page by Patricia Gaines

The Atlantic Monthly Press
841 Broadway
New York, NY 10003

98 99 00 01   10 9 8 7 6 5 4 3 2

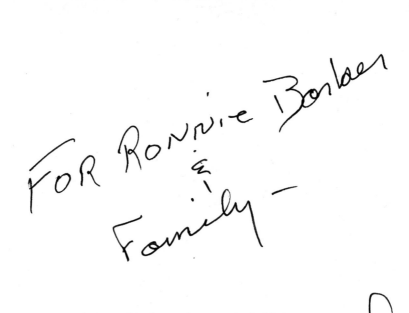

For my brother, Thomas Seybold—
sailor and friend

CONTENTS

FOREWORD

AT ONE TIME or another, each of us has gone down to the sea in ships—if only in our hearts, and even though the sea may in actuality be only a farm pond, mountain stream, or tree-rimmed lake, and the ship a birch canoe or rubber raft. Boats of all kinds have been used to explore, defend, harvest, ponder, and enjoy the waters of the world—from vast oceans to inland seas, remote rivers and suburban streams to benign freshets and rills. That the appeal of the sea and ships is universal and lasting, that it continues to grip our imagination and arouse such passion in our souls is a wonder worthy of celebration, which is precisely the intent of this collection.

Although the stories included here, the majority of which were

written specifically for this collection, deal with a variety of craft—
from canoes to schooners, icebreakers to model ships—it would be
misleading to say this is a book solely about boats and boating. Just
as Herman Melville's classic *Redburn* was about far more than sailing
a three-masted, square-rigged ship from New York to Liverpool, so
too do the stories in *Boats* concern more than the vessels they describe. Indeed, the boats themselves are really secondary to the lives
of those who are connected to them.

This collection includes a variety of literary forms, from short
stories, essays, and reminiscences to reportage and poetry. But although there is diversity of narrative, readers of *Boats* will discover a
similarity and coherence among the stories themselves. For instance,
the emotions in John Cole's essay—which lovingly reviews all the
boats he's owned because he *had* to own them—are strikingly similar to those evoked in E. Annie Proulx's short story about a man who
goes to extremes to possess a certain make of canoe. And when in
Annie Dillard's short story the crew of a ship in a bottle comes to life
under her microscope, we are as convinced of their lives and history
as when we read Peter Matthiessen's nonfictional account of his
journey to Gaspé in 1950, where he studied pelagic birds and survived an attempt to return home in a small sailboat.

However, the type of narrative in *Boats* is not the issue, nor the
kind of vessel involved, nor even the nature of the trip taken. Rather,
the stories in this collection are held together by a fundamental and
underlying sense of adventure and imagination that both informs
and—I hope—entertains. Each piece attempts mainly to convey an
overriding passion for boats and a shared wonder of the sea. And
each piece, in its own way, expresses—specifically, tangentially, or
vicariously—just what it is about boats and the sea that continues to
attract and inspire men, women, and children the world over.

The desire to cast off in a boat is primal, as powerful and ancient as
the ebb and flow of the very tides themselves. And just as powerful
and ancient is our need to expound on why it is that boats and the
waters they ply arouse in us such passion and curiosity and fear.
Hopefully, readers will find *Boats* a welcome addition to that need.

—David Seybold
New London, New Hampshire, June 1990

But I wanted more adventure, and above all
I wanted to be free, as free as a wild sea
bird like the stormy petrel, to sail where
I liked as long as I liked on the great ocean.

SIR FRANCIS CHICHESTER,
The Romantic Challenge

. . . those events of the sea that show in the
light of day the inner worth of a man . . . the
secret truth of his pretences, not only to
others but also to himself.

JOSEPH CONRAD,
Lord Jim

BOATS

MY LAST BOAT

BY JOHN N. COLE

FOR A WHILE THERE it looked as if my affinity for small boats had surpassed mere interest and become a compulsive eccentricity. I had reached the point of maximum accumulation in many of my life's various dimensions: a new home, seven children, cats, kittens, golden retrievers, golden retriever litters, horses, ponies, assorted vehicles, failed power tools, and some hundred acres of woodland in what was then rural coastal Maine—acres that tapered to a headland facing southwest above the silver cloak of Middle Bay dropped there for me by a glacier ten thousand years before.

Mid-life, I suppose: those years when the children are old enough to assert their individuality but still too young to set out into the world; the years when both Jean and I were strong enough to live harmoniously with excess, to revel in the wonder of coastal Maine's glorious opportunities for dwelling in nature's embrace. Of each of the excesses I indulged in, none was more excessive than boats.

Don't be misled. I am not a wealthy man. Those years of accumulation were also years of a mountain range of debt, a threatening presence of fiscal doom which somehow was forever unable to penetrate my consciousness. I was the Happy among our gathering of financial dwarfs, perpetually undaunted by dire letters of collection or the sullen messengers who sometimes delivered them in person. Jean's loyalties to her home are fierce indeed; her hostility to any presence from without was relentless if it posed any dangers to the family within. Even though she was fully aware of the surreal risks our life-style guaranteed, she maintained her serenity—that wondrously calm demeanor that pervaded our home like the silent peace of a vast cathedral.

Except when she stopped to count my boats.

The Banks dory came first, the slab-sided eighteen-footer I had bought even before we moved to the point on Middle Bay. After my haul-seining years on the ocean beaches of eastern Long Island decades before, I wanted a dory in the yard forever. This one had been around a while. Heavily built to start with, she had begun to sag with age; her oak ribs were checked and her knees had fattened with countless years of soak and stress. She had a well installed about two feet inboard of her stern, and I used it to support a seven-and-a-half-horsepower outboard. Running against tide and wind, that dory averaged about two knots; if the chop was heavy, I had to quarter.

By the time we moved to the house on Middle Bay, that dory was moored in a tidal creek off the Kennebec River some twenty-five miles east of our home. In the wake of a massive effort by federal and state leaders, the Kennebec had been raised from the dead. Once rendered mute and useless by the accumulated wastes of the Industrial Age, the river was cleansed at last and its ocean approaches were returned to the schools of striped bass that had formerly gathered there in vast numbers.

The creek where my dory was moored was near the home of an acquaintance who let me park on his property while I used the boat to navigate the several branches of the lower Kennebec in search of reunions with the fish that had sustained my former life. There were glorious dawns witnessed from that clumsy dory, moments of delicate summer awakenings when fish danced for me on salt marsh lagoons silken in a silver mist.

With that dory assigned a river career, I was left without a home boat. But not for long. Frank Webb, a neighbor and fishing friend, was, even in those long ago years, benefiting from the increasing realization in Massachusetts and beyond that Maine coast properties could still be acquired for something less than the cost of three days in a suite at the Ritz. Frank was the steward of quite a chunk of such real estate. He'd bought it because he loved it, but his love was not reckless enough to make him stupid.

As he prospered, like so many who do, he hungered for a newer, larger boat. Which is how I came by his Boston Whaler, one of the first ever made by the builders, who have since earned a national name. Frank's Whaler came with a twenty-five-horse Johnson, a trailer, and a Danforth anchor.

Oh, that Whaler. Of those seven children, five were boys during the Whaler years, and each learned most of what he knows about small boats in that superbly designed craft. They, and their sisters as well, drove it ashore on the tiny islands scattered like seeds of granite and pine on the waters of Casco Bay. They fished from her, made love aboard her, drank their first beers in the safety of her isolation, and, most critically, became aware of the songs of the wind, the chorus of the tides, and the sea's eternal and restless energies.

Middle Bay is like most Maine bays: a sweep of tidal flats held together by a skein of slim channels that eventually unite with the sea beyond the islands. We had a dock like most Maine docks designed for most Maine tidal locations: The far end floated free except for its connection to a ramp, which was, in turn, fast to a huge whaleback of ledge. From the ledge we stepped to the ramp and from there to the float and from there into the boat of our choice—except during the last of the tide. Through the ebb's low point our float rested on the Penobscot clay that is Middle Bay's bottom.

Which meant the Whaler had to be moored in a small channel a short row offshore, which in turn meant that we needed a pram to get from the dock to the mooring, a pram that could be easily hauled onto the float where it would spend the night in relative safety. I found a pram advertised in the local paper. It turned out to be aluminum and had a few lumps, but the woman selling it was leaving Maine and relieved to see it stuffed in the back of our station wagon.

The pram needed oars and a small anchor, the Whaler and the

dory both needed oars (I never completely trusted outboards), and both the Whaler and the Kennebec dory needed mushroom-anchor moorings. Each of the three needed painting in the spring and storage during the winter, even if it was merely a relatively dry space in back of the barn. Add various paraphernalia like gasoline cans, outboard emergency tool kits, life preservers, waterproof flashlights, assorted fishing gear, compasses, and extra oarlocks and you begin to realize why Jean began to wonder about the wisdom of boats—plural.

And that was before the Hobie Cat.

Editing a small weekly newspaper, as I was those days when I wasn't messing around with boats, is a job of several unique advantages—none of them fiscal. I could, for example, get a look at the advertisements before they were seen by the general public. One afternoon, I struck gold. The first catamarans designed by California's Hobie Alter were on their way to Maine. An adventurous entrepreneur in Portland had ordered two, and was about to advertise the fact in our paper.

I have this penchant for being first; combined with my addiction to boats it compelled me to call Portland that very afternoon and commit to a Hobie Cat, sight unseen except for a brief appearance on our television screen during a documentary about surfing on the West Coast.

Oh, that Hobie Cat. When the wind bunched inside great hummocks of clouds in the northwest and hurled across our north–south narrow bay (too narrow for seas to build) the Hobie and I would fly before it, one hull hissing and singing as it sliced white through green water, tilting high enough to hoist its windward twin free and clear as we reached, racing first toward the open sea, then rocketing home into our own cove, where I'd jibe, drop the sail, and glide until the curved bows of the cat's twin hulls nudged the shore's grassy slope and let me rest there for a while, still lost in the exhilaration of my sail.

It is best, I was advised by Mr. Alter's instructions, to moor your Hobie offshore, if that's possible. Of course it was possible, but it meant buying another mooring. It also meant that when someone was using the Whaler, the pram would be fast to the Whaler's mooring. Any of us who wanted to reach the Hobie had to swim, either to retrieve the pram, or to reach the Hobie herself.

We needed still another boat. This one, acquired with the same insane abandon as each of the others, was an inflatable. She would, so the theory went, be light, easily hauled aboard the float. She would not, as it turned out, be able to withstand any but the most gentle hands. Much of our time was spent patching leaks inspired by carelessness, or trying to row a boat that grew wrinkles before your eyes.

As we acclimated to the dory, the Whaler, the Hobie, the pram, and the inflatable, fate lent a hand. Within the next three weeks, two marine derelicts drifted ashore on our very own point. One was a cumbersome great flat-bottomed wedge of a wooden clamming skiff with all the grace of a hog's feeding trough. Built in some digger's backyard from pine planks and common nails, she had the stolid heaviness a work boat should, but lent herself to no purpose we could readily devise. None of the sons I knew had any inclination to dig clams for a living. Nevertheless, we plugged her worst leaks and gave her a home.

The other gift from the sea was a narrow aluminum scow with bow and stern both squared—the sort of boat that's sold via mail order to Arkansas farmers who want to try fishing for largemouth bass in the local swamp. Well, I thought, at least I'd have a way to get out on the bay if the children had taken off in both the Whaler and the Hobie, as they often did.

Seven small boats should be enough for one family, I decided. But what did I know? Even at that moment, more were headed my way.

No one with the slightest affection for small boats could have resisted either one. The first arrived with a comely young woman who walked through the always open door of my office at the newspaper. She had a friend, she told me, an older man, who had begun a late-in-life career as a boat builder. Once a ship's carpenter, he had worked his way through tragedies never revealed to me. Now, with his skills regrouped, he was building a sample of the boat he would produce on order for future buyers.

"Would you," my charming visitor wanted to know, "put something in the paper" that would help her friend by telling our small world about this boat-buying opportunity.

I could, I said, but first I'd like to see the boat.

That was, of course, my undoing. The moment she slid back the door to the builder's shed and sunlight spilled over the Swampscott dory suspended there in its builder's brackets, I knew I could not leave well enough alone.

She was small, probably ten feet along her bottom, maybe four-teen from the tip of her curving bow to the top of her angled stern. Already painted, her lapstraked cedar sides gleamed white and smooth as marble. Her rails and thwarts were varnished, her fittings brass, and her transom hand-carved with flourishes taken from de-tails of an admiral's gig pictured in some naval history. She was breathtaking, clearly a work of genius, the result of the same singular concentration Michelangelo had sacrificed to the Sistine Chapel ceil-ing. This boat was a poem, wrested from the soul of a tormented poet—a once-in-a-lifetime creation that would never be duplicated, in spite of resolutions made or self-promises given.

I set her mooring so she could be seen from every window. When I awakened, I could watch her as I dressed and gauge the tide and wind from her response to the slightest shifts in the balances of her universe. From where I sat at our family table, I could look at her over the heads of guests, family, and friends.

Oh, that Swampscott dory. She swung on her line like a tern in flight, lightly, the waterlike air beneath her narrow bottom. Her movement was an endless ballet, symphonic testimony to the har-monies possible when design, craft, genius, materials, and heart-break combine to produce a marine mobile, a sculpture as pure as David, a sonnet, a song sung each morning and on through dappled afternoons and moonstruck nights.

I loved her more than any other.

I gave her a mutton-leg sail and mast that I could carry, and on September evenings she and I would glide over Middle Bay, the only dancers on the sunset.

So, why yet another boat when I'd found such fulfillment?

Friendship and sentiment, I suppose.

Dick Barringer had helped me build our deck, my life in Maine, and our newspaper. When he told me his oldest son was hoping to earn money restoring an ancient Old Town sailing canoe discovered in an Aroostook County barn, what was I to do but offer to become the buyer. Besides, I had another reason.

Most of my boyhood summers were spent far out on the tip of eastern Long Island in a vast ramble of a shingled house perched like some great blue heron on a narrow strip of sand between the Atlantic and Georgica Pond. Often, as my brother and I ate our supper, an Old Town sailing canoe swept across our view through the west-facing dining room window. Mr. Jewett's white panama and his tanned features would be about even with the gunwales.as he lay almost prone in the canoe, adjusting daggerboards, steering with two lines attached to a tiller perched on a crescent stern, trimming the gaff-rigged cotton sail, and, in general, seeming to be in total and gentle control of his summer solitude. His easy mastery of the Old Town, I thought as I watched, was a skill I would emulate when I grew up.

I grew for almost sixty years before I got the chance. There was no way I could turn down the opportunity.

It was the last I would have for a while. During the almost two decades since I'd moored the Banks dory in her Kennebec creek, the mountain range of debt had moved closer, its shadows made even more depressing because they fell across so many empty spaces in our home—spaces left by children grown to men and women laying the keels of their own lives.

When Sam, the youngest, left, the house became a cavern and even the Swampscott dory on her mooring seemed a bird bereft. Jean and I put the home we had built on the market and when it was sold to a California couple, the Whaler and the Old Town were part of the deal. The Banks dory had long since succumbed; the aluminum pram stayed on the dock; the Hobie Cat was given to Sam and his brother Bob; the old clamming scow and the flat-ended Arkansas bass boat were set adrift, returned to the bay that had brought them. Somewhere in the barn rafters, the inflatable sagged in habitual deflation, an experiment failed.

But I could not let go of the Swampscott dory.

It was November when that house on Middle Bay was truly sold, when, as they say, papers were passed and deeds recorded. We stayed on through most of the winter, Jean and I, because the California couple wanted the place for summer vacations and be-cause the small house we had bought near Main Street was still being made ready.

Along the shores of Middle Bay, the first skim ice traces the marshes during late October nights. By November, when the wind, tide, and temperature are right, the cove can ice over from bank to bank. No small boat should be on its mooring through a Maine November.

But I left the Swampscott dory on hers. I wanted her to be part of my awakenings until the last possible morning. I knew when she came ashore she would have to leave, and she was my last boat, the one I loved most.

In early December, the cove froze and I had to break the ice with an oar to free the dory. I hauled the trailer around to the landing and paddled the dory over. After she was safe in our barnyard, I went to my office at the paper and wrote a "Boat for Sale" notice for that week's classifieds.

The following Sunday a lean and close-cropped woman drove down from Camden. She asked me what she thought were tough questions about the dory, technical nit-picking, making certain I understood how much she knew about boats. She never once said how lovely that boat looked, even on that harsh December day. She bought the dory and the next afternoon arrived with another woman in a truck to pick her up. I shed some tears as they left.

That was almost a decade ago, and I've been boatless ever since. Jean and I live in Key West now, as well as Maine, and one of our sons is living with us. He wants to go halves with me on a small boat we can use to fish the flats, maybe an old Whaler, like the one we had in Maine.

IN A FOG

BY GEOFFREY WOLFF

THE FULL MOON lit Boston shortly before midnight. Precisely: The moon edged over the horizon at 11:27 that eleventh day of July, as good as my pledge to my wife and two sons. I had warranted much, that we'd have fun, for example. The notion was definitely to have a good time. That was always the idea, to take pleasure from doing something just so, from coming through in the crunch (if, God forbid, there should be a crunch), and caring for the boat and your loved ones. Priscilla, Justin, Nicholas, and I had embarked on a routine cruising adventure, a voyage Down East: Narragansett Bay to Cuttyhunk Massachusetts; Cuttyhunk to Wings Neck; through the Cape Cod Canal to Race Point buoy off Provincetown; thence a

11

straight shot offshore, 120 very nautical miles northeast to Monhegan Island, its light visible twenty miles, or so I believed.

Now, just past midnight, we were gurgling downwind across Massachusetts Bay; Nicholas, at the helm, showed me the Big Dipper up there. Seas were moderate, as promised, slapping reassuringly against the counter of *Blackwing,* our Mystic 30 cutter. Hazy, hot afternoon in Cape Cod Bay as advertised, wind sou'west, just what the weatherman had said.

That warm night in the cockpit, aboard a boat I love, with the three people I most care about, doing a thing I cannot get enough of doing, bound for Casco and Penobscot bays, watching my fourteen-year-old boy anticipate the shove of a swell and correct for it, watching him scan the horizon for ships lucky enough to be in the neighborhood that gorgeous night, well, wasn't this as good as it got? Wasn't this, in fact, my *doing*?

Of all provocations for my smugness that soft night, the most urgent was the appearance, precisely when and where it was meant to rise, of the moon's sharp-edged, silver face, like a cheerful, goofy neighbor peering over a fence. *Hey, Guys, what's cookin'?* Eldridge had said it would be so and it was so, benign prophecy, the spheres in their regulated cycles, time and tide, all right with the world, natural law at the helm (and steering sure).

Justin was below, sleeping an eleven-year-old's serious sleep, and Priscilla slept, too. And this was good: They trusted me. I'd said how it would be and it had been that and more. Late afternoon, a couple of hours after leaving Race Point, off-soundings, we had sailed into a pod of humpbacks. I hadn't promised whales, but I'd delivered whales. Now we were talking of them, how they'd simply materialized, not there and then there. We talked about their show-off explosion of water breaching, great theater, a big-scale memory for us.

Now Nick was talking about things more comfortably discussed in the dark, away from home. A girlfriend from sixth grade. Fears and disappointments. Bewilderments. My son was backlit by the moon, and the sea was a most remarkable pewter. We talked about the Bomb, ghosts, What's the Meaning of Life.

And then I was tired. Suddenly and bone-achingly tapped out. I had been on deck twenty hours. Oh, it had been *such* a day! I told Nick to sail another hour while I slept below. Reminded him—he needed no reminding—to look sharp for traffic. Checked the trim, noted our course, noticed the stars fading, overpowered by moonlight. Was halfway below when I thought to say:

"Call me right away if fog comes in."

"Sure, Dad."

I laughed, a little. *Sure, Dad* really meant *Shut up, Dad, trust me.*

In fact, I trust nothing and nobody, including myself. I know a bit about myself, including what I don't know, so I ration trust miserly. I have my compass swung, update charts, tighten what is loose, reef too soon. A thirty percent chance of thunderstorms is one hundred percent to this meteorologist. The only surprise I welcome at sea is a wind shift in my favor. *Uneventful* is my favorite notation in the log. I do not sail boats to pump adrenaline, or to grow an ulcer. When I finally put away the last of many motorcycles, I put to rest whatever compulsion got me speeding tickets. My desideratum at sea is elementary: to cause no harm.

To cause no harm is no passive ambition. It requires an imagination for disaster; it demands that the master of a vessel (or of children, say) not put his vessel (or his family, say) in harm's way, needlessly, fecklessly. I expect to be surprised at sea—I am not a fool (I once thought)—but I want surprise to come of natural law rather than my carelessness.

So you see, the captain of *Blackwing* that moonlit July night in Massachusetts Bay, bound for the Gulf of Maine, was a prudent mariner. Which is why I had felt wounded, unjustly judged, by Priscilla's reservations about this overnight passage, indeed, our first overnight passage as a family. She had sailed with me for twenty years and better than anyone she knew my limits, because we had taught ourselves to sail together, first on day sailers in Chesapeake Bay, then on an Ohlson 35 yawl we owned with Priscilla's sister and brother-in-law John.

I owe my circumspection at sea to John's negative example. To push the envelope was his only purpose. Many an adventure with John, many a laugh, never a dull afternoon on the water with John, many a bump, many a grounding. I came to hate the damned excitement, and soon I was surprised to discover I had translated myself from the quondam Hotspur Priscilla had married into a very clerk of a sailor, fussy, priggish, a look-before-you-leaper. This fever of caution had alarmingly spread inland to other enterprises: I now balanced my checkbook, "maintained" my shoes, did a fall lay-up on my body, would have put a spring coat of varnish on the lawn mower if I could get the Z-Spar to adhere to grease. Bobbing at a mooring in Buzzards Bay, launchpad for the Cape Cod Canal and points Down East, the last thing I had expected to hear from Priscilla was:

"You know, maybe we shouldn't. Maybe this is too much for us."

I couldn't believe my ears! On the eve of jumping off, having voyaged from Jamestown, Rhode Island, to Wing's Neck, having topped the tanks, iced the chest, stocked the larder, having collected and annotated the charts, having *promised the boys*, and Priscilla wondered, *now*, if this was a "good idea"!

She gave lame reasons: I seemed strung out by the profusion of tasks and charts, and I hadn't seemed to take into account that we were—how should she best put this?—*shorthanded*.

"What in the world do you mean, 'shorthanded'?"

(The marine weatherman was broadcasting from Boston.)

"I'm not competent to do this. Justin is eleven years old, Nick is thirteen . . ."

"Mom, don't call me names . . ."

(. . . humid . . . wind southwest . . .)

"You are thirteen, till day after tomorrow."

(. . . twenty-five percent chance of evening thunderstorms . . .)

"You're forgetting somebody." I said this patiently, not wishing my logic to crush my dear wife.

"Well, let's talk about you. You'll be in effect single-handing more than thirty hours. I trust you, but at night? Offshore?"

"You mean you don't trust me."

"Guys," Justin said.

(. . . fog likely by Monday morning in the Gulf of Maine . . .)

"We don't *have* to do this," she said. "Your manhood isn't on the line."

Sure. I saw a picture in my mind's eye, beating home over the course I had just traveled, telling them back in Jamestown I'd be needing my mooring this summer after all, the weatherman had said there was an outside chance of fog Down East and, besides, my wife had reminded me that it's difficult to see in the dark. We'd decided we'd prefer to voyage Down East by Subaru. As Priscilla said, my manhood wasn't on the line.

"But we promised the boys," I said.

"Wow," said Nicholas, with considerable justice.

In fact, I'd promised myself (and a hotel keeper) that come noon the day after tomorrow I'd be swinging at a mooring in Tenants Harbor. That is, I didn't care what Priscilla or a Boston weatherman opined about my plan, we were pushing off next morning at first light.

And so we did. Serene dawn passage through the Cape Cod Canal, Race Point right on the money after a fine morning's sail, humpbacks in the afternoon while we ate an estimable lunch delivered cheerfully from the galley to the cockpit. I kept a meticulous log, made a great show of competence. ("No, thanks, I'll skip that beer, I've got a gang of water ahead.") In fact I felt stretched; I fiddled with the RDF, homing in on Race Point. It gave little assurance, its toy compass poorly damped, the null approximate rather than persuasive. I had considered buying Loran C, but at the time to have bought Loran would have been to sacrifice several necessities: the case of Ruinart champagne in the hold, the rooms waiting our arrival at Tenants Harbor, the tape deck Jimmy Buffett required to sing us downhill to Monhegan.

So, there we were, Nick at the helm, Captain Romance below, dead to the world above.

"It's here, Dad."

Nick sounded grim. Oh boy, oh boy, oh boy. Was it ever there! My sleeping bag was heavy with it. My glasses were wet. I wasn't even surprised. Just before I went below, I'd wiped moisture from the compass dome and, when I'd warned Nick to have a care, I could see my breath.

"Did you see other boats?"

"It came so fast, Dad. It didn't roll in, like they say. It wasn't here and then it was here. Like the whales. I was looking at the moon, so *huge,* and then the moon was gone. It just blinked off."

"Did you see anything?" I willed my voice to hold steady. It was 3:35. We were in the Portland shipping lanes. With any luck we would see the loom of the big light on Monhegan in a couple of hours. Maybe we'd get lucky again? Didn't that seem fair?

"There was a set of fast-moving lights to seaward, heading across our bow. Pretty far ahead."

"How far?"

"I don't know, Dad. It's hard to say at night."

So it was.

"Any other shipping?"

"Something on our course, coming up astern. A sailboat, maybe. I don't think it's moving faster than we are."

But we weren't moving. We were becalmed. Nick and I dropped sails and fired up the sturdy Yanmar diesel, never a missed breath these three years. My chest had already cramped, while I waited for some tanker to crawl into our cockpit. I posted Nick in the bow, resumed 040 degrees, smelled coffee brewing. Priscilla was looking through the companionway hatch.

"Priscilla . . ." I began.

"Just keep your head," she said.

How did it get so cold? The rigging dripped on us. The decks were greased with wet and the gray swells seemed oiled. Nick blew a foghorn with requisite regularity into the dense, wet dark, which swallowed the doleful, coarse noise.

Oh, how I had counted on the loom of Monhegan Island light! To follow the loom of that light home to its source was the First Principle of this adventure. Now the light could be fixed to my damned bowsprit and I wouldn't see it.

Hours later, with Justin in the bow blowing a pitiful warning, with Nick below trying to recover from the night, with Priscilla deep in Duncan and Ware's *Cruising Guide to the New England Coast*, day broke. Day broke my heart. Black, impenetrable obscurity had given way to pearly obscurity. Portland marine weather said it was going to be a great day ashore, sunny and hot, good beach day, maybe a little hazy. Oh, offshore? Fog banks. This was told as though it weren't a tragedy, but commonplace!

Priscilla never said, then or later, "How did you get us into this?" But how could I fail to know what she was thinking as she read (Roger F.) Duncan and (John P.) Ware, whose celebration of the water we now blindly bobbed upon bristled with warning labels of treacherous tides, rocky shoals, evil weather, fog?

Priscilla is neither vindictive nor eager to make a bad situation worse, but she read aloud from the humid pages something she thought I might need to know: " 'The onshore tide set from Portsmouth onward is a major navigation hazard. In spite of the fact that we make a major compensation for this effect, we almost always fall inside of the anticipated landfall. . . .' "

"Does that bear on us?" Priscilla asked.

I nodded. I shook my head. I said, "I don't know." Because the tide sets irregularly along the course we had sailed, in a circular motion, I hadn't the least notion where I was, not the foggiest. Now I favored east over north, the sea over the coast. The good news: I wouldn't (probably) run up on a rocky beach in Muscongus Bay. The bad news: Between us and Portugal were few bells, horns, whistles.

At 10:00 A.M., our ETA for Monhegan, the diesel coughed and then it sputtered. Nick was at the helm and I barked at him, thinking (I guess) he'd adjusted the throttle, which he hadn't. For the first time with my family at sea, I had shouted in panic and my response provoked alarm in the people I had brought here to make happy. I felt sorry for myself; I was ashamed; I was scared.

I'd been in fog before, fog as thick as this. I'd never been in fog thicker than this, because fog didn't get thicker than this, but I'd run buoy to buoy from Pulpit Harbor on North Haven into Camden. That was five years ago, and when I'd missed a mark, I'd known enough to motor the boundaries of a square, shutting off the engine to listen, and I'd found my way. It had been a strain, of course, cramping the neck muscles, all that tensing to hear, that fierce concentration on the compass. We'd been swallowed by fog running from Block Island to Newport, Rhode Island, and I hadn't panicked, just patiently held on course for Brenton Tower and there it was, its monster spider legs rising from the sea, on the button.

This was different. I tried to find Monhegan with the laughable RDF. The null suggested it was abeam, either port or starboard. Gee, thanks. The weather radio suggested a likely possibility of thunderstorms and we prayed for them, to blow the fog away, to part the veil for just a moment. The air was milky, like sour milk, dreadful yellow. The air was thick, morose. We were cold. A slight breeze astern blew diesel exhaust at us.

We didn't speak. I think they were ashamed for me. We listened. Will I ever listen as acutely? I dared not shut off the engine. Why? I can't remember. I believed so powerfully now in entropy—in general disintegration and systematic failure, in bad luck—that I dared not alter anything: course, throttle, helmsman. We motored forward, 040 degrees. . . .

*   *   *

Priscilla heard it first. Then I heard it and throttled back after all, and then we all heard it, a low moan, like someone sick. The delicate lament would come and go. For an hour we sought it, steering every which way, finally finding our way to it. My rational self knew that a whistle had not been placed to tell us where we were but to mark a hazard; I knew no hazard worse than not knowing where we were. Nick begged me to come up on it slow and I did, because I was stalking the whistle and feared I'd spook it. And there it was, fifty feet, anchored. I envied it. Now the deep whistle groaned frankly, excessively.

We circled it while I called the Coast Guard; my voice alarmed me. I had once had a bad stutter and it had come back. Was there an "SL," black and white, near Monhegan?

That was a negative, Skipper. We were circling a marker on the Seal Ledges, a little east of Large Green Island, fourteen nautical miles east-northeast of Monhegan, which we had missed by a mile (as they say). We were in bad water, with a foot between our keel and a kelpy rock slab, and the Coast Guard suggested we get ourselves out of there, pronto, to Matinicus Island, three miles east.

Looking back, I guess we should have felt rescued. But our least desired course that afternoon was a course to seaward that would leave behind us the one thing we knew, yonder moaning whistle.

The weather radio was undecided between thunderstorms and dense fog, growing denser. We went for Matinicus and its sister a little to seaward—Ragged—trying to pick up a nun on the Foster Ledges, missing it (big surprise). We should have been near Matinicus. Priscilla was reading:

" '. . . the region should be approached with caution. There are no really snug harbors . . . unmarked dangers are frequent and tides are swift. In fog or storm the careless or inexperienced can get into real trouble. . . .' "

Justin was on the bowsprit, shouting, "Look at those thunderclouds!"

I looked up and saw black. Umbrella pines on a cliff. And then we were among the rocks and a rocky beach materialized yards ahead, and I swung the wheel over while Nick yelled directions, and we *didn't* tear open the hull, or ground, or even stub our toe.

We anchored. I got on the radio (and this hurts to repeat):

"Anybody on Ragged Island or Matinicus. Please come back. This is *Blackwing*. I am off a rocky beach on the west side of one of your islands. We are tired and lost. I repeat, we are frightened. Please come back.''

And bingo, back came a lobsterman. Said he was pulling pots, he had us on his radar, would drop by in a jiffy, lead us into Criehaven, the harbor on Ragged. He had an extra mooring, he said, we could use it. Drink a cup of coffee, he suggested. Take it easy. Welcome to Maine, he said.

I don't think Priscilla will mind if I tell she fell in love with that lobsterman before she met him. Did I resent how Priscilla and my sons felt about the man with radar and sense enough to find his way (and ours) to a safe haven? I did not. My manhood, poor pathetic thing, was back there in the Portland shipping lanes, or where I'd lost my wits somewhere near Monhegan, when I forgot how to use an RDF, where I'd gone plumb dumb, numb with senseless dread.

When the lobsterman came alongside and saw how it was, heard my voice and saw my hands shaking, he suggested, seeing how thick o' fog it was, that he would *tow* us in. That seemed to me a capital notion, just the brightest idea anyone ever had. He towed, I pretended to steer, the boys fished off the stern and hauled them in, laughing.

We hung on a mooring in Criehaven two days, two nights. It's a snug harbor, but till the fog lifted we never saw land from *Blackwing*. That night it cleared and we saw the Northern Lights. Next morning: fog. We stayed put. If the fog hadn't lifted we'd still be there, believe me. But the fog did lift, as it does, and we moved along, and Maine showed us a dandy time.

So now? I feel less and less like a fool, which is striking evidence of foolishness. More and more it seems fine and sensible to try it again. Next time I'd like to creep up on Matinicus Rock at dawn and surprise the puffins. With Loran, of course. Matinicus Rock is almost as easy a chance from Race Point as Monhegan. After all, *Blackwing* came through. We did. Where was the harm?

COLLECTOR

BY E. ANNIE PROULX

1.

THE TELEPHONE DOWNSTAIRS in the kitchen was ringing. He knew it was his ex-wife; he could tell by the dizzy ring. He sat up on the side of the bed. Bambi moaned, "Answer the goddamn phone, will you?" and jerked the blankets over her head as though she were harpooning a shark. He stood up. The phone was ringing. He felt two hundred years old.

"Hello, Dede."

"Hello, Horsie. I saw one last night." She talked in her normal voice.

"Saw one what? And where's Seacroft or whatever the hell his name is to let you wander around calling people up at"—he slewed

his eyes at the onyx clock on the stainless steel wall—"five twenty-
one on Sunday morning before it is even light?" The dim reflection of
his face in the polished metal resembled a flour tortilla.

"His name is not Seacroft and you know it. It's Sealey. And it's
none of your business where he is. He's in Chicago. And he doesn't
'let' me do anything; I do what I want. I call you up to tell you
something important and you start in with the sarcasm. I don't need
it, Horsie."

"I don't need it either, Dede. What I need is another six hours'
sleep. I'm freezing. I'm standing on a cold tile floor in my bare feet.
Tell me the important thing and I'll be grateful."

As he talked he opened the door of the custom burgundy enamel
refrigerator. Dozens of jars, pots, and Tupperware bowls with dabs
and fragments of leftover food crowded across the shelves. A dried-
out piece of paté on a saucer had shriveled and curled until it looked
like a cat turd. Beside it was a nearly full bowl of salsa.

"Last night I saw what you're always looking for. On the top of an
old car, an old De Soto that had not been restored. I copied down the
license number for you. We may be divorced, Horsie, but I still think
of your interests."

Sure you do, he sneered to himself.

He dipped a slightly withered hot dog in the salsa. As soon as it was
in his mouth he remembered the salsa was dangerously incendiary,
crammed with 10/10 jalapeño peppers. His lips, mouth, and throat
burst into flames. He spat half-chewed fragments into the sink,
turned on the cold water faucet and plunged his mouth into the
bubbled stream.

"What are you doing, Horsie? Are you in the bathroom?"

"I'm getting a drink of water. In the kitchen," he croaked like
Edward G. Robinson with a crushed larynx. "A Rushton? You saw a
Rushton? How could you tell?" He was awake now.

"Because, in my long term of imprisonment in your life I saw so
many canoes, from birchbark to titanium, that their forms are permanently imprinted on my memory circuits. It's an embarrassment
these days. Sealey and I will be somewhere and I'll see some filthy
thing on top of a Winnebago and I grab his arm and scream 'Oh
look!' and he shrinks away. Literally shrinks away. It was small,
couldn't have been any more than ten feet long."

He had a clear vision of her gibbering into the receiver, her taffy-
colored hair puffed into curls, the pale eyes fringed by false eyelashes

coming unstuck at the ends. "There's a lot of canoe builders out there now making replicas. What'd the driver look like?"

"Horsie, there were so many Garfields stuck on the back window I could hardly tell if the driver had a head. Do you want the plate number or not?"

He wanted it. And back in bed, when Bambi mumbled, "It was her, wasn't it," he said no, it was the answering service but Groats was taking care of the problem.

"Liar," said Bambi.

2.

BAMBI was six feet tall and as flat as a cupboard, as elegant as black silk. She called her fingers "little servants." She dressed like a quetzal bird. It was hard to believe she had been a U.S.D.A. meat inspector when he first met her. She had limped into his life three months after Dede had left him for retired tennis ace Sealey Books. Bambi was suffering shinsplints from years of trekking through Pennsylvania scrapple processing plants. Even before they were married she switched the full headlights of her interest from scrapple to canoes. Horse was thrilled with her eagerness to learn every detail of his latest Rushton find.

At the height of their romance she treated him like a doll, stuffing him into Charvet shirts and Giorgio Armani suits, bought him a gold expansion-bracelet watch that tweaked the hairs out of his arm and a briefcase of mink leather strips that ripped apart the second time he used it. But on his most recent birthday the present was a polyester jogging suit and an enormous rowing machine with two accompanying video tapes, one titled *Rough Weather off Cape Horn*, the other, *Caribbean Hurricanes*. He began to spend more time at his father's camp on Lake Strangles, where he could eat jelly doughnuts without censure.

When his father bought the camp in 1973, Horse was still in medical school. It was the time, then, of the Doctor-Adventurers. Interns vied to climb Nanda Devi, cross the Empty Quarter, paddle the Nahanni. Some were drawn to a maverick new specialty, wilderness medicine, derided by old doctors as the art of staunching bear claw lacerations with wads of moss. Horse went in for hiking and climbing and river trips in a mild way but stopped far short of wilderness medicine.

His few colleagues who eschewed ballooning across the Cordillera collected things. Bob Vint collected urine specimen bottles and had a sixteenth-century blown glass flask with an authentic residue in the bottom. Menlove Edwards collected signed first editions of gastroenterology texts. Wallace Turban went in for Bugatti axles. Podiatry was a dull field, but Horse melded the call of the wild and the cachet of collecting and began buying old canoes. In no time at all he had two dozen aged hulks, all gray wood and rotten canvas, suspended from hooks in their apartment ceiling.

A family of mice came with one of the wrecks and spread into an aerial city of rodents who squeaked and rustled and gnawed. At one of Dede's Sunday afternoon get-togethers, thin flakes of paint and shreds of canvas dribbled down onto the hot crab puffs, and Dede, looking up, saw bold, beady eyes returning her gaze. "Get those fucking crates out of here," she growled at him out of the corner of her mouth.

The camp on Lake Strangles was a godsend. He could keep his canoes there and paddle them without the bother of dangerous and exhausting trips, for, after a few years, he found collecting more satisfying than scrambling up Napes Needle. After one visit Dede never bothered to come out to the camp again. There was a downside; his father was often there, tearing out walls.

"Don't expect too much," Whitebread, the real estate agent, had mumbled, steering onto a dim track. And all at once he had expected everything, feeling the woods rise around them like ground fog, tasting the floury pink dust coming in through the driver's window, ready to advise the old man to buy the place before they even saw it.

His father sat in the front seat. Carvel Horpse was a close-lipped homicide detective with eleven years to go before retirement, and constantly irritated by the inconveniences related to his hereditary mancinism. His thin white hair was parted in the middle, giving him the look of a religious fanatic. A severe case of acne in puberty had left his skin lumpy and coarse, and with the heavy tan he kept up at the tanning parlors his face resembled an enlarged walnut. He held his little leather notebook. Whenever he wrote something down with his left hand, his elbow brushed Whitebread's shifting arm and he gave an annoyed twitch.

"Now this road," said Whitebread, "this road is a private road so the town won't do nothing. You want it improved, it's your road. As I told you. You will have to pay for your own gravel." His father made a note in the little leather-bound book. Horse could read it. "Gravel." Whitebread left the track and drove into the brambles, the limber stems flailing like circus whips, the thorns squealing across the car fenders.

The camp looked like an enormous brown cupcake. The dome roof flowed into the exterior walls without a break. A rail fence circled the strange building like an asteroid belt around a planet. Thickets of wild raspberry rolled away to the edge of the lake, a sea of silvery leaves and thorned purple stems. A gray wall of dead spruce stretched out onto the point.

"Man that built this place back in the thirties was supposed to had a dream about domes, about dome houses. This is one of the first ones ever built in this country. Some famous architect. I forget his name. When he died he deeded it to the Boy Scouts and they tried to get it listed as a national landmark but they didn't bite. So they used it a couple seasons then put it up for sale. As I told you."

"Where's the boathouse? The ad said there was a boathouse."

Carvel wrote "Architect? Boathouse?" in the notebook.

"That's the one thing the Boy Scouts added to improve the property. Right over there." Whitebread gestured toward the point, and Horse saw that what he had mistaken for a stand of dead spruce was a severely weathered building.

"You can put fifty boats in there on them racks. There's like a little workshop in there for repairs and stuff."

Horse reached around the passenger seat and jabbed surreptitiously at his father's short ribs as a signal of pleasure. Carvel crossed out "Boathouse?" and jerked his elbow back in complicitous answer. They bought it without getting out of Whitebread's car.

Carvel had always wanted to get into interior decoration and the camp was his chance. He tore out the plywood cubbies the Boy Scouts had nailed to the walls, tore out the cheap wallboard the famous architect had installed himself. He had a hundred ideas for refinishing the place. Over the years he replaced the wallboard, first with imported olive oil cans hammered flat, then with mosaics made from broken Fiestaware, then with stretched deer hide panels, and most recently with pecky cypress at twelve dollars a board foot, whitewashed and flagellated with chains for a distressed look.

3.

HORSE had known about Rushton's canoes since his early collecting days, but after a hundred years, surviving craft were so rare the builder seemed more of a mythic Canoe God than a collector's specialty. Then, on the way to a tennis tournament, he dragged Dede into the Adirondack Museum for a few minutes. There was the *Sairy Gamp*. She seemed to float on invisible water. Tears came into his hardened doctor eyes as he walked around the taut and perfect little canoe, while Dede tugged at the sleeve of his sports jacket and whined, "Let's get out of this mausoleum. This isn't getting us to the tennis."

The little canoe was an exquisite marvel, a cedar eggshell, weighing only ten and a half pounds in her nine feet of length and beam of twenty-six inches. The flexible planks were a mere three-sixteenths of an inch thick. Rushton had built her in 1883 for George Washington Sears, the strange and tubercular Pennsylvania cobbler better known as Nessmuk. Nessmuk ordered five go-lights in the last years of his waning life: the *Wood Drake*, the *Susan Nipper*, the *Sairy Gamp*, the *Bucktail*, and the nine-pound *Rushton-Fairbanks* for adventuring along the sharky waters of the Florida coast. Of the canoes Rushton made for Nessmuk, only the *Sairy Gamp* had survived, though Rushton sold other go-lights through the catalogue—the Nessmuk models. Horse bent close to read every label in the museum, and a sense of physical bonding came over him when he read that Rushton barely cleared five feet in height, while Nessmuk was his perfect match at five foot three. Brothers.

He sold his rodent-riddled fleet in one lot to a Texan at the annual convocation of the American Canoe and American Paddle Collectors American Association (ACAPCAA) and started looking for Rushtons, the most beautiful canoes, he told Dede, ever built. And of those fine cedar lapstrake canoes with oak keels and stems, red elm ribs, spruce gunwales, and clinched copper nails, of those floating works of art, he thought the sweetest were the little lightweights, ten-foot peapods weighing less than twenty pounds but sturdy enough to carry a man and his gear deep into the wilderness. That is, if the man was small and his gear light.

But lately the collecting was tough going. Whenever he tracked down a purported Rushton canoe it turned out to be something lesser, or another collector had beaten him to it. In five years he had managed to collect only five Rushtons, and he suspected that one of them, the Ugo, was a fake.

4.

HORSE liked to know what his patients did for a living. The information came in handy sometimes, as when Carvel was able to redo the camp bathroom in pink marble, purchased at an excellent discount from a quarry owner whose hammertoes Horse had treated. And Mrs. Eugenia Sturgis, still grateful for her successful bunionectomy three years ago, was a clerk/supervisor in the Motor Vehicle Department records section.

"Hi there, Mrs. Sturgis. Doctor Horpse here. How's that little foot of yours? Good! Well, I've got a funny request for you. We had a gentleman in the office last Friday and I'm afraid he had quite a wait. As you know, the place gets mighty busy sometimes. This fellow went off before I could see him. And darn it, Marie never even got his name . . . she was so tied up with the phone. She tried to catch him when he left, but it was too late. He was already pulling out of the parking lot. Fortunately she managed to get his license plate number. I really want to get in touch with him. Marie said he limped very badly and I'm afraid he needs our help. Could I prevail on your kindness? The license plate number is JJ444."

"Why doctor, I'd be glad to help. Just let me bring it up on the computer here. Here we are, a 1960 De Soto sedan, dark blue, registered to Karl Dovebeak, Rural Route Two, Box Fifty-five, up in Waxton. Phone is 989-8809."

"Mrs. Sturgis, you're a sweetheart. Keep in touch, now. In fact, you might come in for a checkup in a few weeks. Here, I'll switch you over to Marie. She can set up an appointment."

He dialed with a felt marker, deepening the blue circle that scored the numbers.

"Hello? Mr. Dovebeak? This is Dr. Horpse from downstate, and I'm hoping you can help me out." He gave a little chuckle and waited for the usual flattering acquiescence.

"What with? Brain surgery?" The voice was creaky and coolly amused.

"No, no, no. It's a little hard to explain. But let me try to explain. My ex . . . a friend of mine noticed your car a few nights ago with what she thought was a canoe on the top possibly made by J. Henry Rushton. I should explain that I'm a canoe collector—I specialize in Rushton canoes—so of course I'm pretty interested. In your canoe. If it is a Rushton."

"No."

"No what?"

"She didn't see a canoe. A pig trough. I lugged a pig trough home the other night on top of the car. Made by my nephew Sidney. I'm just a simple farmer. So I'm afraid you wasted your nickel." He hung up.

5.

THAT night, as Bambi lay in bed watching *Return of the Vikings*, Horse called Dede from the phone in the winter conservatory at the back of the house.

"You are a real birdbrain. I tracked down that license plate. You want to know what the driver was carrying on the top of his De Soto?"

She was almost whispering. "A canoe. A little Rushton canoe."

"A pig trough. He told me it was a pig trough. Made by his nephew Sidney. Not even a canoe, for godsake. Were you drinking? And how come you're so helpful all of a sudden?"

There was a silence. In the background Horse could hear a deep roupy shout, "Who is it? Is it for me?"

"No, it's not for you. Well, Horsie, that takes the thirteen-egg cake. I was *not* drinking. I've been cold sober ever since Sealey and I did the Maple Sands dryout. It *was* a canoe. I swear to you it was a canoe and I'm sure it was one of those baby Rushtons. And I still think of you fondly. I thought you'd appreciate the tip."

"Who is it?" cried the deep voice.

"For heaven's sake, it's my sister," shouted Dede, then whispered, "I've got to go. I'll call you up again someday even if you are a horse's ass."

Back upstairs, Bambi glared at him straight on like an insolent *toro* in the plaza. "That was her, wasn't it?"

"I called the office," he said.
She snorted and tossed her horns.

6.

ON Friday he left the office early and drove up to the camp on Lake Strangles. White glinting pieces of water showed through the trees. Horse could smell wet rock, foam-scummed backwater, raw mud flat shining like patent leather, and the smell of the lake itself, strongest in the rain like a wet dog or like the deep animal odor of Bambi's dripping hair underlying the perfumed shampoo, and the bitter smell of broken willow stems and rank weeds, pale juice as slippery as spit, and the rocks under the water, the brown cloudy coating like wet fur.

He meant to stay for three days, paddle each of the five Rushtons he owned—a Rob Roy, an Indian Girl, an Arkansas Traveler, a Saranac Laker, and the Ugo—oil them down and put them away under the rustling dustcovers. Turning off the long dirt road, he noticed tire tracks in the lane—vandals, or perhaps his father with the raw materials for a new decorative scheme. Now that he was retired and on a good pension, he had all the time in the world to mess around with chintz and Art Deco clocks.

Carvel was unloading heavy flat cartons the size of pizza boxes. "Granite," he huffed, stacking them on the floor. "Beautiful." Horse helped him carry in dozens of them and then went down to the boathouse.

The Arkansas Traveler was fast but unstable because of her narrow beam and sharp rise, as anxious to roll on her back as a dog in rotten clams. It took skill to hold her level. He paddled down the lake, proud he could keep her in steady balance, cutting through the early evening, the paddle hitting gently now and then against the gunwale. Swallows skimmed the water, and as the light thickened, the bats came, pinwheeling through the soft air. He stayed out until the early stars were smeared by the vapor rising from the lake, and at last paddled slowly toward the far shore, toward the camp where the lamp was shining through the windows to guide him back. This was the life.

"What do you think?" asked his father, on his hands and knees in the corner. The granite tiles, arranged in complicated patterns of gray and black, gave the three-dimensional illusion of pits opening into the cellar. Horse felt dizzy, looking into them.

"I got them from an architect. The client changed his mind and wanted walnut parquet. They weren't cheap. Cleaned my bank account out." But Horse was silent. There was plenty on his mind.

"Dad. I need a favor. I need your professional advice on something."

"I always knew my family would draw on my experience one day. Who did you kill, son? Bambi?"

Horse said it was a matter of investigation, of finding something out, not help on the far side of a deadly crime. He explained Dede's call, Dovebeak's denial, and his persistent feeling of something awry. Although his father seemed disappointed, he agreed to run his eye over the problem. The next morning they headed for Waxton.

7.

DOVEBEAK'S place was easy to spot. The mailbox was shaped like an enormous bird beak that opened when the mailman pulled a lever on the side. The house was Victorian, sporting crenellated towers, cutout latticework, gingerbread trim, and colored glass panes around the entrance door. The shaggy lawn was crowded with overgrown spirea, syringa, mock orange, snowball, and smoke shrubs. The two-car garage door gaped open, the inside empty except for a stack of liquor boxes. Then they were past the place and around the bend.

"That didn't do much good. I didn't see a damn thing but shrubs," said Horse.

"You don't have an expert's eye, son. I saw plenty. That big addition on the house with no windows and double doors opening on to the drive—that's an exhibition space with concealed lighting if I've ever seen one. In the back of the garage there was a flotation cushion of the kind most often used in canoes. All those gin and bourbon cartons spelled do-it-yourself moving in, probably with a U-haul trailer. And, if I'm not mistaken, the door knocker was in the shape of a paddle."

"That's amazing, Dad."

"The trained eye. And you also have to look for the things that aren't there. For example, there was no sign of a pigpen or a pig trough or the presence of pigs. I'm afraid you're up against a very wily collector, son."

"Why would anybody be secretive about a canoe collection?"

His father's laugh was bitter with knowledge of the evil ways of men. "For the same reason most of the great jewel collections are secret, the reason they never tell you who owns those big houses full of art objects in the Deco mags. Because the collection is full of priceless, irreplaceable stuff. Or full of hot treasures stolen from tombs and museums."

"Well, I'd like to know if whoever it is did have one of the go-lights on the top of a De Soto last week, where he got it, where it is now, and if it's for sale," said Horse. "I've missed out on every Rushton I've tried for in the past two years. Missed them all."

"Son. Just let me see what I can find out. You go do your doctoring and let me look into this."

8.

IT was a stunning week for podiatrists all over the city. In one of those strange outbreaks of similar accidents that plague the medical profession from time to time, hundreds of people injured their feet with brush hogs, electric shoe polishers, roller belt foot massagers, ill-fitting hunting boots, string trimmers, exercyles and, of course, lawn mowers. Friday evening Horse was so exhausted he couldn't finish his Lobster Diabolique and fell asleep on Bambi's shoulder during *Virgin Spring,* the opener in a Bergman revival. It was Sunday before he could drag himself up to the camp.

For once his father was relaxed. He swung in his Sea Island hammock while sipping a Rolling Rock and staring at gnats. The look on his face was that of a man who has scored a triumph.

Horse threw himself into the matching hammock on the other side of the door. "What a week," he sighed.

"You said it."

"I've never seen anything like it."

"You said it. Crazy."

"So, did you find out anything about Dovebeak's operation?"

"You bet. I found out plenty. But first go inside and take a look around. You're in for a surprise."

Horse heaved to his feet and went into the camp's main room. The granite trompe l'oeil floor was gone. So was the wooden floor beneath it. He was standing on a narrow deck overlooking a sunken garden, an exact but miniature replica of the Zen Buddhist Ryoanji garden in Kyoto. Groups of jagged black rocks rose out of the raked quartz gravel. On the other side of the garden he could see the kitchenette, forlorn and cut off.

"Jesus, Dad, how do you get in the kitchen?"

"I've got a ladder outside. In and out the window. But it's only temporary. I'm going to put in a catwalk. The men are coming tomorrow."

"I thought you were strapped. That garden must have cost a fortune."

"It all worked out," Carvel said, smoothing his hand through the air. "Now. About that Dovebeak thing. I called up some of my old contacts in the department, and out of the department, if you know what I mean. At first I thought Dovebeak might be part of an international canoe-smuggling ring. But he was clean. So I started to dig around. Dig, dig, dig. What I come up with is this: Dovebeak comes from Wellsboro, P.A. He's the grandson of a guy that used to have a pig farm next door to a guy who knew Rushton and owned some of the little canoes."

"Nessmuk? My God, could it have been Nessmuk?"

"Some guy named Sears. Dovebeak's grandfather was James Hurdle. He was the one lived next door to this Sears."

"Sears was Nessmuk. Go on. Then what?"

"Well, Sears picked up his laundry in what, 1885, 1886? Where your stuff goes when you die is a surprise sometimes. It don't always go to the next of kin. In this case, it seems that some of the canoes might of ended up in the neighbor's barn. Now, like I said, the Hurdle family farm down in Wellsboro was a pig farm. They raised pigs for the scrapple trade. And what we find out next is that this farm stayed in the family until five months ago, when it was taken by the state for highway development. The grandson, Dovebeak, is still moving stuff up here." The old man paused for effect. "And I want to tell you," he said, looking hard at Horse, "that he has got a collection of wooden Rushton canoes that would make you puke in your shoes. I know, because I saw it."

"My God!"

"I just went right up to the door, told him I knew all about his grandfather and the pig farm and the canoes. He was surprised at first, but he calmed right down. I didn't have any trouble with him. In fact, we got along real good. A very interesting man. Very persuasive. He showed me the canoes. Just like I thought, they're out in that addition. One hundred and two Rushton canoes. He's got everything. He's got the first one, a trial 1872 Rob Roy that wasn't ever paddled because it was only five inches deep. He's got the last one they ever made, December 1916. You know, Dovebeak wasn't ever a pig farmer. He was a used-tractor salesman. Retired, now. The man is seventy years of age. He said the pig-farming trait died out in the family except for his granddaughter." He looked sideways at Horse. "Seems she became a meat inspector. Specialized in pork products."

"What! Not Bambi!"

"I always said you were smart, Horse. You got it right away. And I hope you're ready for this. You know, life is full of bad news. We just have to take it the best we can and hope for tomorrow and a brighter day."

"What the hell are you trying to say, Dad?"

"Blood is thicker than water. Or I wouldn't of told you. And she wouldn't of done it. Bambi was the one tipped old Dovebeak off whenever you made a good find or an auction was coming up. So you did the work tracking them down, and he got there first."

Horse was breathless with shock. Dovebeak, the grandfather of Bambi! Bambi, a spy for Dovebeak! That charming interest in the old canoes. She must have betrayed him from the beginning, because he remembered her excitement when he was on the trail of a matched pair of decked Vespers. Both of them had been bought and taken away only minutes before he arrived with a certified check in his pocket at the Chicago warehouse where the owner had stored them.

Horse left his father on the porch and walked down the path to the boathouse. He'd feel better in the company of the few Rushtons he owned. He thought of the beautiful little Huron he'd expected to find in a Mississippi garage after a two-year exchange of letters. It had turned out to be a fiberglass monster that didn't match the owner's earlier descriptions in any way. And the Navahoe in perfect condition that he'd raced to buy, only to see it speeding up the thruway on the top of a car in the northbound lane while he was in the one heading south. Had the northbound car been a De Soto? He opened the door to the boathouse. It was empty. Even the Ugo was gone.

His father wasn't on the porch. Horse took the steps two at a time and, breathing like an accordion, burst onto the walkway above the sunken garden. Carvel, wearing a kimono figured with mountains and clouds, was raking the gravel into a new pattern.

"Dad!"

"This is incredibly beautiful. I ordered it shipped by air from Japan. It came with two workmen who installed it yesterday. Including the rocks. I drove them back to the airport. The workmen, not the rocks."

"Dad. Where are my Rushtons?"

"For Christ's sake, Horse. Didn't you get the drift of what I was saying? Dovebeak is a professional collector and a practiced sales-man. You can't stop him. He persuaded me. He showed me how you'd be better off if he had those canoes. I mean, he's got almost everything else. You just had a few, and he said one was a fake. It was hopeless. This garden, Horse. It's yours, son. I bought it for you. With the money Dovebeak paid for the canoes. You're better off with this. There are esoteric mathematical relationships in the arrangement of the rocks, and these are the key to underlying harmonies and a complex series of echoes that link the observer to the abstractions of nature. Don't you feel something standing there looking down on it?"

"Yes," said Horse. He could almost hear Dede and Bambi snig-gering.

VOYAGE

BY JOHN B. PUTNAM

IN THE LATE 1940's, you could walk the length of Boston's Atlantic Avenue on a winter Saturday morning and not see another living being. A few fishboats rocked at their moorings, dwarfed by the night boat to Nova Scotia, but of humankind there was no trace.

I was no stranger to the waterfront; Pop and I had prowled there together since I was small, and our ferry trips to East Boston and the occasional treat of the steamer to Nantasket Beach let us look at the city from seaward like the explorers I fancied we were.

This particular snowy day was different, though: it was my first solo trip, and I was on a mission. Somewhere ahead, buried among the buildings that teetered at the water's edge, was Bliss's, the old chandlery that still reeked of pine tar and hemp and Brasso. I'd been there before with Pop, of course, but never long enough for me. There was something special there I had to spend some time with: models of old sailing ships, and drawers of fittings and cordage, and boxes of plans.

I skittered down the icy cobblestones, tugged open the door, and stomped the snow off my boots. A gray-haired woman looked up from behind a counter: "Morning. Can I help you?"

"I just wanted to look at the model stuff."

"Well, you go right ahead. Let me know if you need any help."

I have no idea how long I stayed, or what we talked about; there was just too much to take in. All I remember is leaving: "We're closing up now," she said. "Take this, and come back again." She handed me a catalogue; I mumbled some sort of thanks, and stepped out into the storm.

It was the first of many visits I would make over the years to come, and the first of many catalogues I would literally wear out in the process of becoming a model builder.

The more I learned of ships and the sea, the more I wanted to know. It wasn't enough just to read about them, or to look at pictures and plans; I needed their presence. And much as I admired the tugs and ferries and colliers that still plied the harbor, it was the ships of the great days of sail that I longed for; but they were gone. I was born too late—fifty years, a hundred, two hundred. Models would have to be my window on the ships of other days; I would have my own fleet to carry me into the worlds of Horatio Hornblower, Jack Hawkins, Richard Henry Dana, or even of my grandfather, who had sailed here from his native Nova Scotia on lumber schooners.

It wasn't all that easy; I had to learn that it took more persistence than patience. You had to stop just before you heaved the damn thing across the room; then you had to come back to it. After the first attempt, I would never try to carve a hull from oak instead of pine, or substitute basswood for boxwood when making blocks. My grandfather helped: "You need less rake in the foremast and more steeve to the bowsprit." A deft twist of the jibstay around the bowsprit, and the mast leaned forward while the bowsprit tilted up ever so slightly. "Not perfect, but it'll do." "Shave off a bit under the transom; that's a barge you've got, not a Grand Banker."

Years passed, and with them came more lessons: what woods were best for hulls and which were for spars, why linen was the rigging cord of choice, and why beeswax was the best stuff for laying the fuzz and keeping the moisture out; why many coats of thin lacquer were better than a single coat of enamel, and why bronze wire was better for stropping blocks than brass; how to weather a hull so that it looked like a working vessel rather than a toy, and how to make and paint a tinfoil flag that fluttered in an imaginary breeze.

Two college summers collecting garbage on Nantucket gave me hours of reminiscence from old geezers who had gone in search of the whale in the early days of the century, and Naval Engineering One and Two unraveled the·mysteries of lines, plans, and construction drawings—half breaths, waterlines, buttock lines, diagonals, inboard elevations. I came to know what did what, how, and why.

I even parted with some hard-earned cash to begin building kits. By my junior year in college, my fleet embraced the colonial schooner *Sultana* from Model Shipways and Marine Model Company's whaleboat. I applied my hard-won skills to William Webb's jewel-like merchant brig *Volante*, also from Model Shipways, and learned that by leaving the braces slightly slack, and then taking up on the main backstays along with the spanker sheets and vangs, I could keep the proper rake of both masts, rather than letting the strain on the braces pull the mainmast upright. One day, in that adult life of leisure that was sure to reward all the hard work of youth, I would bring all this seasoning and wisdom to a truly worthy project—one of the great nineteenth-century American clippers. I even knew the vessel I would build: Donald McKay's legendary *Flying Fish*.

I finally went to sea on my own, to learn the ways of modern warships: aircraft carriers, destroyers, submarines. I learned that seafaring meant being cold, wet, hungry, tired, bored, and, occasionally, exhilarated or scared out of my wits. I encountered the perils posed not only by an uncaring ocean but by my own inattention and lack of experience. Learning to stand top watch while under way threw new light on competence, responsibility, authority. I survived; I began to grow up.

The years passed and I came ashore again, to edit scholarly books at a university press. Along the way I had collected a wife, a very small child, a charming but temperamental French automobile, monthly rent payments, doctors, dentists, shoe repair shops, and a number of other things that had not occurred to me during those carefree college years. The years at sea had allowed no time for model building, and the subsequent scramble for a civilian job and learning a new profession did not encourage anything so frivolous and expensive as tackling a large clipper. Or so I thought.

Somehow, I found myself one hot Sunday afternoon in the hand bindery at the Press; it was about a hundred degrees as I gingerly gave another quarter turn to the handwheel of the binding press. If I didn't tighten enough, there would be gaps in the sandwich of pine planks; too much and all the glue would squeeze out, or, worse yet, the planks would skate across the film of glue and hydroplane out of position, leaving me with a useless and costly stack of lumber. In my haste to get on with it, I had forgotten that a few one-inch brads judiciously placed at the center of each lift would have avoided the glue-skating problem, and I need not have been in this swivet of anxiety. As it was, I was lucky to work in one of the few publishing houses with its own bindery, where in the idle weekend hours I could avail myself of the luxury of this giant clamp.

The glue seemed to be squeezing out nicely, but not too much, and a swipe with a damp rag showed my pencil marks neatly lined up: all seemed well. Already she looked like a ship, the lifts—each a horizontal section of the hull at a given height above the keel, sawn out and laid atop the one beneath—creating a rough but recognizable approximation of her shape. Many hours with rasps and gouges lay ahead before that shape emerged, but I was on my way. I could not foresee the importance that epoxy auto-body putty would hold for me as I sought the elusive fair curves denied by the whimsy of natural wood grain and my own impatience. Nor could I imagine the sheets of basswood I would butcher before finding just the right shape for the bulwarks and the wales beneath them. Least of all could I reconcile the frivolity of such an undertaking with the need to get serious about being a grown-up. The ghost of the Puritan battled half-heartedly with the Yankee adventurer—and lost. The project was launched.

I would make my way to the bindery early Monday morning, before the crew arrived, and liberate my creation. A good afternoon's work, heat or no.

So began a peculiar voyage—a career just under way, a family starting, a small woodpile struggling to become a ship. As the ship emerged, its builder grew, too, and the world itself was changing. By day, I diligently blue-penciled scholarly manuscripts, stealing bits of the night from my family to build deckhouses, flatten brass wire to strop deadeyes and make chainplates, and ponder how to simulate the copper sheathing that would protect *Flying Fish*'s hull from the ravages of the shipworm.

As the hull approached completion and spars began to take shape, the New Frontier called us to Honolulu, where a new publishing venture would open doors between the U.S. and Asia. *Flying Fish* got a plywood shipping container only slightly smaller than a piano and every bit as awkward to move. For months she plowed the oceans catching up with us, then sat atop my chest of drawers—the only place safely out of reach of two tiny pairs of hands. In the Islands, she acquired masts, stays, shrouds, and a fine coating of volcanic and coral dust that weathered her every bit as effectively as four passages round the Horn and provided a home for generations of exotic forms of mildew. I learned the fine art of shipkeeping with throatswabs and diluted Clorox even as I tapered her spars and tinkered with parrels, trusses, and jackstays. The romantic notion that *Flying Fish*'s proto-type had perhaps parted these very seas was only slightly tempered by the difficulty of finding the exotic lacquers necessary to finish her top-hamper.

Thrashing back the jungle that surrounded our house and regu-larly rushing our youngest child to the emergency room seventeen miles away over the mountains for relief from myriad vegetation-induced allergies added excitement to life and consumed enough time and energy to slow the pace of construction. Relief mingled with regret when a new job lured us to the shores of Lake Michi-gan. Back into the crate went *Flying Fish* for her second major crossing.

Even my growing responsibilities could not in the end prevent her final launching, however, and four years after that murderous Sun-day in the bindery, I took a final hitch on the starboard spanker sheet to put just a bit more tension on the mizzenstays and braces, raised the house flag, and stepped back for a look at my very own clipper.

She was beautiful. Everyone said so, I knew they were right. At the party attending her launching—ostensibly a cocktail gathering for faculty authors and my colleagues from the Press—she sat proudly atop the hi-fi cabinet as I modestly accepted compliments on her behalf. I cringed inwardly as less attentive guests brushed by her yardarms, which jutted into the room at kneecap level. A fast-moving skirt set the whole works vibrating like a harp, then moved off harmlessly into the room. I had never liked putting my models in cases; after all, the idea was to see the damn thing, get your eye right down at deck level and look this way and that, as you'd look at a real ship. Perhaps I was wrong?

No. All she needed was a safer perch. Tomorrow I'd see to that. Now I wanted her down here for all to see.

Next day she moved to the piano. We had no livestock, and the kids were well behaved in general and kindly disposed toward *Flying Fish*, despite the hours she had stolen that should more rightly have been spent with them. She became a beloved member of the household, the sort of character you don't find in every family.

From time to time I pondered other models, even went so far as to dredge up old plans and cut lifts for new hulls. But none went very far; too many responsibilities at work, I said to myself, need to spend more time with the kids. A new house—our own—with lawn, garden, decaying woodwork, and fading wallpaper.

I knew these were excuses, not reasons. The fact is, I was tired of building models, of the process, of the frustrations, the delays, the things that took too long and produced so little. I realized that it was not so much model building that I liked, but having the model itself before me; not the issue of hours of agony over years of doing, but the image, the icon, of the ship itself, freighted with its power and the dream of those who built and sailed her. *Flying Fish* would always be there, testifying to skill and persistence. She was my metaphor of accomplishment: This is what I could do! Now it was time to move on to more important things, time to get serious about life.

I was creating a reputation now: beginning to travel, to write, to deliver papers, to advise, to consult—in short, to succeed. Life was full, and very good. The years flew on.

The house was deathly quiet. The kids had taken a powder, and my wife sat disconsolately on the living room couch as I surveyed the wreckage.

"I had no idea she was even in the house. God, I could have killed her! Sara yelled at her, but she threw it anyway."

"She" was the youngest neighborhood tomboy, barely seven, a tiny terror trailing disaster in her wake. "It" was a rubber ball that had just that afternoon sailed through the rigging of *Flying Fish* in what had seemed a relatively secure mooring atop the piano. The mainmast was snapped off neatly above the maintop and now pointed straight down at the deck in a hurrah's-nest of spars, sheets, shrouds, stays, and braces. The fore was relatively intact, but the mizzen topgallant had been sheared off as the mizzenstays carried away the main. All in all, a thorough job.

The first phone call at the Press was only a mild shock, followed by anger and depression. Only at home, viewing the disaster for the first time, did I comprehend its scope and its meaning. I had never calculated the hours I gave to the building of the *Flying Fish* any more than I had counted the times I had looked at her with pleasure ever since. All gone! Too saddening and too difficult to think about undoing and redoing all that loving work. No time for that now; the house—our first—needed far too much work. Pride of ownership demanded fresh wallpaper and paint, and prudent stewardship dictated the replacement of much of the board-and-batten siding on the north side. More paint, and of course there were the lawn and garden. Not to mention the growing demands of an increasingly responsible job.

The father came to apologize, commiserate, consult. Good-hearted soul, who only a few weeks before had murdered my one good chisel in removing putty from the window broken by the same kid.

"You could sister it up, tighten those lines up, she'd probably be all right." We both knew better.

"No big deal," I said, and suddenly I realized I meant it. No one had been hurt; far worse things had happened, and would happen, to me. I was, after all, a mature adult, and as Mom always said, "Blessed be nothing." *Flying Fish* was only a thing, after all, and things could be fixed. But first, there was the job, the family, the house, the lawn . . .

We shook hands, agreed that kids would be kids, and I put *Flying Fish* atop the tool cabinet to deal with another day.

That day was long coming: another step up the professional pyramid took us back to the East Coast, the crippled clipper hiding in her case. I took her out for a look, reaffirmed my judgment that I had neither the time nor the inclination to deal with her, and consigned her once more to the top of the tool cabinet.

The new job was all an aspiring young publisher could ask: a heady taste of real challenge and leadership, opportunities to see and be seen in the great wide world of books. I had paid my dues, moved up through the ranks, done my thing. I lunched with Important People, sat on government committees, traveled to obscure nations that no tourist would even think of visiting, consulted for movers and shakers from all over. Long hours, difficult commute, more time stolen from those close to me. But that was the price of success, wasn't it? Life at the top was a perpetual struggle against the law of gravity. To lose one's balance was to fall.

The pain was the worst I had ever felt. I was half sitting, half lying against the cellar wall amidst the remains of the stool on which I had been standing when the steel window frame I was trying to replace crashed through it. The toe it encountered briefly on its descent was not the first I had broken, but it was certainly the most painful—a bright icy point of pain beyond comprehension; it was the surrounding foot that, in sympathy, really hurt.

I was alone. My wife had gone to fetch help from the nearest neighbor, a quarter mile away on our country hilltop. In advancing shock, I stared about me, and suddenly became aware of *Flying Fish* just beneath the floor joists, where she fit perfectly by virtue of her missing main topgallant mast. You too, pal, she seemed to say; it can happen to anyone.

But this was not supposed to happen to me; I was not meant to self-destruct replacing steel cellar windows. In that seeming clarity of mind that sometimes comes with shock, it came to me that I had lost touch with other things that mattered. Like the canary in the coal mine, *Flying Fish*—a crippled, inanimate bundle of sticks and string—was telling me of my danger: too many birthdays missed, too many mistakes made, too many relationships untended to. That she remained dismasted, dusty, disowned was but a symptom of my larger losses and failures. With the chill of shock came the certainty that I was adrift, off course, disoriented by my own delusions of success. Somehow, despite all I had learned, all I had accomplished, I had forgotten those simple lessons all seafarers learn: vigilance for others as well as for oneself, attention to detail, however mundane, readiness for the unexpected, the certainty that the worst could happen at any time.

My wife returned with help, and administered Scotch, the all-purpose remedy, which deadened the pain enough for the three of us to get me onto my functional foot to tackle the stairs one at a time. *Flying Fish* receded into the gloom below, a sobering reminder of all that had not been done.

The toe mended in time, a useful harbinger in later years of important changes in weather, as well as a reminder of past failures and uncertain future.

It is not falling that hurts, goes the old saying; it is the hitting the ground. There came a day in my drifting when I sailed into an abyss—off the edge of the world, it seemed; I could scarcely believe that the collision with the ground had not utterly destroyed me. In one breathtaking, breakneck, stormy year, everything seemed to carry away—job, marriage, belief in self. Being adrift had been bad enough: being on the beach was worse.

The last box stacked chest-high, right up to the door of the tiny storage room, leaving just enough room for *Flying Fish*. Shaking almost uncontrollably from the exertion, I hoisted the old clipper from the floor, where she waited patiently, and neatly snapped the tip of the jibboom off against the doorjamb. It seemed not to hurt a bit after all the rest of the hurt. Life was mending now, like the toe all those years ago, but it seemed I had not lost my touch at inflicting damage. I gently lowered *Flying Fish* into her new anchorage, and somehow coaxed the bits of fractured jibboom back into place before closing the door on the debris of a lifetime.

There were friends, of course; a few old ones who stood by me, and new ones, casualties like myself helping each other sort out the debris and fashion jury-rigs to get under way again. A plank here, a piece of line there, some fittings, long-forgotten in some locker now pressed into life-saving use. And, derelict though she was, dusty and dismasted, *Flying Fish* too came to my rescue.

A strange turn of events, this: In short, interminable years I had traded the big desk, the telephone, the corporate lunch for a scarred old workbench, a tackle box crammed with the magic clutter of ship modeling, and an uncertain future in the business of building, repairing, and restoring ship models at New York's South Street Seaport Museum. In a few days I would begin another career as a bookseller in the museum's bookstore, blending at last my two greatest lifelong interests—ships and books. Along the way I had reinvented myself many times over—as cat and apartment sitter, executive recruiter, carpenter, and, of course, consultant. I rediscovered old values, found that responsibility and competence were better measured by the satisfaction, rather than the income, they produced; I polished long-abandoned skills, and found that they could still help me earn my keep. Some of these incarnations were fun, if strenuous, such as being the bartender closest to the festivities on the occasion of the Brooklyn Bridge's hundredth birthday party. Others were ironically humbling: being fired as a nightshift proofreader in a magazine composing room because I could not stay awake and kept losing my place. A few, such as running a book club for pilots and aviation buffs in a commercial publishing house, were downright miserable. I was still afloat, though, and now another leg of the voyage lay before me as I applied the finishing touches to *Flying Fish* for her relaunching.

She looked a little naked with all the debris removed, but at last, after more than fifteen years, something was happening. The museum was reopening after a major rebuilding and restructuring, and *Flying Fish* had been invited to join the party as a performer—one of a number of models from the museum's own collection, I had renewed my ties to this old friend. It was not easy, but it had been as full of hope as any healing process, both for me and for her. After all the years of neglect, we were tending to each other again, I applying my rusty but returning skills to her wounds, she by assuring me that while I could not repair my past, I could mend the present and improve the future. We had learned that the dues are never paid, that there are no life memberships, that you pay up every day.

The restoration was a hurried process, urged on by the bustle of workers on the restored buildings outside the back window of our temporary shop. I had to dispense with jackstays on the replacement yards and there was no time for some of the running rigging—sheets, clew lines, downhauls: but at least she would be able to hold her head up, and her black topsides and copper bottom were as beautiful as always; they had never lost their luster under all the grime.

At last, days before the deadline, she was ready, from six feet away every bit as handsome as she had been nearly twenty years before. She rested now in the huge case along with her sister *Flying Cloud*, the packet *James Monroe*, and a good dozen other immortals from the mid-1800's. In a few days, and for months after, thousands would stream past her and others, admiring a shadow of the great fleets that once lined the piers a block away. I felt good for her—good for myself. We had come a ways, and there were new courses open to us now.

Things are still not perfect, but *Flying Fish* and I have long since accepted—indeed, embraced—the imperfections of life. Her jib-boom tip requires more frequent adjustment these days, and parts of her head rigging are held together by loops of thread, casualties sustained in her new public life. One lifeboat periodically attempts suicide and hangs drunkenly from one fall. Neither am I what I once was; arthritis and failing eyesight mean I can no longer do the kind of work that brought her into being. But we are both very much alive, and looking forward to the next leg of the voyage.

THE MAKING OF
AN ADVENTURE

BY PETER MATTHIESSEN

IN LATE JUNE of 1950, when scarcely twenty-four, I engaged myself to marry. Much as I loved that beautiful girl, I also knew I was setting aside, perhaps forever, a longing to travel light and see the world. And yet so thoroughly did I enjoy the engagement party in Gloucester, Massachusetts, that I gave offense to my fiancée, her imposing aunt, and her widowed mother, whom I harangued from the foot of the stairs at an early hour of the morning until she came out, affrighted, in her nightgown and threw me down the key to the liquor closet.

A few hours later, not well rested, I departed for six weeks on Bonaventure, a small island off the Gaspé Peninsula in Quebec, accompanied by my college roommate and old friend, Sheridan Lord. We were avid students of ornithology, and the purpose of our journey was to visit the huge colony of pelagic birds on the seaward cliffs of Bonaventure. From there I would set off, some six weeks later, on the first real adventure of what would turn out to be a life of travel.

Between Bonaventure and the Gaspé shore at L'Anse-au-Beaufils (Son-in-Law's Beach, pronounced in the local French Canadian "Lance-o-Buffies") there rises a remarkable high rock or skerry like a detached cliff, pierced by a great sea-carved window on the rude Atlantic. Bonaventure is an ocean rock that looks even higher than it is because its cliffs are so steep and its plateau so small; the fields and forest above the cliffs extending more than three or four miles in any direction. Washed by the long sea swells, it appeared all but inaccessible, despite the "welcome" that its name suggests. Even in the island's lee, an almost constant heavy surge rumbled in the boulders beneath the cliffs. But in the corner of a steep rock beach was an open cove where a small boat, expertly managed, could be brought ashore. Old Captain Will Duval, who took us from the coastal village of Perce out to Bonaventure, arranged for our lodging at the house of a young fisherman named Walter Paget, where we were fed by his kind family a relentless diet of salt cod and boiled potatoes.

Despite French family names, the language of Bonaventure was English, suggesting that the little band of islanders had been isolated from the French-speaking mainland clans for a long time. In 1950, there were only a few households left, one of which had degenerated sadly; yet even the island madwoman made us feel welcome, coming to sing songs for us at Walter's house. She had a strange, plaintive, and quite beautiful voice, well suited to the old sea chanteys and railroad ballads of Canada's frontier days. Of all her songs, I remember the melodies of two, the refrain of one:

> Gathering up the shells from the shore, Maude,
> Gathering up the shells from the shore,
> When we were young on the beach, Maude,
> Gathering up the shells from the shore.

Most of our evenings were dead quiet; we breathed with the sea surge under the cliffs below the house. Television had not yet come to Bonaventure, I recall no radio, and we read and listened and studied our bird notes and books. Every morning, in early sea fog, rain or shine, we packed the sandwiches prepared by Julia Paget, bid our adieus to baby Ivan, and set out uphill through the fields toward the evergreen stands on the island ridge, where we entered the wet gloom of the spruce forest. On all sides sang warblers, thrushes, crossbills, tiny kinglets, and where the soft root path opened out on the fogbound cliffs that overlooked the gray Atlantic we were met by sharp gull cries and the eerie growling of the alcids, the acrid odor of guano. On this high side of the island, with its shrouded ocean prospect, the forest extended almost to the cliff edge. Within minutes we were among thousands of the bare stick nests of the gannet, a magnificent blue-billed gold-headed white bird that represents the great booby clan of the southern oceans in the North Atlantic.

Scattered among the gannet nests were bare scarps of razor-billed auks and murres. Another alcid, the guillemot, black with white wing patches and red legs, flew in and out of the rumbling sea caves far below. Here and there, around the rocks below, we saw the oceanic gulls called kittiwakes, or a harlequin duck, or the bright-billed puffin. In burrows in the bare white ground, under the spruce roots and tussocks, nested small black seabirds of the albatross family called Leach's petrels or "Mother Carey's chickens"; to avoid drawing attention to their nests, the petrels were nocturnal in their feeding habits, and we came at night with a big torch in order to see them flicker in from the open sea. The fog, the eerie wind-borne cries, the boom of the cold seas on the rocks—the sounds and smells stay with me to this day.

I had not been on Bonaventure long when I hit upon a plan to acquire a nineteen-foot codfish smack from Walter Paget and sail her back south around Nova Scotia to New England and Long Island; such an adventure, I thought, would reconcile me "tying myself down." And I had actually bought the boat when my beloved turned up on Bonaventure to inform me that due to my churlish behavior at the party and my failure to maintain communication since, we were no longer engaged to be married. Next day she departed, leaving me stunned as well as stuck with my great plan. A fortnight later, well plied with lore and warnings about winds and currents from Walter and old Captain Will, I found myself alone on the high seas, headed southwestward off the Gaspé coast.

The first leg of my proposed journey was to take me as far as Grande-Rivière, on the peninsula from where I would head south

across the Gulf of St. Lawrence to Prince Edward Island and Nova
Scotia; Sherry Lord would take our car back south to the United
States. My craft—christened the *Maudite* (Cursed One), as a symptom of my drastic mood—was a small, beamy double-ender, so
rough-hewn that the inner layer of her double hull of yellow pine
still had the bark on it. Forward, there was a small cuddy just large
enough to crouch in and a short mast for the gaff-rigged sail; the deck
was entirely taken up by fish hatches, with a tiny cockpit and stern
tiller. In the after hatch, Walter had installed a one-cylinder Acadia
engine that made the earnest *put-put* (in this case, *pot-pot*) sound of
gentler days. This engine was started by hand cranking a flywheel
and stopped by yanking the wire off the single spark plug; there was
no such thing as idle or reverse.

To accommodate the maximum number of codfish, the level of
the fish hatches was scarcely three inches below the level of the
gunwales, and the pinched cockpit where the stern drew to a point
was very shallow, so that in these rough seas, on this bright, windy
day, the peril of going overboard was imminent. The Atlantic north
of Nova Scotia is very cold, and since I was old-fashionedly attired
in cumbersome and very heavy fisherman's oilskins to ward off the
constant spray over the bow, and since one voyaged for hour after
hour off this steep and inhospitable coast without seeing any sign of
another boat, there would be little prospect of surviving a fall overboard unless the *Maudite* came to a quick halt, and meanwhile this
high blue sea seemed to grow higher with each passing minute. The
problem of stopping the *Maudite* with a man overboard was quickly
solved by securing a light line from around my ankle to the wire on
the spark plug; and the swim would be short since the *Maudite*
would yaw as soon as my hand left the tiller. But as the island fell
away astern, cold dread (as they used to say) descended as remorselessly as the cold spray over the bow. I was inexperienced in navigation, and knew that were I caught at sea by storm or fog, I would
be in trouble.

Of that first day, my fondest memory is the sight, as it withdrew, of
the great rock of Bonaventure, so warm and welcoming in aspect by
comparison with the dark stone blue of the northern ocean. The
green meadow of its plateau, its dark ridge of forest, rose and fell on
the ocean sky over the wake. To starboard lay a steep, forbidding
coast, its lace of white water visible from miles offshore. The coast
was broken here and there by a wave-swept cove where the steeple

of a fat white church rose among gray houses of a weathered settlement. The exhilaration of the wild blue day was dampened by big ocean swells that loomed up implacably on the port bow to buffet the boat. They lifted her high and rolled out hissing from beneath the hull on their way to their collision with the Gaspé coast.

In late afternoon, after some maneuvers, my craft rode the back of a big sea past the breakwater at a small fishing settlement and swung around into the lee. I was so exhausted after a long day of hanging on for dear life to the tiller, and so relieved to be in out of the wind, that I lay down on the seawall in my oilskins, arms spread, flat on my back, while the afternoon sun crusted the salt onto my face.

The second day was similar to the first: hard sky and high seas, fatigue and loneliness. My one-lunger engine was so small and the double-hulled boat so very heavy that, bucking the wind, the *Maudite* made little progress. At Grande-Rivière that evening, I was told by local fishermen (who took it for granted that I knew my navigation) that in a codfish boat, small and crudely made, I was *fou* (crazy) to head out across the Gulf of St. Lawrence toward Prince Edward Island, much less to attempt to sail the wild and desolate outer coast of Nova Scotia. Toward the end of the third day—just as rough as the first two—the *Maudite* entered the outer harbor of Port Daniel, Quebec, scarcely sixty miles by sea from Bonaventure.

The inner harbor of Port Daniel—or so it appears through the prism of forty years—lay on the far side of a bridge over an inlet, beneath which the short mast of the *Maudite* would scarcely pass. It certainly made sense to step the mast, but on this primitive craft, with the mast built in, the operation would demand more tools, skill, and energy than I could muster after a long day of sun and sea. Surely a merciful Providence would let me pass.

Black against the sinking sun, the silhouettes of hook-and-line fishermen on the bridge cried and gesticulated like demons— outraged, as I thought, because this strange vessel was making them reel up their rotten baits. Too late I recognized the note of warning. Having no reverse, nor an outgoing tide to slow her down, I yanked the wire to the spark plug, but the bow slid remorselessly into the arch, and the mast tip touched—only an inch or two. As the boat disappeared beneath the fishermen, there rose to their ears a satisfying *cra-a-ack* as the timber broke off at the deck and mast and sail fell heavily upon the helmsman. The spry among them crossed the bridge in time to see this outlandish craft emerge on the far side, its hapless captain floundering in lines and canvas. Ears ringing with loud and rural laughter, I clung futilely to the useless tiller as the *Maudite* beached herself on a broad mud flat, there to remain until the next high tide.

Through salt-crusted glasses I glared at my tormentors, then threw out the anchor and stomped off the boat, sinking instantly to the low crotch of my oilskins in the mud. With the strength of rage, I thrashed mightily ashore and forged on without a backward glance, for on the hilltop I had seen some sort of inn, and where there was an inn, it was only just that there should be a bar.

At the bar stood *un bon homme* named "Logger" Journeaux, who had arrived considerably earlier and made the most of it. This large-hearted man concluded upon short acquaintance that despite my outlandish appearance and boggy odor, I was surely the finest speci-men of mankind ever to fetch up in Port Daniel, and that rather than see his new *copain* disappear in the rough seas off Nova Scotia, at incalculable loss to all humanity, he would sling the *Maudite* onto the bed of his huge timber truck and take her south to Massachusetts as soon as first light put our celebrations to an end. In a slurred delivery of his slurred language, I warned him that he was taking on a three-day round trip, at the very least; Logger gestured expansively for another round. And at dawn, just as promised, the biggest truck I ever saw winched the *Maudite* out of the water at the base of the bridge and took off with a loud growl and snort of air brakes for Massachusetts.

With his stubble beard and massive hangover, my comrade, even that first dawn, was more black-visaged than I remembered him; he was scowling with the terrible suspicion that a serious error in judg-ment had been made. But he traveled with the same ferocity with which he drank, deterred by neither dead of night nor dread of day, and the following afternoon, in a boatyard in Manchester, Massa-chusetts, he tied her anchor line to a tree and drove out from under the *Maudite*. As she crashed to earth, he kept right on going without so much as an adieu, the huge truck venting a last loud disgusted wheeze of air brakes as it headed north.

A few months later, that beautiful girl decided on marriage after all, and a few years later she decided on divorce. I set forth at last on the long series of expeditions that would carry me all across the world.

THE FIRST BOAT

BY LOUIS D. RUBIN, JR.

1937

I GREW UP on salt water. Charleston, South Carolina, was a peninsula with rivers on two sides. When I was eleven my parents built a house up near the northwest boundary of the city, at the foot of a street named Sans Souci for the old plantation house that still stood there. (Like all French names in Charleston it had long since been Anglicized, and was pronounced *Sands Suey*.) Together with Sans Souci, our new house was on a bluff, the only such along the entire Ashley River shoreline, with a sloping dropoff to the edge of the salt marsh. From our front porch, through a line of water oaks, we had a view of the Ashley River.

An expanse of marshland lay between the shore and the river, with a creek winding through to the river's edge beyond. Cattails fringed the border of the marsh along the shore. In the winter and early springtime at low tide the marsh was brown-gray. As spring progressed the blades of reed grass began turning green at their base, the new life creeping upward until by full summer the brown was all gone and the reed grass was a thick carpet of green from shoreline to river. When the tide was high the water often covered all of it except along the edges, with only the tips of the reed grass visible, as if it were a lake, which on sunny days reflected back a prickled image of the sky overhead in a kind of *pointillisme.* The river itself was perhaps a quarter-mile wide at that juncture. Beyond it lay the dark green western shoreline of St. Andrews Parish.

A mile or so upstream, and out of sight behind a grove of trees, were docks belonging to some fertilizer and lumber companies. Several times a week ships passed by along the channel, preceded by a tugboat of the White Stack Towboat Company. The Seaboard Air Line railroad trestle spanned the Ashley a mile downriver to the south, and the hoot of the tug's klaxon signaling for the swinging drawspan to open, followed at once by a deep-throated blast from the whistle of the ship, alerted us to the imminence of traffic out on the river. My father bought several pairs of cheap binoculars when we moved up to the house, and whenever we heard the sound of a ship's whistle we hurried to retrieve the glasses from his bottom bureau drawer and went out onto the porch to watch. If the oncoming ship were of any size at all I was not satisfied with that, but ran down the steps into the yard, through the gate, and across our neighbor's property to the high point of the bluff to watch from closer up.

From the shoreline below the bluff to the river, out past the reed grass, was a distance of at most only several hundred yards. Yet for all that mattered, it might have been a thousand miles. For without a boat there was no way to gain access to the edge of the river. But my father was utterly uninterested in boats, sailing, or fishing, and I showed no aptitude for them. I did not even know how to swim.

I would have been thrilled to go aboard a tugboat, to look on from the pilothouse as it churned its way out to the entrance to the inner harbor, to make fast a tow line to an incoming freighter, then proudly lead that freighter up the channel off James Island, northward along the Cooper River waterfront past the High Battery and

Adger's Wharf to an assigned berth, then patiently push, nudge, and tug the ship alongside the dock where it could be made fast. But this was beyond all probability. I was no youthful Francis Drake, growing up at Plymouth on the Devon coast, listening to the tales of old mariners and plotting out the voyages he would make when he grew to manhood. I knew no mariners, ancient or otherwise. I only watched them from afar, admiringly, down at Adger's Wharf at the head of Tradd Street, where the shrimp boats and small craft berthed. If I dreamed of sea voyages it was in the most fanciful and remote terms, unconnected with any actuality that I could foresee.

All the same, I should have liked to go out into the marsh that fronted our house. The edge of the Ashley River seemed so near. If only I were able to get across those acres of reed grass that lay between the shore and the river, and when a ship came along to view it from up close . . .

My friend John Connolly owned a set of the *Book of Knowledge*, and once when we were twelve, I came upon a picture in it of a small boy seated in a boat, with a set of paddlewheels attached to the sides. The boat was wooden and blunt ended, with uncurved sides. Thereafter I thought about that box-shaped boat with the paddlewheels. With such a boat I would be able to go out onto the creek and into the surrounding marshland.

Then one day the idea came to me. *We could build a boat.* Why not? The boat pictured in the *Book of Knowledge* was nothing more or less than an elongated open wooden box. Surely John Connolly and I could build a boat like that! We could take it down to the little dock behind Sans Souci, launch it, and go paddling along the marsh creek in fine fashion. We could go exploring along some of the other creeks and pathways that led through the marsh, and at high tide move out onto the lake-like expanse of water that covered all but the tips of the reed grass.

I knew better than to mention any such notions to my mother in advance, for she would at once bring up the fact that I could not swim, and had no business on a boat. But if after the boat was built I was questioned about it, I could reply that all I had in mind was to paddle about in the creek itself, staying close to shore, where the water was no more than a few feet deep and the thick marsh grass close by.

Securing the materials for building the boat constituted no problem whatever. Although when we had first moved into our house there had been a half mile or more of open fields between us and the nearest built-up area off to the east, other homes were now being built, and there were several of them now under way just up the street. When the workmen were finished for the day lumber was left lying about everywhere. As for nails, there would always be a half-filled keg or two of those left open on an upper floor.

We did not think of it as stealing; what could the taking of a few boards matter, from among so many? It would not be appropriate to be seen carting such things off in broad daylight, but, having cased the joint by day and earmarked what we would need, we would wait until after dark, then visit the building site with my younger brother's wagon and haul home what we required.

To be sure, there were ethical considerations. It was improper to remove planks from off stacks of unused lumber. But once any portion of a board had been sawed off, then what was left, whether two feet or ten feet in length, became fair game. The same applied to nails. To pry the lid off an unopened keg would be unthinkable, but to requisition one already opened was permissible.

We began the boat the next morning, setting up operations on a pair of sawhorses underneath the side porch. It was to be eight feet long and three feet wide. The sides would be made of two ten-inch-wide boards each. Rather than making it completely box shaped, the lower part of the bow would be slanted inward in order to let it move through the water easier.

By noontime we had sawed the lumber and nailed together the sides and the bow and stern, and begun sawing the planking for the bottom. The tide was scheduled to be high in the late afternoon, and we were bent upon finishing the boat and launching it that day.

My father soon noticed what was going on. The night before he had observed us bringing in the lumber, but had said nothing; he, too, had occasionally paid visits to houses under construction. My mother, however, when she became aware of the project, had remarks to make along the lines that I had anticipated. I could not swim; therefore I could not go out on the water. My argument about sticking close to the shore and near the marsh grass did not convince her. Still, she did not positively say no.

John Connolly and I got on our bicycles, rode down Sans Souci Street to King Street and then over to the Chasonoil station at Mount

Pleasant Street, and asked whether there were any old inner tubes we could use for floats. The service station was one that John's father regularly patronized, and the proprietor was obliging. Not only did he locate a pair of inner tubes for us, but he proceeded to inflate them, place them in a tub of water to find where they were defective, and apply patches to the leaks. With the inflated inner tubes slung over our shoulders, we bicycled happily back to my house.

We had sawed the bottom planks, which were to run crossways, to approximately the proper length, and were preparing to nail them into position, when another boy who lived nearby, Billy Mucken-fuss, came over to observe for a few minutes. "It's going to leak like a sieve," he predicted. "You have to cork the seams."

"What are you talking about?"

"If you don't use corking, water comes in between the boards. I know, because my old man told me that's what kept boats from leaking. He said the corking swells up and keeps the water out."

This was a new problem. There were some bottle corks in the pantry, but slicing them up thinly enough to line the planks would be difficult, and there wouldn't be nearly enough to do the job, either. I decided to consult my father, who was out in the garden working on his temple orange trees.

"Not corking," he explained. "C-a-u-l-k-i-n-g. It's a kind of string. It's made out of something called oakum." It was sold at marine stores such as J. W. Luden, on East Bay Street, he said.

"Is it expensive?" I asked.

"I don't know. I've never bought any."

My father returned to his pruning, and John Connolly and I went into the house, looked up the telephone number for J. W. Luden, and called to ask the price of caulking. We were told that it sold for twenty-five cents a roll. Not only did I not have twenty-five cents— my weekly allowance was fifteen cents, and it was all spent by now—but even if we could assemble such a sum, to travel all the way downtown to the store on the Rutledge Avenue trolley car and then back home again would take up most of the afternoon, and we were eager to finish nailing on the planks and get the boat down to the dock and afloat.

We went back outside, and I reported the news to my father. "You'll have to save up your allowance," he said.

"Do we *have* to use caulking?" I asked.

"You could tar the seams."

"Have we got some tar?"

"No," he said, "but you could probably find some tar paper scraps over at one of those houses they're building."

We wasted no time in proceeding to the nearest construction site. I asked one of the workmen whether there were any scrap pieces of tar paper around, and was told to look over next to the toolshed. We did, and soon returned home with several armfuls.

By that time my father had gone inside for his afternoon nap. I thought of waiting until he woke up to ask for advice on how to apply the tar paper, but that would mean a delay of several hours.

"Do you think we're supposed to nail it over the seams?" I asked John.

"No, I don't think so. The water would come in all around the edges of the tar paper."

Our decision was to cut the tar paper into narrow strips, place the strips between the planks, then while one of us pressed the planks together as tightly as possible the other one nailed them in place across the sides. The planks were not quite the same length, so we sawed off any protruding ends flush with the sides. Then we lifted the boat down off the sawhorses, turned it right side up, and nailed two boards across the sides for seats fore and aft. With my father's brace and bit I bored a small hole an inch below the edge of the topmost plank at the bow, found a length of clothesline rope, and tied it to the boat.

What had especially intrigued me about the boat pictured in the *Book of Knowledge* were the paddlewheels affixed to each side, with two little handles for turning them. I was not sure just how to build any such devices for our boat, however, so we decided that for the present we would use paddles to power and guide the boat. My father had some lengths of one-by-one-inch boards stored underneath the front porch, so we nailed pieces of flat wood to the ends of two of them.

I had read somewhere that when a boat was launched it was considered proper to break a bottle of champagne across the bow. We had no such, but my sister was making some Kool-Aid and, because John Connolly was involved with me, offered to pour some of it into a milk bottle for the occasion, so we decided to settle for that.

The boat was weighty, but we managed to load it atop my brother's wagon, and with the paddles and the inner tubes placed inside we hauled the boat out from under the side porch, around the house to the front gate, and then across our neighbor's oak-lined property down toward the wharf at the foot of the bluff behind Sans Souci. My brother and a friend of his from up the street came along to watch, and my sister brought along the milk bottle with the Kool-Aid. It was slow going, because the grass under the oaks had grown high. I glanced back at our house to see whether our departure had been noticed. My mother was standing on the porch, watching.

When at length we reached the slope leading down to the water it became necessary to hold back the boat to keep it from sliding off the wagon. Finally we drew up to the dock.

I looked around, as if to fix the scene of the event firmly in my mind. It was a bright late afternoon, and the water, though not at flood tide stage, was well up in the creek and marsh. The yellow-green reed grass, the tall brown-furred cattails along the shore, the high sky overhead with a cluster of cumulus building to the south-west, were all in place.

In the seventh grade at James Simons School we had memorized stanzas from Longfellow's poem "The Building of the Ship." I remembered its words:

> *She starts,—she moves,—she seems to feel*
> *The thrill of life along her keel,*
> *And spurning with her foot the ground,*
> *With one exulting, joyous bound,*
> *She leaps into the ocean's arms!*

While it was true that our boat had no keel, the general principle held.

We removed the inner tubes and the paddles, slid the wagon from underneath, and dragged and pushed the boat onto the dock. Smashing the milk bottle of Kool-Aid across the bow, we decided on second thought, might not be a good idea after all. All of us were in bare feet, and there might be pieces of glass left about. Moreover, we did not have one of those bags of meshed cord that were used to swing the bottle of champagne against the ship's prow on such occasions, and if I held the milk bottle by its neck and tried to break it, I might very likely cut my hand. So we agreed to settle for pouring the Kool-Aid over the bow. "I'll do it," John Connolly said, straddling the bow at the edge of the dock. "Give it here."

My sister reached over and handed him the bottle.

"I christen thee—Hey, what are we going to name it?" John Connolly asked.

"I don't know." The idea that the boat should have a name had not occurred to me. "Call it *First Boat*," I said.

"I christen thee *First Boat!*" John Connolly declared, and poured the Kool-Aid out of the milk bottle and onto the bow of the boat. It was grape-flavored, and stained the unpainted wood purple.

He stepped back and out of the boat. With the end of the clothesline rope tied to my wrist, together we manhandled the boat off the edge of the dock into the creek. It plopped into the water and slid across the surface of the creek into the reed grass beyond. With the rope I hauled it back to the center of the creek, from where it drifted against the dock, as if it were saying, Let's get going!

It floats! I thought exultantly. It floats!

I looked down into the interior of the boat. There was a little water coming in along the sides.

"We need a bailing can," I said.

"Go get a couple of those empty tomato cans from under the basement steps," I told my brother, who had been watching the procedures silently and with great seriousness. He and his friend set out for our house, running up the slope at full speed.

"Well, let's try it out," I said. John Connolly collected the inner tubes and paddles from where they lay on the shore, while I sat down on the end of the dock with my feet hanging over into the boat.

"Give me the rope," John said. I removed the loop from my wrist and handed it to him. Then, with the inner tube looped around my neck, I stepped down into the boat, one foot first, then the other. The boat slid away from the dock and I grabbed on to the sides to keep from falling. Then I took a seat on one of the cross planks. The boat was a little wobbly, but gave no signs of upsetting.

"Here, grab this." John reached out with one of the paddles, I grasped it, and he hauled me back alongside the dock. Then he handed me the other paddle and stepped down into the boat, too. We swung away from the dock. Before I knew it the stern of the boat, where I was seated, had nosed into the reed grass. I thrust the paddle over the side to move us out. John did the same, and we turned into the creek.

"Hey, it's leaking!" John said. I looked down. Our combined weight was pushing the hull down into the creek, and the water was jetting up from between the planking in little fountains. Not only that, but the strips of tar paper, far from impeding its entry, had been forced up from the seams and were now floating around inside the boat.

"We better get back to the dock," I said.

About then my brother and his friend came back with the bailing cans. We maneuvered the boat alongside the dock and took the cans from them. After some minutes of urgent bailing we had scooped out a goodly part of the water from inside the boat, getting thoroughly drenched in the process. But the respite was only momentary; more water was swiftly coming in through the seams in its place.

There was no doubt about it, our boat leaked like a sieve, just as Billy Muckenfuss had predicted. Still, with frequent pauses for bailing, we could venture down the creek a little. So we paddled our way fifty feet along the marsh, until we reached a place where the creek forked. Several times as we moved along, marsh birds in the adjacent reed grass, frightened by the unexpected visitors, vaulted upward and soared off, startling us. The tide was high, so that we could see over the top of the reed grass, and observe the expanse of marsh and water on either side. "Boy, this is great!" John Connolly said, and I agreed. However clumsily and wetly—and by now we were fully soaked—I was afloat, on the water at last.

It was a hot afternoon, and the constant bailing soon became a chore, so we headed back to the dock and climbed out, leaving behind the paddles, the bailing cans, and the inner tubes, which by now were floating in the water inside the boat. John Connolly departed for home. My brother and his friend were eager to try out the boat. I was afraid to let them go off in the creek by themselves, but I let them climb inside and paddle around near the dock while I held on to the end of the rope. As for my sister, now that John had departed she was of no mind to try her hand at it.

That evening at supper I recounted the events of the day, and reported the failure of the tar paper that my father had suggested to keep the boat from leaking. "You mean you just cut the tar paper up and stuck it between the boards?" my father asked.

"We didn't have enough to cover the whole bottom with it," I explained.

"What I meant was you could build a fire and heat the tar paper,

and get some liquid tar that way, and then pour it along the cracks,"
he said. "The way you used it, you'd have been better off without the
tar paper at all."

But the likelihood was, he predicted, that the wooden planking
would swell from being left in the water, and within a day or two the
boat might not leak so badly.

John Connolly came over on his bicycle the next morning bearing a
ball of heavy twine. "My father says to wedge it in the cracks with
this"—he extracted a putty knife from his pocket and showed it to
me—"and it will help keep the water out."

When we went down to the boat we found it a dozen feet away
from the dock across and down the creek, high and dry on a mud
bank, with the clothesline rope extended to its limits. The tide was
going out, and there was less than a half foot of water in the creek. If
we could have pulled the boat off the bank and into the water we
could have gotten to it, but it was so heavy that it was impossible to
dislodge by tugging on the rope. We had to wait until early afternoon
when the tide had turned and enough water was flowing back into
the creek to float the boat off the mud bank. When we did we found
eight inches of water inside it.

"That's why we couldn't move it," John Connolly said. "That
water must have gone in there from the last high tide, early this
morning."

"I guess so." I thought about it for a moment. "But if it didn't drain
when the tide was out, then the seams must have swelled up some
overnight."

So they had. My father's prediction had been correct. When we
climbed down into the boat and bailed it out, some water came back
in because of the additional weight of our bodies, but far less copi-
ously than the previous day. It still remained necessary for us to bail
from time to time, but not nearly so often. Emboldened by the
development, we headed down the creek and this time did not pause
at the fork, but continued on toward the river.

It took us a while to get close to the creek mouth, both because the
creek doubled back on itself several times as it wound through the
marsh, and because we were bucking the incoming tide. At length
we came to a point where the creek executed a sweeping bend and,
more than a dozen yards wide now, ran parallel to the river, sepa-

rated from the open water by no more than a twenty-foot strip of reed grass.

Not only was the water in the creek flowing strongly, but there was definite wave action, so that our boat rose and fell as we paddled on toward where the creek broadened into a wide enclave and fronted the Ashley River itself. As we drew close, prompted by an identical impulse we lifted the blades of our paddles from the water and rested there to allow our boat's forward motion to cease, and drift in the current.

We did not stay in place for long. The powerful incoming tide quickly swung the blunt bow toward the edge of the marsh. Broadside to the current, the boat rolled perceptibly as the low waves moved against the sides and then slipped underneath us. In an instant we were being propelled swiftly back into the creek. Seated in the bow, John Connolly dug the blade of his paddle into the water to straighten us out, and I did the same. We were now moving rapidly with the current, and no longer in control of what our boat was doing. I reached down to where the inner tube lay around my feet and lifted it across my knees.

"Paddle for the marsh!" John said. Working strenuously, we were able to angle the boat across the creek and up to the reed grass. The current was flowing strongly through the grass, the tips of which were no more than a foot above the surface of the water and bending with the flow. John reached over and caught hold of a clump of reed grass, and I tried to shove the blade of my paddle into the mud at the base of the grass. For a second we hung there, but then the stern swung upstream with the current, the reed grass slipped from John's grasp, my paddle pulled loose from the mud, and the boat, now almost parallel with the edge of the creek, slid inexorably out into the creek again, this time stern first. Paddling hard as we bowled along, we succeeded at length in turning the boat, so that, bow first now, we went scooting up the creek until we reached the bend. The marsh grass was thicker and taller there. This time we let the boat be carried well up into the reed stalks, where after a moment we came to a halt.

"Boy!" John said. "That current was something!"

I was sweating from the effort of paddling, my breath was coming in gasps, and my heart was racing. I looked around. For now, at least, we were out of danger.

"Let's catch our breath," I said after a minute. "Once we get around this bend we'll be out of the river current."

So there we were, our boat caught in the reed grass, and the Ashley River no more than a few dozen yards away, flowing along powerfully, the mottled green surface flashing in the afternoon sunlight. We could see the docks upstream quite plainly, less than a mile distant, with a freighter alongside one of them. Downstream the black horizontal profile of the Seaboard railroad trestle was in full view, stretching from shore to shore. To the west, across the river, the far shore, which from our front porch had seemed so distant, was now visible in detail, the edge of the marsh distinct from the dark green trees on the land.

Eastward, back where we had set out, was the grassy bluff of Sans Souci, and atop it the house itself, white with red roof. To its right the line of oak trees partially obscured the sight of our house, but I could make out the front porch. Was my mother watching from it? It was too far off to tell. I hoped not.

This was where I had wanted to be, at the river's edge. How many times had I yearned to be able to reach it, so that when ships passed up and down the channel I could watch them from close by. Yet now I glanced anxiously upstream and down, to satisfy myself that none were approaching. The last thing in the world I wanted was for a ship to come along. When that happened I wanted to be well back into the creek, safe from any wake that might be thrown up.

What I had not anticipated was the force of the current. I had assumed that the river would be placid and still, like the water that made a lake of the marsh at high tide. Instead, once we drew near the creek mouth and encountered the flowing water of the river, the boat we had built for ourselves, which had seemed so completely adequate and sturdy back in the confines of the marsh creek near the shore, had rocked and swayed from side to side unsteadily, and we had been unable to keep it steered properly.

John Connolly must have been thinking along the same lines, because after a moment he said, "It's too bad we didn't make the boat wider, and put a keel on it."

"I don't think a keel would be much good in the creek," I said. "We'd be snagging it in the mud all the time."

"I guess so, but it sure would help out here."

We waited a few minutes longer, then after bailing the water from inside the boat we pushed against the roots of the reed grass with the paddles until we were out in the creek again, then set out for home, rounding the bend and then back up the creek, moving beyond the reach of the river's flow, along the creek. Another turn, and we were pointed toward the bluff.

Stroking along almost without effort as the incoming tide bore us with it, I felt proud of our boat and what we had done. However uncertain and even perilous the edge of the river itself might be, I was satisfied that the marshland and the creeks that led through it were thoroughly within my competence. No longer would I have to stand on the shore at flood tide and watch the water cover the reed grass. I could go out on it. And on our voyage down and up the creek and back again, I had seen that there were all kinds of smaller side creeks leading off into the marsh. Where did they go? From now on, when the tide permitted I could travel anywhere I wanted in the marsh.

We moved up the creek toward the dock. When we got there we pulled the boat up into the marsh grass next to the dock and tied it close, so that tomorrow morning when the tide was out we could try pressing the twine into the seams. But now that the boat was leaking only moderately it was no longer so important. A little bailing here and there was no trouble, not for a boat that could take me to the edge of the river or wherever else in the marsh I might want to go.

If my mother knew or suspected what we had done, she gave no indication of it. I told my father about the way his prediction about the planks swelling had worked out. He made no comment. Matters having to do with boats were without interest for him. In a box of old photographs up in our attic there was a yellowed picture of him, my Uncle Manning, and their friend Octavus Roy Cohen, who became a famous writer, in a fishing boat of some kind, taken when they seemed to have been in their late teens. I asked him about it, but he said only that they had rented boats occasionally and gone fishing out in the harbor. He must long since have ceased to take any pleasure in such activities, because I had never known him to go fishing or boating.

John Connolly soon lost interest, too, but I did not. As the summer went on I came to be much more adept at handling the little boat. Not only did I explore all through the marsh, following the numerous side creeks and on flood tides cruising out upon the tidal lake that covered all but the tips of the reed grass, but on several occasions I went back to the mouth of the creek and even out onto the river itself. But it was always, and only, at times of slack tide, and only for brief periods. On one such expedition I even attached a wooden pole vertically to the boat and fashioned a crude sail—out of very porous burlap material, fortunately, for without a keel the boat would certainly have been capsized by the first good gust of wind. That day I made my way along the edge of the marsh for several hundred feet before turning and paddling back to the creek.

That day, too, my mother was watching. I can only guess what anxiety she must have known when she saw me out there by myself on the Ashley River, in a tiny, keelless, coffin-shaped wooden boat with a sail, in twenty-five feet of river water—for the ship channel led close to the marsh's edge at that point. Yet she never said anything to me, never gave the slightest indication that she was aware of what I was doing with the boat! Was it stoicism on her part? Did she feel that she ought to allow me, as a boy, to take chances on my own? I doubt it; my mother was otherwise in no way reticent about expressing her opinion about my activities. It may have been that she, too, did not realize just how dangerous what I was doing was.

Whatever it was, I am reasonably sure that she was more than a little gratified and relieved when a large pea-green-painted U.S. Army Corps of Engineers dredge showed up in the Ashley River that fall. In the months that followed there was much tooting of whistles, blowing of sirens, ringing of bells, and shifting of suction pipes as the dredge worked methodically away at deepening and widening the ship channel. In so doing, it pumped out thousands of tons of white sand all along the edge of the marsh, creating a chain of small islands and completely sealing off the mouth of the creek behind Sans Souci.

Years were to pass before I was able to acquire another boat, but thereafter I have never been without at least one, and usually several at a time. Yet the clumsy wooden boat that John Connolly and I built more than half a century ago meant most to me of all. Every boat I have ever acquired as an adult, whether old or new, sail or power, has represented, in a very real sense, an attempt to reproduce that one early experience.

A GOOD
WORKING BOAT

BY GEOFFREY NORMAN

THE TRIP I had in mind was . . . well, unusual. And the man I was calling was a total stranger. I had his name, on a business card that also carried his telephone number, and I had seen his boat earlier in the day, down at the dock. I liked the look of the boat. It was not graceful by any means, or lavish in the fashion of the big sport-fishermen and cruisers that have become such a common sight along the Gulf Coast in the last decade or so. But the *Quester* had the kind of beauty that is a by-product of utility. Sports cars have one kind of beauty. Pickup trucks have another. In the world of boats, *Quester* was plainly a pickup, but a stepsider with big tires, a rebuilt engine, fifty thousand miles on the odometer and a gun rack in the cab. Just the right boat for what I had in mind.

Question was, would the owner, one Captain Joe Madden, agree. That's what I was calling to discuss.

"Hel-LO." The voice at the other end was full of enthusiasm. I took that to be a good sign.

"Captain Madden?"

"You got him."

"Captain," I said, sounding, even to myself, like a man trying to sell shares in some oil lease scheme. "I picked up your card this morning and I want to talk to you about a charter."

"Great. When do you want to go?"

"Well, before we get into dates, maybe I'd better tell you exactly what I have in mind." Now I sounded like somebody who was about to suggest some smuggling.

"I'm game for anything," he said, "so long as its legal."

"It's legal," I said.

"Then tell me about it."

So I explained. "What I want to do is a little snapper fishing and a little diving."

"No problem, long as the divers are certified."

"Well," I said, "there are three divers and we are all certified. My wife and I have a fair amount of experience. I'd say we are competent intermediate divers."

"Sounds good."

"The third diver, my sister, is open water certified but she has not been diving since she got her certification. That was a couple of months ago. She'd like to have someone who is instructor qualified to go with her as her buddy."

"That would be me," Madden said. "And I'd be proud to do it."

"Good," I said. "That's fine. Now let me tell you about the rest of my crew."

"All right."

"I have two children," I said. "Girls, six and nine years old. They won't be diving, of course, but they'd like to get some snapper fishing in and see some sights."

"No problem. We've been running across a lot of turtles the last few days. I expect I could give them a look at one of those."

"They'd love that," I said. "And to round things out, there is my mother and a friend she'd like to bring along. They are in their sixties. But game."

"Sounds like a great trip," Madden said. He still sounded enthusiastic. If there was any insincerity in his voice, I couldn't detect it.

This made me wonder about the man.

On the morning of our trip, I checked the dive gear and loaded it. Then I went into town, first to a dive shop where I rented tanks, then stopped by a Popeyes, where I bought a couple of buckets of chicken, one spicey and one mild. I loaded two coolers with ice. Filled one with beer and the other with soda and fruit juice. My wife packed a boat bag with towels, sun block, seasickness pills, and other necessities. The girls helped her make some potato salad and a batch of chocolate chip cookies. They were excited about the trip and eager to get on with it.

"Do you think we'll see a whale?" the younger one asked. I had seen one a couple of weeks earlier, when I was fishing for marlin with an old friend in his boat.

"I wouldn't count on it," I said. "I've only seen one in my whole life."

"And he's a lot older than you," my other daughter said, sounding wise.

The younger daughter seemed disappointed.

"But we might see some other things."

"What?"

"Well, the captain said they'd been seeing some turtles."

"Turtles?"

"Yes," I said. "The big ones that live in the ocean."

"How big?"

"Bigger than that table," I said.

"*Really?*"

"Really," I said.

"Have you ever seen one that big?"

"Sure," I said. "Lots of them."

"Wow," she said. Her eyes were wide with anticipation. "If we see one, can we catch it and keep it for a pet?"

My older daughter rolled her eyes. "Even if you could catch one," she said haughtily, "where would you keep it?"

"Maybe in a swimming pool?"

That discussion continued until it was time to grab sunglasses, visors, and boat shoes and leave for our adventure.

Captain Joe Madden was waiting at the dock. He was a burly man but nimble, like most people who have spent a lot of time around boats. His skin was so tanned that it could have been stained and he had a quick smile and plenty of chatter.

"Morning, morning," he said happily, "looks like we got us a great day for it, doesn't it. There'll be a little roll in the pass but after that it ought to be nice and calm. Here, let me help you with that."

We loaded the tanks and the rest of the gear. Then he helped my mother and her friend aboard. He called them both Darlin'. Called my daughters Miss Hadley and Miss Brooke. My sister, Miss Brenda. Introduced us all to his mate, another burly, friendly man whose name was Pete. Captain Joe called him Pedro.

When we were all aboard and the gear was stowed, he said, "Pedro, you want to slip that bow line so we can get out of here and go fishing."

He climbed up the ladder to the fly bridge, threw the engine into gear, and eased the *Quester* out of its slip, down the line of boats, then out into the channel, which was a portion of the intracoastal waterway. We were about fifteen miles from the mouth of Pensacola Bay and the Gulf of Mexico.

There was something reassuring and familiar about the short cruise to the pass. I have spent a lot of time on that stretch of the Gulf Coast between Destin, Florida, and Mobile, Alabama. Parts of it were still legitimately wild when I was growing up. I remember one island some six or seven miles long, totally uninhabited except for rattlesnakes, feral pigs, and other kinds of vaguely threatening creatures. I liked going out to that island by myself, or with a friend, in a small skiff, to explore and fish and imagine myself in the sort of roles boys used to dream about—pirate, shipwreck victim, solitary hunter.

In those days, it was plain even to a kid that these upper reaches of the Gulf Coast lacked glamour. In the American consciousness, Miami Beach was a real beach. Certain California beaches also qualified. And some on Long Island. But a beach that could not be reached by automobile, where there were no dwellings, and no places to buy a drink and a meal . . . that was just "coastline" or something. Certainly it was no beach.

I, of course, loved the Gulf Coast for its lack of cachet. And nothing spoke more eloquently of its backwardness than the boats people used to work its waters. Commercial fishermen and shrimpers, oystermen and a few charter captains managed to make a living along our coast. And they did it from the damnedest-looking collection of old locally made wooden boats that has ever been seen. These were the days when mahogany was the material of choice in boats. But nobody along the Gulf Coast where I lived had the money to make a boat from mahogany. So they used local juniper and cypress. They painted the bottoms with red anti-fouling paint. They used all manner of engines for power. Some diesels were designed for marine use. Others had been pulled from farm tractors and jury-rigged beyond recognition. A few captains chanced gasoline engines and, every now and then, a boat would blow up and burn to the waterline.

The boats were tubby and inelegant—especially when stacked up against the Chris Crafts that people in Miami favored and which we knew about chiefly through pictures in magazines. But as I learned about the boats along our coast—and spent some time around the men who ran them—my feelings about them changed from defensiveness to pride. They may not have been long on looks but they could do any job you could imagine. The captains routinely went out into the Gulf, way offshore, and found limestone banks with a lead line. They'd anchor over these banks and, using hand lines, load the boat with red snapper, which in those days was still pretty much our secret.

Some of the boatmen, I learned, had hauled rum during Prohibition—you can imagine how much that did for their esteem in my fevered imagination. Some of them would charter for the occasional rich man and take him out to catch tarpon or marlin or big king mackerel; catching that kind of fish was nothing to them.

My favorite story about one of these boatmen was the one about a cow. Seems this man, in addition to fishing, was running a few head on whatever open land he could find and decided to put a couple out on a little island like the one where I used to go exploring. Things went along fine until one day there was a storm and the thunder and lightning frightened the cows so badly that one of them ran into the water and started to swim for it.

Well, the cow got sucked down into the pass where the current carried her out past the breakers and into the sea, maybe half a mile offshore. By this time, the poor animal was so disoriented and frightened that it started swimming *south*, away from the shore.

"Damned animal was heading for Cuba," the man who owned it told me.

Somebody had seen the cow as it was being swept, bawling insanely, through the pass and had driven over to the owner's dock to tell him about it.

"Nothing I could do but fire up the engine and go out looking for that cow. If a rattlesnake had bitten that cow, on the island where I put her, that wouldn't have bothered me. But for some reason I couldn't stand the idea of sharks getting to her."

So he steamed out through the pass and, calculating winds and tide, decided where to look for his lost cow. He spent the rest of the day looking and didn't find her until last light, when he was two or three miles from shore.

"I was by myself and there was no way I was going to get that cow on board, even with a snatch block. So I just lashed her to the side and turned for shore. She was too tired to make a sound. I worried about sharks until we were back inside the pass."

The breadth of skill and competence represented by that story was, to me, undeniable. The man was not just a first-class seaman but also something of a cowboy. Crunch and Des *and* Shane all in one. Or maybe Harry Morgan. I might have been reading Hemingway by the time I heard that story.

It seemed self-evident that Gulf Coast boat captains were the best in the world, and for a long time I wanted to grow up and be one. And if they were the best captains, then it followed logically that theirs were the best boats—even if they looked like overworked tubs. Their dowdiness became an essential part of their appeal.

That was a long time ago and, for several years now, the empty island where I used to go exploring has been filled with lavish, half-million-dollar homes. There may be one or two rattlesnakes left out there but no feral pigs and no free-ranging cattle. The Gulf Coast is still the forgotten stretch of the American seashore—every fifteen months, the *New York Times* travel section "discovers" this hitherto unknown beach—but it is not what it was when I was a kid and felt like I owned it.

Since they could never see it as it had been, my daughters have had to endure my telling them about it, the way it was. Telling them over and over. I often get the look that lets me know they've heard the cow story before, more than once, and don't think it is all that special, anyway. Still, when I decided they were old enough to go out on a boat for the day, they were keen for it.

But all the old boatmen I had known were either dead or retired, so I went looking for someone who seemed to be carrying on in the old tradition. I decided on Joe Madden because I liked the look of the *Quester*—broad beamed, sturdy, no chrome or brightwork, plainly seaworthy and built for work (made of fiberglass like they all are these days)—and on the way down the intracoastal, I told myself I had done right. The fifty-foot boat with the brute Cummins marine diesel would plainly do whatever needed to be done along this coast, right up to rescuing a panicked cow. And Joe Madden, who had built her, was a captain out of the old school.

I stood next to him in the cockpit and asked him where he planned to go to find fish.

He had a few places in mind, he said, spitting snuff into a coffee cup, where we could catch some snappers and get some good diving, maybe even get our hands on a lobster or two.

"Natural or artificial?" I asked.

"I got one of each, to start with," he said. "I built one, two winters ago, out of an old barge. The other I found one day when I was trolling for kings and had the recorder on. I saw the fish and got the numbers. Day or two later, I went back and checked it out. Put on a tank and dove it. Guess what it is?"

I shrugged.

"Airplane. I looked it over real good and took some pictures. Then I went to the library and did some research. I'm pretty sure it's a Navy trainer. An old one, from back around the Second World War. There were fish all *over* that wreck and a couple of lobster down inside the cockpit. I don't think anyone had fished it, or been diving on it, before I found it."

He unrolled the chart and showed me the location of the old plane wreck, about fifteen miles offshore. Then he pointed to some marks on the chart in the area around the plane wreck.

"All of them," he said, "are trash reefs I made in the last three or four years. They ought to all be good if we don't have too much company.''

Trash reefs are not unique to the Gulf Coast but nowhere are they more vital or built with more gusto. Along the coast, boat captains like Joe Madden have made a study of trash reefs. Their livelihood as boatmen depends on it. Without trash reefs, most of them would have to get a job on the beach, and a man will do a lot to avoid that. Certainly he will take to hauling car bodies and other debris out into the Gulf and sinking them.

Trash reefs became a necessity when more and more people started going out into the Gulf looking for snapper. In part this was because there were just more people fishing and partly it was because restaurateurs had discovered the red snapper and learned what a fine fish it was. Snapper wasn't merely a wonderful food fish, it was also just about the most durable thing that lived in the sea. You could put them on ice when you pulled them out of the water and, as long as you kept adding ice, they would still be good to eat long after any other kind of fish would have spoiled. A Gulf snapper could be shipped anywhere, and fetch a good price when it got there, even if it had been out of the water for a month.

The limiting factor, when it came to snapper, was habitat. They lived around limestone reefs, of which there were a few, all well known and easily found once electronic depth finders and Loran navigational aids became available and a fisherman no longer needed to know how to use a lead line and take bearings from the beach. The natural reefs were easily and quickly fished out. This was also true of the known shipwrecks that existed in the Gulf.

Before there could be more reefs, there had to be more bottom structure, so enterprising fishermen took the obvious step of making their own reefs. Old cars being generally abundant and cheap, captains took to buying up a few, loading them onto barges and taking them out into the Gulf, where they would sink them and mark the location by the Loran numbers. In a few weeks, the car bodies would no longer be rusting eyesores with kudzu growing over them, but productive deep water reefs.

Cars tended to rust and disintegrate quickly, so fishermen began roping a few dozen old tires together and sinking them with weights. They also used old, cracked sections of concrete culvert and discarded appliances such as washing machines and refrigerators when available. The enamel on the surface of an old stove would keep it from rusting for a while.

Just about any kind of junk would do, and a man with ambition and a reliable source of junk could scatter reefs all over the Gulf in a couple of years' time. Every location would be carefully—and secretly—recorded in a notebook, and the numbers in that notebook would be worth a lot. You heard stories, now and then, about somebody stealing another man's numbers. People have been killed for a lot less.

On our way out, Joe Madden and I talked about the reefs we would be diving and fishing, until we came to the pass. Then I went aft where my daughters were sitting. I wanted to point some things out to them.

They were not especially impressed with the old brick and mortar coastal forts that defended the pass. When I explained that the one on the low barrier island, right at the mouth of the bay, had been held by Union troops throughout the Civil War, while the one on the mainland, on the distant high bluffs, had been Confederate, they nodded the way kids do when they are indulging adults. Too young, I told myself, to appreciate any of that. Best to wait another three or four years on the Civil War.

So I showed them the lighthouse. "Neat," the younger one said, doing her best. The older one merely nodded. We saw a large flight of pelicans, that Pete, the mate, identified as "the whole Cuban Air Force." My daughters did appreciate *that*.

The water in the pass was green and clear enough that you could make out the shape of the bottom, forty feet down. There were large swells rolling through the pass. *Quester* rode over them sturdily. My older daughter leaned over the gunwales and took the spray full in the face. That was a good game.

As we cleared the pass, we were followed by half a dozen porpoises, three on each flank. They kept the pace effortlessly and when they rolled for air, it was perfectly synchronized. They could have been a drill team. The show went on for ten or fifteen minutes, until Madden gave the engines a little more throttle and the porpoises all shot out ahead of us and jumped, six of them simultaneously, about one hundred yards from our bow.

It was an hour's run to the wreck Madden wanted to check out. We settled down for the ride. The heavy throb of the diesel was too much for normal talking. You could shout, but it was more pleasant simply to sit and watch the horizon and the occasional seabird that drifted across it.

Captain Joe, however, was working. When he found a large patch of jellyfish, he eased back on the throttle and changed course.

"What's up?" I asked.

"Well, turtles like to eat these jellyfish, so I thought I'd just check this place out and see if we could find a turtle for your kids to look at."

So we circled the area. The jellyfish were thick and white and made you think, strangely, of snowflakes. There were hundreds and hundreds of them, drifting indifferently on the slow surge of the tide.

"There's one," Madden said.

He pointed and we all saw the big, sorrowful head of a large leatherback riding on the waves like a misshapen basketball. Some of the large carapace was also visible. But it was the head, with the beak like an old man's nose, that we watched raptly, until the turtle dove to devour a few more jellyfish.

"Neat," my older daughter said.

The younger daughter was speechless for one of the few times in her seven years.

"I really appreciate that," I said to Joe Madden.

"See 'em all the time," he shrugged. "Especially this time of year."

The turtle sighting sustained us for the twenty or thirty remaining minutes it took to reach our first fishing and diving location. This was the old plane wreck that Madden had discovered and identified in some seventy feet of water about fifteen miles offshore.

"What I thought we'd do," he said, "is anchor over it and fish for a while. There ought to be some triggerfish and maybe a few snapper down there. Then we'll bring in the lines and the divers can go down and take a look. Like I say, we're liable to find us a couple of lobsters, too."

"Sounds good to me," I said.

"Okay then, let's do her." Madden throttled back on the engine and shouted, "Hey, Pedro, you want to handle the hook. Just get up there and let her go when I tell you."

Pete gave him a salute and walked around the cabin to the bow. Madden watched the Loran and when the numbers lined up he cut the engine back almost to idle and hauled the rudder all the way over. As *Quester* made a series of tight circles, he watched the bottom as it printed on his depth finder.

"Probably see the fish first," he said to nobody.

He watched for three or four circles and then shouted, "There it is. Throw it, Pedro." Pete dropped the anchor. I looked at the monitor on the depth finder and saw the black streaks indicating fish, about twenty feet off the bottom.

Madden killed the engine and the silence was a startling relief.

"Okay. Let's catch some fish."

Pete broke out the rods and began cutting chunks of bonito for bait. I helped my younger daughter with her rod. Older daughter did not, by God, need any help and didn't care who knew it.

"Dollar for the first fish," I said, violating my own beliefs about tournament fishing.

My mother caught the first fish. A red snapper. About three pounds. I gave her a dollar.

Before long, we all had some action. More triggerfish than snapper. In the days when men were using boats to round up cattle, nobody had bothered to keep triggerfish. They are hard to handle and hard to clean and, besides, snapper were plentiful. But as snapper became more precious, fishermen learned how to skin out triggers and a lot of people discovered that they are a first-class food fish.

After thirty or forty minutes, the action fell off. It doesn't take long to catch all the fish on a small reef. Captain Joe told us all to reel in and get ready to put the divers over. The kids jumped on the food and soft drinks while my wife, my sister, Captain Joe, and I put on our gear and went overboard and down the anchor line, into the warm clear water. The temperature was in the high seventies at the surface and the visibility was probably one hundred feet. Diving conditions are seldom better in the Gulf.

Joe Madden led the way down the anchor line and the rest of us followed. Halfway down, we swam through a large school of amberjack. This was a sure sign that we were above some kind of structure. Thirty feet or so from the bottom, I was able to make it out. It was about the size of a pickup truck, covered with coral and vegetation, surrounded by dozens of school fish. As I dropped down on it, the shape plainly became what it was—the fuselage of an old airplane. Almost without realizing it, I was a few feet above the cockpit, looking down at the seat, the stick, and the instrument panel. I wondered, fleetingly, what had happened to the last pilot to fly this plane.

At least two lobsters had made a home inside the cockpit. But they retreated deep into the wreckage and we could not get them out. I swam off, hoping to find a big grouper. I was carrying a Hawaiian sling because Madden had told me there ought to be some big fish on the wreck.

I found a grouper that looked to be about ten pounds but never got close enough for a shot. Also, I was distracted by the schools of bait, the dozens of large starfish around the wreck, the anemones that had fixed themselves to the plane's surface, and the other marvels that you see only when you dive. I was too much the rubbernecking tourist to be a good hunter.

Madden gave up on the lobsters so he could serve as a guide and instructor for my sister, who had never been on a dive this deep. He stayed close and pointed out the small tropical fish and the other sights worth noticing. This is the best way to overcome your initial hesitation—stop thinking so much about the fact that you are diving and concentrate, instead, on the environment you have entered. Even underwater, with everyone's face obscured by a mask, I could see my sister was becoming less tentative.

When I was down to seven hundred psi in my tank, I began to look for the anchor line. On the way up, I speared a medium-sized amberjack for the smoker. My wife brought back starfish and some broken coral, which impressed the kids a lot more than an old amberjack.

"That was a fine dive, Captain," I said to Madden when we were all back aboard.

"It's a beauty, isn't it," he said. "I keep that one for myself and a few good customers."

Madden got rid of his tank and while he was drying off, said, "Okay, Pedro, let's pull the anchor and get to another spot."

We ate Popeyes chicken and drank Coca-Cola while Madden ran a few miles to a new spot. My mother and her friend fussed over my sister, making a lot of how brave she was to make that dive and worrying about the slight mask squeeze she had experienced, leaving one eye a little bloodshot. My kids wanted to know all about what we had found down on the bottom and how soon they could start diving.

"Not long," I said. "Ten years or so."

"*Ten years*," the older one said. "Come on, Dad."

"Well," I said. "In your case, it might be more like seven."
"*Seven* years."
"Be here before you know it."

I asked Captain Joe about his next spot and he said, "I believe it's a couple of Chevrolet trucks, but I'm not sure. Could be Fords." Pete dropped the anchor, cut up some more bonito and we cranked in some more snapper and triggerfish. When the action slacked, Pete brought in the hook, and we ran to another place, leaving chicken bones for the seagulls in our wake.

The cockpit on *Quester* was spacious enough that we spread deck chairs and relaxed. This was something I'd always liked about the old Gulf working boats. They were long on cockpit space and short on cabin. Plenty of room for work and not many of the amenities. In the case of *Quester*, there was a small head below and a couple of V-berths. But no galley or lounge such as you would find on the big custom cruisers and sportfishermen. This boat spoke of utility.

As we moved from trash reef to trash reef, we saw flying fish, solitary birds, and huge schools of bonito. The sun had reached that point along its afternoon descent when the color of everything changes. Where the glare had been too much for unprotected eyes, there was now a warm orange glow that made the surface of the water seem restful and serene. Ashore, at this time of day, you would be thinking about cooking something on the grill and having a drink while you waited for the coals to burn down.

Captain Joe caught the mood. "How about one more short dive, then we'll ride in on the sunset."

"Sounds good to me," I said.

So we ran inland for a few miles and anchored over an old barge that had sunk in forty feet as the result of some unremembered misfortune.

"Nothing secret about it," Captain Joe said. "Everybody on the coast knows how to find it. But there might be something worth looking at and you may get your grouper."

So we put on the tanks again and swam down the anchor line. The visibility, in the shallower water, was not very good. Thirty or forty feet. But I could see fish, including a grouper that was large enough for its face to assume human properties. It looked like Edward G.

Robinson, all lips and scowling eyes. I never got close with the Hawaiian sling.

There were jellyfish all over the wreck and I was stung in half a dozen different places while I went back up the anchor line, empty-handed. Back on board *Quester,* I treated my wounds—externally with Adolph's meat tenderizer: internally with Meyers's rum and Schweppes tonic. Within minutes, I was feeling no pain.

Captain Joe let the kids take turns steering while he and I talked. My younger daughter enjoyed the job and stayed with it for several miles. She kept her eyes on the compass, resting in its binnacle next to the wheel. Occasionally, Captain Joe would interrupt himself to call out a slight course correction. "Watch your compass now, sugar. You're drifting a little too much to the north. Bring it around. That's it."

Our first sight of land was the thin, abrupt profile of the lighthouse. Then, gradually, the high-rise buildings that had grown up along the coast over the last decade came into view. By the time we reached the sea buoy indicating we were in the ship's channel, the sun had set. Captain Joe made a game of shining his spotlight on each of the buoys to startle the cormorants that were roosted there. The kids loved it. At the mouth of the bay, he took the wheel back from my daughter.

"If you want to do some interesting diving," he said to me, "right here is the place."

"In the pass?"

"Yep. You've got to catch a slack tide. But you can find all sorts of things on the bottom here. A lot of Civil War stuff. Cannonballs that missed when those forts were firing back and forth, every day. Anchors. Anchor chains. I've brought up a lot of stuff from right around here. I take it down to the historical society and research it in the books they've got. It's sort of a hobby with me. When you think about history, you realize there were a lot of boats working this coast before this one."

"But none finer," I said.

"Nosir," he smiled. "Not a one."

It was long after dark by the time we had run back up the intracoastal and reached the dock. Long past time for the kids to be in bed. There were a few dozen fish to clean. Tanks and dive gear to hose down. A boat to be washed. Tackle to be stowed. I offered to help.

"Nah," Joe said. "You need to get those young 'uns home. Me and Pedro can take care of this. Come by in the morning, we'll have those fish cleaned and on ice. Just pick 'em up and take 'em on home."

"Well, I want you to take some of those fish."

"All right," he said. "But I'll be sure to leave you that amberjack."

It is impossible to imagine any distinct coastal area without the boats that work it and the men who run them. When you think of the Eastern Shore of the Chesapeake Bay, you see skipjacks and the men who dredge oysters and tend crab pots. Maine is not conceivable without lobster boats and the durable souls who work that trade. The Gulf Coast is semitropical, vast, and various. There is no one boat design that is unique to this area because there is so much that any boat must do. Captain Joe Madden, for instance, advertises himself as available for billfishing, snapper fishing, trolling, and diving. No doubt he would do a little salvage work, too, if the price were right. A less scrupulous man might do other kinds of work with a boat like *Quester.*

Likewise, the boatmen do not precisely fit a stereotype. They are, however, almost unanimously resourceful, capable, independent, and possessed of a sense of humor. Madden certainly belonged to the breed and I was pleased that my daughters had met him and spent some time on his boat. They might, as a result, better appreciate the story of the cow who tried to swim to Cuba. It was, after all, part of their heritage.

As for me, I hope to go out again with Madden someday and anchor in the pass and dive for artifacts from the Civil War. With luck, I might recover a piece of shot from some pointless artillery exchange. All these years later, I thought, and my imagination was still invariably seduced by the thought of days spent on boats.

THE SHIP
IN A BOTTLE

BY ANNIE DILLARD

ON THE BAY SIDE of Cape Cod, my husband and I own a summer cottage and a seventeen-foot Thistle. A Thistle is an old-class boat, a racing sloop; it is open, so you can pile in families for picnics.

A year ago July we were embarked upon such a picnic when I found the extraordinary ship in the bottle. We had sailed into fog. The pale bluffs of Wellfleet's Great Island—our destination—seemed lower as we approached them. Then we saw the bluffs blur in fog and vanish. When the fog covered our boat, the wind died back and the children began to gripe. "Look—" my husband started to say to distract them. But there was nothing to see. Beyond the boat the air in every direction glowed. We could see each other in sharp focus—

this friend scrambling for a jacket, that friend with a white strip of zinc oxide on his nose. And we could see a circle of waves, dark and crisp around our hull. We heard the boat move through the water.

We sailed in a moat of clarity, a floating island like a flat galaxy of matter in a void. When a corked bottle floated by, I reached over the side and let it slide into my palm. It seemed something was in it, something hanging in shreds like torn cloth. It was a ship in a bottle; we all could see when I brought it aboard. The children, predictably, were not interested.

The bottle was sixteen inches long, blown of glass green at its base. It could have held thirty-six ounces of rum, say, or molasses. Its cork was tight. Someone had cunningly fashioned a ship inside it: a three-master, classic ship-rigged, beamy and round-hulled, and rather heavily decked over. The ship's intricate rat lines looked to be varnished black carpet thread. Her maker had so brilliantly miniaturized the rest of her hull, deck, and rigging, and each glowing canvas sail, that no one could guess its origin; you could see the ship only in its whole perfection and imagine a real ship shrunk. Every detail of her rail was carved walnut, it looked like, and her masts were spruce the size of matchsticks. Even the weave of the billowing canvas sails was in scale, so those furled on the yards did not bulge; and the grain of wood on the decks was in scale, as if lumbered from bonsai trees. On the transom, brass letters spelled FRAM. This perfect ship floated, as it were, on a crude blob of plaster painted blue.

I trust you have seen ships in bottles. I mention this one and its provenance only because it proved itself unusual six months later, long after I had forgotten about it.

Our summer cottage has no insulation; we close it every fall and flee. We draw the curtains and drain the pipes. The cottage abuts Black-fish Creek, a tidal estuary that empties into Wellfleet Bay. The mean tide range is ten feet; twice a day our moored Thistle careens itself on a mud flat, and twice a day it floats in the basin of water the tide brings. We have often heard that ice piles up on the tide line in winter—we have seen snapshots of muddy, spongy ice lining the beach below our cottage—but we had never seen it until last winter.

Last winter, my travels took me to the Cape in January. It was only a short jog to visit our own empty cottage. I was alone. Daylight was fading when I got there. On the windy beach I saw the shore ice heaped in broken slopes. The tide was out, but the yard smelled like ice, not mud flat. I entered the cottage and stumbled into the porch furniture piled inside. Because the house was no warmer than the yard, it seemed colder. The familiar paintings on the walls, the red end tables, the frozen couch, the junky lamps—all of these things looked haunted and dear, like beloved objects people put in graves with corpses, to accompany them.

I opened the front curtains. My eyes fell on the ship in the bottle, which lay mounted on the windowsill. My husband had carved for the bottle a wooden stand. We had bored guests all that August with the bottle's small story, what we knew of it: We found it floating in the bay, in a fog.

Now, standing at the windowsill, I saw something I will not forget or ever explain. The bottle's blue water had frozen to white ice. On the ice were many men and dogs; they lived and moved. I could make them out in the bottle's dim blue light. The yellowish Samoyeds fought on their tethers; men dressed in fur parkas stroked the dogs and faced each other, gesturing, with lively expressions and open mouths as if talking on an ordinary occasion. Wooden cartons—on the same intricately small scale—lay strewn about the ice, as did sledges, a potbellied iron stove, and debris too small to recognize. The ship listed on the ice, undamaged. All her rigging was bare; no canvas was in sight. A rough gangplank bridged her deck and the ice.

The men alone interested me. I smiled at them and hazarded a wave. They stood in twilight, unseeing. I resisted, barely, the impulse to knock on their bottle—only because I remembered chastening public aquarium signs to the effect that it drives the animals and fish mad if you knock on their glass, which is so precisely what I wanted to do that it seemed almost worth it. Down on the white ice in the bottle, one man beat his gray mittens together. He was talking, apparently, with two bareheaded men, both brown-haired, with iced-up beards. I could see their breaths. I could see my own breath, too; it was an effort to keep it from fogging on the bottle. The men, ship, and spars cast no shadows; it was too dark.

Two men—glistening fur parkas, dark leggings, high fur boots— stood at one edge of the ice and simultaneously tore off running to the other edge. When they reached it, they both fell on their backs and laughed. I could see the startling cuts of white that their teeth made in their opened beards. A cloud of white vapor appeared over each tiny face. The two men stood and made their way up the gangplank and into the ship; one of them opened a hatch on deck and walked into it. The other man followed, and so did everyone else; the men were clearing the ice. They climbed the gangplank, ducked into the ship, and vanished; I watched each last fur boot step over the hatchway, and watched the hatch close. The ship did not twitch. The ice held it fast.

Now it was dark, inside and out. The chunks of shore ice on our familiar Cape Cod beach held the last light like clouds. In the cottage behind me, I could see only a black heap I knew was porch furniture. My hands were cold. I looked from the window again and saw Jupiter north of Orion's bare shoulder.

Inside the dark bottle, over the ship, in the bottle's sky, dimly, a fabric of dark colors hung and moved. I could see stars through its spread. The lights waved and billowed across the sky; their low edge curved like a hem.

A little snow was blowing across the wooden ship; it blew across the wood cartons and iron stove on the ice. The dogs lay fanned out at the end of their traces, each curled, each facing the wind, each with its nose under its tail. A stovepipe on the ship's deck let out a thread of white smoke, and the wind took it.

Last week—in mid-May—when my husband, daughter, and I opened the summer cottage together, I walked in first and spread the living room curtains. On the windowsill the ship in the bottle looked just as it had when we first found it, just as it had last August: a wooden ship bearing many bright square sails, a rounded hull, a blob of plaster painted blue.

We settled into our summer routines. Last night I was reading on the couch beside the windowsill, as is my habit. My husband was out, my daughter asleep. I finished a book (*Great Heart*, the story of a Labrador canoe expedition) I enjoyed so much that when it ended in my hands, and I looked back through it and studied the maps and read the beginning again, I put it down in sorrow, and, rather than rise and find another book so betrayingly soon, I picked up the ship in a bottle.

As so often during this past week, I turned the bottle over in my hands. I searched the ship's wooden deck for sign of the hatch that led belowdecks. Again I sought in the rigging for men, and tried at the wheel, and the rail, and the peak. I searched the blue plaster sea. I looked under the sea, even—between the plaster and the glass, as if for bodies. But it was on the surface of the sea that I saw something new, a cylinder the size of a splinter. It was too regular for a splinter, however; both ends were flat. The cylinder tumbled when I turned the bottle.

It was with pliers, finally, that I uncorked the bottle. The cylinder slid into my palm. It was a log of cork; age or water had blackened it. A seam circumscribed it. With care I pulled both ends; the cork parted at the seam and revealed a wooden cylinder within. This inner cylinder was the size of a chocolate jimmie, of the sort children sprinkle on ice cream. In the scale of the ship in the bottle, the cork log was the size of a hand telescope and the cylinder within the size of a cigar case. I saw with something akin to disgust that this small cylinder was itself a case; a seam disclosed its wooden cap. I have no patience with small things and, frankly, no interest in them. Still, having come this far, I had to open the wooden case. Two pairs of tweezers did the trick. Inside the case I found two sheets of yellowed paper curled lengthwise. Written on the papers was a small text.

I have just spent the morning reading this wretched text under a microscope, with my husband, and transcribing it. I keep my only microscope at the Cape Cod cottage; in recent years I have looked through it only at sand. I laid the papers side by side on a glass slide and covered them with another glass slide. My husband and daughter stood by my study desk interested and eager. When my neck wearied of this sore work, however, and my husband took it over, the words came out so slowly. The words did not explain in any way what the ship called the *Fram* was doing in the bottle, or in the ice. In fact, there is no clear inference—given the peculiar nature of this bottle—that the cork case came from the ship. The cork case and its broken text could have floated into the vicinity of the *Fram* on the surface of the great intermingled sea all ships share. (Except, of course, that the bottle's sea is a pouring of plaster corked off on a windowsill. Every theory has problems.)

Under the microscope I saw a clear, smooth script—brown ink on yellowed paper. I expected a broken grain to the magnified handwriting, because magnified ordinary writing or print shatters under magnification and reveals flaws. But in this case magnification merely restored the document's original scale. I could make out eleven or twelve lines of script at the same time, before I had to nudge the slide.

12th There was so much visibility last week on the 8th [it began] that we bottled some extra visibility in flasks and stored the flasks, tightly stoppered, in one of the forward holds. Today, our first day of no visibility, a day of blinding fog, we made our experiment. The captain signaled me, and I signaled the mate: He walked forward into the bows, uncorked the first flask, held it in an outstretched arm, and released its contents into the air.

At once blue sky streaked from the flask and ripped across the fog. It was a banner of clarity, and it floated. In it, I could see a petrel dashing along the top of the water, and I could see calm seas to the horizon. I climbed the rail and looked down. Through the banner of clarity I could see several inches into the water, which was green, and filled with jellyfish.

The banner-shaped patch of visibility was ten feet long and as narrow as the flask's neck. As our ship drew along slowly (for there is rarely great wind in a fog), all aboard realized that we should soon lose the visibility over our stern. The captain gave an order, and a man, Larsen, on the afterdeck reached out with a belaying pin and snagged it. He moved it with care, rolling the pin until the center of the clear patch wrapped around it. He lowered it from the air, gingerly pinched it at a corner, and, trailing it from his fingers like a Chinaman's kite, carried it to the captain.

We were hard-pressed to keep the men from feeling of it, for we suspected, and rightly, that touching it would smear the visibility with fingerprints, or, worse, tear it. Accordingly, the captain held it by the same corner Larsen had used, and waved the men away. Slowly he brought a shred of it before his eyes. He looked through it thoughtfully, out to sea. He passed the flowing thing, as if it were an angel, to the sailmaker, who sat and brought his curved needles to bear on its corners. He fashioned delicate grommets there, and whipped their edges with cod line. Then the mate lashed the visibility on the lee bow between forestay and shroud. There it cut a slash of clear and colored vision in the fog. It revealed the sea and the sky, far and near in their proper colors. The pale fog lay all around the slash like a limed wall.

We sent a man forward for another flask. The ship possessed

altogether two dozen flasks of visibility. The captain will decide how many we might use now, and where he will hang them. We hope to sight Spitzbergen after dawn.

The pages ended here, at one paper's lower edge. My tale ends here, too, as my story converges on the present, and finds me at my desk. I have stored the small papers in the slide case between two glass slides, so the papers do not blow away. This cottage is old and loosely made. Even here at my desk I can smell the muddy scent of low tide visible beyond this upstairs window; the west wind carries it.

BOAT RIDE

BY TESS GALLAGHER

SINCE MY GIRLHOOD, in that small boat
we had gone together for salmon
with the town still sleeping and the wake
a white groove in the black water, black
as it is when the gulls are just stirring and
the ships in the harbor are sparked with lights
like the casinos of Lucerne.
That morning my friend had driven an hour
in darkness to go with us, my father
and me. There'd been an all-night party.
My friend's face so tired I thought, *Eskimo-eyes*.

He sighed, as if stretched out
on a couch at the back of his mind.

Getting the bait and tackle. What
about breakfast? No breakfast.
Bad luck to eat breakfast before fishing, but
good luck to take smoked salmon to eat
on the water in full sun. Was my friend's coat
warm enough? The wind can come up.
Loaning him my brother's plaid jacket.

Being early on the water, like getting first
to heaven and looking back through memory
and longing at the town. Talking little, and
with the low, tender part
of our voices; not sentences but
friendlier, as in nodding to one who already
knows what you mean.

Father in his rain-slicker—seaweed green over
his coat, over blue work-shirt, over cream-
colored thermal underwear that makes a white V
at his neck. His mouth open so the breath
doesn't know if it's coming or going—like any
other wave without a shore. His mind
in the no-thought of guiding the boat.
I stare into the water folding
along the bow, *gentian*—the blue with darkness
engraved into its name, so the sound
petals open with mystery.

Motor-sound, a low burbling with a chuckle
revolving in the *smack smack* of the bow
spanking water. *You hear me, but you don't
hear me*, the motor says
to the fish. A few stars
over the mountains above the town.
I think *pigtails,* and that the water under us
is at least as high as those mountains, deep
as the word *cello* whispered under water—
cello, cello until it frees a greeting.

We pass the Coast Guard station, its tower
flashing cranky white lights beside
the barracks where the seamen sleep in
long rows. Past the buoy, its sullen red bell
tilting above water. All this time
without fishing—important to get out of
the harbor before letting the lines
down, not time wasted but time
preparing, which includes invitation and
forgetting, so the self is occupied freely
in idleness.

"Just a boat ride," my father says, squinting
where sun has edged the sky toward Dungeness
a hazy mix of violet and pink. "Boat ride?"
I say. "But we want salmon."
"I'll take cod, halibut, old shoes, anything
that's going," says my friend. "And you'll get
dogfish," my father says. "There's enough
dogfish down there to feed all Japan."
He's baiting up, pushing the double hooks
through the herring. He watches us
let the lines out. "That's plenty," he says,
like it's plain this won't come
to much.

Sitting then, nothing to say for a while,
poles nodding slightly. My friend, slipping
a little toward sleep, closes his eyes.
Car lights easing along Ediz Hook, some
movement in the town, Port of the Angels,
the angels turning on kitchen lights,
wood smoke stumbling among scattered hemlock,
burning up questions, the angels telling
their children to get up, planning the future
that is one day long.

"Hand me that coffee bottle, Sis," my father
says. "Cup of coffee always makes the fish
bite." Sure enough, as he lifts the cup,
my pole hesitates, then dips. I brace

and reel. "Damned dogfish!" my father says,
throwing his cigarette into the water. "How
does he know?" my friend asks. "No fight,"
I say. "They swallow the hook down
their gullets. You have to cut
the leader."

No sun-flash on silver scales when it
breaks water, but thin-bellied brown, shark-
like, and the yellow-eye insignia
which says: *there will be more of us.*
Dogfish. Swallower of hooks, waster of hopes
and tackle. My father grabs the line, yanks
the fish toward the knife, slashes twice,
gashing the throat and underbelly so
the blood spills over his hand.
"There's one that won't come back," he says.

My friend witnesses without comment or
judgment the death and mutilation
of the dogfish. The sun is up. My friend
is wide awake now. We are all wide
awake. The dogfish floats away, and a tenderness
for my father wells up in me, my father
whom I want my friend to love and who intends,
if he must, as he will, to humor us, to keep
fishing, to be recorded in the annals
of dogfish as a scourge on the nation of
dogfish which has fouled his line, which is
unworthy and which he will single-handedly
wipe out.

When the next fish hits my friend's line
and the reel won't sing, I take out my
Instamatic camera: "That's a beautiful
dogfish!" I say. "I'll tell them in New York
it's a marlin," my friend says. I snap
his picture, the fish held like
a trophy. My father leans out of
the frame, then cuts the line.

In a lull I get him to tell stories,
the one where he's a coal miner in Ottumwa,
Iowa, during the Depression and the boss
tries to send the men into a mine where
a shaft collapsed the day before. "You'll
go down there or I'll run you out of
this town," the boss says. "You don't
have to run me. I'm not just leaving
your town, I'm leaving your whole goddamned
state!" my father says, and he turns
and heads on foot out of the town, some
of the miners with him, hitching from there
to the next work in the next state.

My father knows he was free
back there in 1935 in Ottumwa, Iowa, and he
means you to know you don't have to risk
your life for pay if you can tell the boss to
go to hell and turn your heel. What
he doesn't tell is thirty years on the docks,
not a day missed—working, raising
a family.

I unwrap smoked salmon sandwiches and we bite
into them. It is the last fishing trip
I will have with my father. He
is ready to tell the one about the time
he nearly robbed the Seminole Bank in
Seminole, Oklahoma, but got drunk
instead and fell asleep.
He is going to kill five more dogfish
without remorse; and I am going to
carry a chair outside for him
onto the lawn of the Evergreen Radiation
Center where he will sit and smoke
and neither of us feels like talking, just
his—"The sun feels good."
After treatments, after going back
to my sister's where he plays with her baby—
"There's my gal! Is the Kiss Bank

open?''—in the night, rising up in the dream
of his going to say, "Get my billfold," as if
even his belongings might be pulled into
the vortex of what would come.

We won't catch a single salmon that day.
No strikes even. My friend and I
will share a beer and reminisce in advance
about the wonderful dogfishing we had.
My father wipes blood from his knife
across his knee and doesn't
look up. He believes nothing
will survive of his spirit or body. His god
takes everything and will not be
satisfied, will not be assuaged by the hopes, by
the pitiful half-measures of the living.
If he is remembered, that too
will pass.

It is good then,
to eat salmon on the water, to bait the hook
again, even for dogfish, to stare back at
the shore as one who withholds nothing, who,
in the last of himself, cannot put together
that meaning, and need not, but yields in thought
so peacefully to the stubborn brightness of
light and water: we are awake with him
as if we lay asleep. Good memory,
if you are such a boat, tell me
we did not falter in the vastness
when we walked ashore.

RIPRAP

BY ALLEN PLANZ

For a long time I had to come up with the equivalent of migration. By late November I was off the water, the boat in its cradle, and I into my dreamtime. Some of my neighbors on eastern Long Island, summer people, went south for the winter, but most folks I knew stayed put and took their rest in the months of cold and darkness.

One summer for a few weeks I had a slip next to an eleven-foot dinghy which Willard Willis, a wiry sailor in his seventies, had sailed across the Pacific and was now preparing to sail across the Atlantic. During his interminable cruises he relied on yoga practiced on his perch on the transom in calm weather; in rough water he slipped into the coffin-like cabin and stayed watertight, praying. On his departure I towed him out of the harbor and around Montauk Point. A month later the empty dinghy was found floating in the North Atlantic. Sometimes when I get to cursing I think of him. I'd get that way, I reckoned, after a long life. Meanwhile I had a lively wife and family for many years, and the long nights of winter were lovely and intimate and you could still get up before dawn.

After my wife died in 1977, I kept to my yearly routine even after my daughter started college. There were plenty of women, but none of them worked out, and winter was a little more desperate. I got south a few times, delivering boats to Jacksonville and the Keys, where I could have stayed on since in those days a licensed powerboat captain with insurance had an open field to play. But I always came home.

In 1983, when I was forty-five, I was hired to captain a boat to the Thousand Islands in Lake Ontario via the Hudson River and Erie Canal. The trip was to be, the woman who hired me explained, an outing on the family boat, a forty-eight-foot Chris Craft Commander, then upwards of thirty years old. Miss Buono, a New York City lawyer about my age, was attractive and straightforward. Our pace would be leisurely, with overnight stays at yacht clubs or towns, and our guests would be various family members joining the trip up and down the route. The Chris Craft, named *Riprap* after materials made by the family construction business for jetties, was the boat children like Miss Buono had grown up on, and the trip was to be a reunion. She expected to dine ashore most nights, and I could join her or stay aboard. Though it was close to November, fall foliage was still on display and the weather mild.

When I arrived at the City Island marina on a pleasant morning, there were three nieces waiting aboard the *Riprap* with Miss Buono. I checked out the boat quickly, stowed my gear, and started a ship's log. We got under way before noon and picked a course through hundreds of moored craft toward the Triborough Bridge, whose span neatly framed Manhattan Island in the background. Then we slipped into the Harlem River, the *Riprap* with her newly installed twin Ford 225's handling the strong currents of the narrow passage with ease.

The *Riprap*'s bridge was arrayed with an amazing variety of electronics: four radios, three autopilots, two Lorans, two radars, three depth finders, a computer terminal, a course plotter, synchronizers, banks of gauges, hailers, searchlights, binoculars, telescopes, and compasses. I learned that family rivalries kept the *Riprap* well maintained and that everyone refrained from removing an instrument someone else installed. Overhead, the flying bridge held a slightly smaller array. In the engine compartment other devices were stored: tools, technical books, spare parts, scuba gear, and fishing equipment, most of it untouched. There were also two generators serving thirty-six batteries in three banks. But I understood the need for gadgetry. It kept one's hand in.

The women wore dresses and leaned on the rail to take photographs. The *Riprap* was clean, newly painted, her canvas white, her rich woods recently varnished. Under the bridges of Harlem we passed through brisk sunlight and cool shadow, then, without faltering, through the rips of Spuyten Duyvil. To the south, the Hudson rolled away in a bright haze that obscured the lower bay. To the north, under an arctic blue that stretched toward Canada, the river gathered the bulk of the Palisades into a darker shining. We turned and stood for Albany.

Two hours later I had troubles. Increasing roughness in the engines led me to check the ignition. I found pitted distributors and burned plugs. I replaced them with handy spares and got more roughness and backfiring. Barely moving ahead, with several stops and starts, we made it into Yonkers Yacht Club many hours later. There the women left for dinner and I scuttled into the engine room, where I despaired until a mechanic, summoned by the dockmaster, took charge. He diagnosed the trouble and reported that somebody had replaced the stock ignition with high-performance Mallory components. He fixed it and, at my request, inspected the power plant and electronics and declared them fit.

The next morning we shoved off with four more guests, kids and adult relatives. The day was calm and fair and river traffic was light and heading in the opposite direction. The view ahead began to display the scenery for which the river is famous. When we passed structures that looked like castles and the ruins of great estates, a guest commented that the Hudson is known as the American Rhine. Past the Tappan Zee Bridge the river began to narrow even though it was still tidewater. We were in the vicinity of the wintering grounds for the striped bass we caught off Long Island's East End, so I switched on the recording depth finder and watched the stylus stroke marks above the bottom that I took to be large bass.

In the late afternoon we pulled into a marina near Kingston and had drinks and then strolled into town to meet four other family members. We dined at a restaurant that was crowded with boat people. The place was a rendezvous for those with one goal: to go south. And the informal atmosphere was charged with their intentness to get there. I was amazed by where they all came from: Montreal, Chicago, Thunder Bay—the American heartland intersected by rivers flowing to the Great Lakes and traversed with canals. They talked of Florida and Caribbean highs, the Yucatán and South America. They were in a hurry, winter was on their tail. They were people fleeing the fierce dumb season of cold who thought we were crazy to be heading north this time of year.

Later, walking back with the girls, we saw the moon rise above the hills and shine down upon the Hudson, the lights of boats in the channel, and I felt a pang of loss. Stopping to listen to the valley wind work its way on the hillside, I realized how much I studied the weather when I fished through the hours of darkness in a small boat on tide race shoals. The sound of a gust could tell me the shape of the sea and the strength of the blow to come. On those nights, the rougher the water, the blacker the sky, the better the fishing—if you could stay out. Now a gust came toward us, stirring the leaves into an exaltation till some rose and fled against the moon, and I recalled many nights with many gusts and how toward winter you were always trying to beat the weather but never could. You got wet and stayed wet. You worked cold and slept cold. Then the sea closed down your business in storm and you were free and ready for winter. I was going to miss that this year . . .

The next day on the Hudson it was raining. The nieces departed with Miss Buono, who would meet me upriver. I made the most of the short passage by making some runs, figuring the best speed with rpm's, adjusting the compass by turning 180 degrees on my wake and noting discrepancies. I didn't really need a compass, though, because the computer worked, as did the autopilots and most of the electronics. In heavy downpours I stuck my face into the radar hood to see what I was about to collide with.

It was strange motoring up a deserted waterway, strange to see clouds sweep east out of the dark wedge of the Catskill mountains and drop down across the river in squalls. And it was strange to run a boat with land so close on either side. But when the rain stopped and the mountains fell behind, the Hudson opened on a postindustrial landscape, sparsely populated with abandoned piers, workboats, factories, and, behind them, exhausted farmland and orchards.

The bad weather continued and Miss Buono decided to meet the

Riprap in Albany for the weekend. I had given myself plenty of chores to do but still spent most of my time daydreaming about the boat and playing with the stuff stored in the engine room. One of the pleasures of being a freelance captain is that you get to drive different kinds of boats and handle fancy equipment. The drawback is that you have to learn to handle it fast. Very fast. There's a lot of improvisation in keeping the show going when, for instance, a 150-pound mako shark leaps into the cockpit or the boat next to the half-million-dollar Hatteras that you're in charge of suddenly explodes.

The *Riprap* was a hoard of marine artifacts and memorabilia. The library held everything from maritime classics to videos. The engine room featured a set of Snap-On tools, cordless power drivers and drills, various engine components, devices like a Mallory ignition, for souping up *Riprap*'s performance, and any number of navigational aids. I imagined Buono family members ordering various nautical devices from catalogues while awaiting their turn on her. And most of it was never used. There was a set of Penn Senator fishing reels still in their boxes, matching fishing rods and tackle representing thirty years of angling fashion nested in custom-built cases. (I came away with a rigging set—a stainless steel knife, pliers, and marlinspike in a leather holster that Miss Buono had seen me moon over and given me at the end of the trip.)

In Albany two days later I joined Miss Buono and other family members in a round of parties in the state capital. The family construction company did a lot of work for New York, and this is how they drummed up business. The weather turned mild again and we took a group of politicians and bureaucrats to a barbecue at a riverside park.

We turned west at Albany and entered the Erie Canal. We moved upland through a series of locks and the going was easy. You tooted your horn and the gates opened. Then you slid in and idled against the wall as the gates closed and water was pumped in. Slowly the boat rose between steel walls, and the slot of sky above widened. That was the best part, that rising into brightness. You felt privileged that the state went to all that trouble for you. Then the doors opened and the boat slipped forward into the Mohawk Valley, an ancient, gently rolling land that seemed empty, devoid of foliage and people. There was little traffic on the waterway, and what boats we did pass were heading south, their helmsmen bent over, intent on flight. We overtook a state workboat towing a log, the pilot vague behind the windshield. The locktenders themselves were a dreamy lot, waving from behind little shacks above the gates. I was dreamy myself, slowly breathing with the boat up an American canal, a remnant of a hydraulic civilization, like the canals on Mars.

Though the leaves were gone, the light was golden as the *Riprap* moved upriver in a soft Indian summer. The canal was solemn and barely moved. Once in a while the six-lane New York State Thruway pitched into sight, its cars and trucks speeding along while the *Riprap*, which was confined to ten miles per hour through the bottomlands, cast a crisply curling wake onto the banks. A few hawks swayed over the fields and, though most migrations were over, ducks barreled by on their way to coastal flyways. No herons stood on the banks and no fish jumped. Mist coming off the river in the mornings smelled of cinnamon and wet wood, and in the evenings ice crystals formed in the lines.

At this point the *Riprap* had six guests aboard, a family of four plus two students from Syracuse University. One morning the women were in the galley preparing lunch and a birthday party for one of the kids. The students horsed around with the kids and regaled us with adventures of trips on the *Riprap* when they were growing up. When the dinner bell rang, we gathered on deck and around a table that was heaped with food and a birthday cake. Before I joined in, I asked a cheerful Syracuse senior named Mark to take the helm while I went to the head.

Water made music on both sides of the forepeak as I relaxed and read an article in a yachting magazine about early Chris Crafts. The Chris Craft Commander, which I now captained, was a classic out of my youth, and it reminded me of when my father had a marina in Long Beach, New York. Though the marina was too small and too ratty for big Chris Crafts to moor at, they often fueled up at the dock. The *Riprap* was as beautiful as those on the glossy pages I was looking at, and I imagined the both of us well into the next century, each a little stiff but still elegant and exquisitely maintained in our old age.

Then the hull suddenly lurched and there was yelling and screaming aft of my precarious position. As I bent to gather my pants, I was thrown forward from my perch into the door. I knew we were aground before I glanced out the porthole and saw nothing but trees. I danced downhill shouting as loud as I could that everything was all right, that I was on the way.

Mark had accidentally hit one of the automatic pilot buttons and the *Riprap* had swung ninety degrees and roared up the bank and into the forest. Struggling with the wheel the boy could do no more than throw the engine out of gear and throttle back before the boat hit. The two kids—unhurt and in lifejackets—bobbed with the birthday cake below the stern. The rest of the lunch was smeared over the deck.

We retrieved the kids and settled down. I checked the hull for structural damage and found the mud bank had been kind and absorbed the impact without causing any. The props seemed clear of the bottom, which was also mud, and I could see no reason why we couldn't continue on our way. All we needed was muscle enough to push the *Riprap* off the bank. Nobody, however, wanted to go for help.

When I was the captain of a yacht club's flagship—another goofy job like this one—I often ran aground while chasing bluefish over tidal flats with a boatload of kids and parents. Then I would order everyone to the bow or stern while I powered the boat off the shoal or, that failing, jumped over and pushed it free. The passengers loved it.

That's exactly what I did with the *Riprap*. I ordered all passengers overboard to push while I handled the throttles. The maneuvering and teamwork took the shock out of Miss Buono and her guests and soon enough we were under way again. There was a bad vibration from under the stern, but there weren't any leaks. I decommissioned the autopilots and everyone had a safe and eventless turn at the wheel. Ten miles down the canal we found a marina with a travelift and arranged to have the *Riprap*'s props and shafts replaced. Needless to say, there were spare props and shafts on board. While the *Riprap* was in dry dock undergoing repairs Miss Buono and her guests departed and I took a room in a nearby motel. The weather turned cold and a storm came down.

Over the next few days I learned a few things about lakes and my nautical charge. While *Riprap* was on the hoist I inspected her hull and saw to my great surprise that it was flat, even a little hogbacked, and with no forefoot to the bow. For all her size, the *Riprap* was an old-fashioned speedboat, which meant that in a beam sea her only hope at seaworthiness was her weight. I also learned the Great Lakes were no place for pleasure boats in early winter and that the Coast Guard recommended against sailing them. The weather, and the weather reports, were notoriously unreliable. The marina operator gravely told me if I got across Oneida Lake I could take on Lake Ontario. Then he laughed.

Oneida Lake. I'd heard nothing about it, yet there it was a day later—all fifty miles of it stretching northwest. I tied up at Sylvan Beach, the southern outlet, to await the weather.

Next morning the wind slackened to a breeze and I came out juking the throttles past 3,500 rpm's. *Riprap* rose vertically, like someone stepping from a puddle, and I brought the bow down with the trim-tabs. The seas were close packed, steep, and breaking. *Riprap* bounced off them. Hard. I slowed down but she still bounced. I quartered, tacked, ran parallel—all with the same results. *Riprap* continued to bounce and careen. So be it, I thought, and plowed on.

Once, near the submarine buoy off Montauk Point, a new Bertram I was working on was taken over by its owner, who wanted to see what his boat could do. He went racing through a few walls of green water, the famous tough hull airborne, while I went below and held on for dear life. Then I started yelling up to him that I was seeing daylight, an ever-widening view of it, between deck and hull. The entire superstructure was shearing loose from the brutal pounding. I felt something like that might happen now to *Riprap*.

I swung *Riprap* about and felt a motion close to rubbernecking overcome her. We made it back, though, and that night I shuddered when I pissed blood. The next morning it was snowing and I was sore. The forecast called for clearing and winds ten to twenty mph. Nice and easy, I thought. Then I went about tying down and tightening anything that might come loose. When the sky cleared in the afternoon, I accelerated past the jetties.

The wind was out of the north and the waves were once again steep. I took them ten degrees off the bow, parrying them with the throttles. I couldn't stop the slamming and jarring, though, and was forced to turn on all three bilge pumps. *Riprap* was getting one God-awful concussion. But if she could take it, so could I. The summer before, a boat I was working on had a narrow entry to the tuna tower. The first time we had a hookup I ran up the ladder to chase the fish and butted my head on the underside of the platform. I managed to hang on, swaying through an incredible moment of light and pain while I pursued a remnant of consciousness. I made it and was glad no one noticed. At the second hookup I did it again, and we lost the fish, a marlin, while I disentangled myself from the ladder. This time, on *Riprap*, it was the overhead VHF radio that crashed onto my skull and, momentarily, did me in.

I was out, I guessed, less than a minute. But when I came to and picked myself up I noticed two things. I had no neck and *Riprap* had an extra motion to its wallow, meaning only one thing: water in the bilge. Once again I gave up and brought her about and headed back.

At the dock the pumps cleared the bilge. I found no holes; water apparently came in as the planks flexed the seams. I got warm and swallowed some aspirin and went to bed.

Later I found the only restaurant in Sylvan Beach, dined in an empty room and later sprawled against the bar, slightly concussed, watching the TV weatherman predict fair skies. I slept lightly that night, waking regularly to listen to the wind, ready to bolt to the cockpit and head north. When I got up the next morning, expecting "fair skies," I was greeted by the first raging of winter. I spent the day painting the cabin.

That night I called Miss Buono and told her that despite the nor'easter I was still committed to the trip. She was grateful but also sorry, for something had come up and she had to cancel the rest of the trip. Would I bring *Riprap* back to New York? Would I, in fact, take *Riprap* to Florida?

That was all I needed to hear. I think I had *Riprap* headed south before I hung up the phone. I don't remember much about the trip downriver, only that there was rain and snow, dismal skies, cold and wind. Lots of cold, lots of wind. But coming around Sandy Hook the weather lightened and *Riprap* was sweet in a following sea. So sweet, in fact, that I stayed offshore until North Carolina.

Off Georgia I trolled and caught blackfin tuna, and off Jacksonville I had a sailfish on for a while. I even caught a bull dolphin off Cape Canaveral. It was green and gold and furious to have been caught, and I let it go. Then I delivered *Riprap* to her home in Palm Beach.

I didn't stay long then, there was my winter routine, my months of dreamtime on eastern Long Island to get back to. But a few years ago I started fleeing the fierce and dumb season of cold myself. Now I head to Florida every winter and even have a lady friend in Miami Beach who has a home and a boat. And *Riprap* is still in Palm Beach, where I hear she now boasts scanning sonar, SatNav, and a new autopilot. Apparently family rivalries are as strong as ever when it comes to outfitting *Riprap*.

Barring disaster, it seems *Riprap* and I really will make it to the next century. We might be a little stiff and require more maintenance, but we will be elegant.

THE CAPTAIN

BY JOHN HERSEY

WE WERE ON DECK making up gear that morning, tied up to Dutcher's Duck opposite Poole's, when the new hand came aboard. Caskie, the skipper, seated on an upended bucket, was stitching some new bait bags, his huge, meaty fingers somehow managing to swoop the sail needle with delicate feminine undulations in and out of the bits of folded net. You could buy bait bags, but would Caskie? He had a closed face, signifying nothing. We knew he must have been hurt by Manuel Cautinho, who had served him as mate nineteen long years and had suddenly walked off on him, but there was no reading Caskie's face, any more than you could read the meditations of a rock awash at high tide off Gay Head. His was a tight-sealed set of features, immobile and enigmatic in their weather-cracked hide. His eyes were downcast, the hoods of the lids the color of cobwebs, unblinking as he steadily worked. We never knew what he thought; sometimes we wondered if he ever needed to think.

I had been bowled over with the luck of being given a site as shacker on Caskie Gurr's *Gannet*. I was an apprentice, I got all the dirty work, I was salting stinking remains of pogies and yellowtail for bait with a foul tub between my feet that morning, but it didn't matter. (You could buy frozen bait, but . . .) Caskie had the best reputation of any of the offshore lobstering skippers out of either Menemsha or New Bedford. Everyone said that he cared, more than most, whether his men got decent shares, and that he knew, better than most, the track of the seasonal marches of the lobbies on the seabed of the shelf out there. *Gannet* was known as a wise boat. Caskie's regulars had been three senior islanders, who had been with him through a great deal of dusty weather—till Cautinho walked off for no apparent reason.

Pawkie Vincent, the engineer, sat far aft rigging a new trawl flag on a high-flyer—a marker buoy with a radar reflector on it, for one end of a line of pots. Pawkie had only nine fingers, yet he was so deft with them that it sometimes seemed he had three hands. He had lost the index finger of his right hand when it got mashed, one time, while he was shipping the steel-bound doors of a dragging net. Every once in a while, as he worked, he would shake his head slightly from side to side, as if some troublesome doubt had occurred to him. Pawkie was tentative; his pauses to think things out in moments of intricate teamwork were sometimes dangerous to the rest of us.

The cook, Drum Jones, was fastening bricks into some new oak pots that had not yet become waterlogged, to hold them in place on the bottom. He had, beneath a railroad engineer's cap, the gaunt face of someone who has seen a ghost, and he sported an odd little mustache that looked like a misplaced eyebrow and accentuated his habitual look of alarm. This made it all the more surprising that he was always cheerful, always optimistic. When we pulled up a lean trawl of pots, he'd always say the next string would be better. But it seldom had been on recent trips—so Drum's dogged good humor was often annoying.

No one had much to say that morning. Our shares had been slim of late: Pawkie, who had a cranky wife and three wild sons in high school, had said that except for the shame of it, his family would do a

damn sight better on welfare. I was an outsider, but I could see that
Cautinho's departure had suddenly ruptured a brotherhood of these
older men, a closeness rich with memories of many years of risks and
scrapes and injuries and quarrels, to say nothing of a never-
mentioned pride in the way they had handled together their very
hard life under the discipline of their cruel and inscrutable mother,
the sea. They were laconic. The only words they used were about
tasks. Their tongues could not possibly have given passage to nouns
like trust, endurance, courage, loyalty, or, God forbid, love. What
stood in jeopardy now, with Cautinho gone, leaving a gap like that of
a pulled tooth, was the sense of the serene and dependable teamwork *Gannet's* crew had enjoyed, the delicate meshing of Caskie's
understated but revered and absolute captaincy with the known
capacities—and weaknesses, such as Pawkie's hesitations—of the
other three, all working together as parts of an incarnate machine,
each one knowing exactly what was expected of him and what the
others could and would and wouldn't do in moments of critical
stress. One linchpin was gone now out of that smooth-running
machine, and I couldn't help wondering if it might fly apart under
the strain of breaking in a new man. But of course no one could talk
about any of that.

There was another thing we couldn't talk about: The Company.
That meant Sandy Persons, the owner of *Gannet*. Persons, a sharp
little creature, only about thirty years old, in a snap-brimmed felt hat
and a double-breasted suit and what looked like patent-leather
shoes, *was* The Company. He reputedly owned six draggers, ours out
of Menemsha and the others based in New Bedford. I was aware of
the hushed voices with which Pawkie and Drum and Cautinho had
always talked about Persons, each time we steamed into New Bedford and tied up and unloaded our catch, after which Caskie walked
off with Persons to settle up—our captain shuffling away on the
stone pier with a slack pace and a bowed head. The crewmen's voices
were muffled then, I inferred, by their sense of Caskie's everlasting
humiliation that he couldn't afford to be his own man on his own
boat; that he was just another captain on broken-forty shares with a
Company embodied in this little peewee, who, we suspected, in our
conspiratorial sympathy for Caskie, could not really be the owner but
must be some kind of mob underling. We had a sense that vast,
unfair, and probably crooked forces controlled our lives. You could
never read on Caskie's face, when he returned from those confer-

ences, how he felt about this little muskrat of an owner, and you certainly wouldn't dare ask him.

We worked in silence that morning. It was a hot September day, with fog burning away to silvery haze before noon. Our heads were lowered over our jobs. All four of us were startled by a sudden thump, and our downturned eyes swept the deck to see its cause—a backpack thrown down onto it from the dock.

"Cap'n Gurr?" a voice asked.

I looked up and saw a fair imitation of Goliath. That package of beef would certainly have no trouble fetching the pots in over the side as they came up from the deep. This was our new mate. He had a big red beard, full lips, a nose as wide as a fist set in cheerful ruddy cheeks. But it seemed to me that there were empty places where the eyes should have been. You could not tell, looking at those hollows, that he was *there*. There was a flicker of something like a smile—or was it?—tucked in his beard around his mouth. My first thought was: He's on something. This isn't going to work.

But Caskie said, "I'm glad to see you. Come aboard."

His name was Benson, he wanted to be called Ben. He'd heard about the site on *Gannet* from someone at Poole's, and Caskie, in need of a hand, had accepted him over the phone. This was the first time the skipper had laid eyes on the man. Caskie had told us that Benson said he'd served in the fishery off Nova Scotia—out of Lunenburg, Port Medway, Ingonish; rough, cold, sloppy work, the fellow must have liked it. Now Caskie's unreadable eyes searched Benson's vacant ones, and all Caskie said was, "We're shaping up to go out tonight. Bear a hand, would you?" He set Benson to splicing gangions into a new ground line—the short lengths of rope, branching off at intervals from the mile-long line of a trawl, to which individual pots would be tied. Not another word between them. I guess Caskie wanted to see if Benson knew anything. He did. His splices were perfect.

When we'd finished our chores about noontime, Caskie said he'd tune in to the 5:00 P.M. weather forecast, and if it sounded all right he'd telephone to each of us to come aboard. Pawkie and Drum went to their houses, and I to the stark roost I had rented in West Tisbury with a couple of other young adventurers, whose rites of passage involved hammers, Skil saws, stapling guns. Benson stayed aboard; had no place to go, he said.

At supper time, Caskie phoned and said the weather report was, as he put it, "on the edge of all right," and he guessed we'd better take our chances and go out—the trawls had been set out there for nearly two weeks as it was. That statement had, wrapped in the folds of its succinctness, an unspoken rebuke to the vanished Cautinho for having caused several days' delay while Caskie filled his site. I was young and brash, and before Caskie hung up I asked, "Is the new man going to be okay?"

I should have known better. There was a long, long pause—which I took to have a meaning: Mind your own business. "We'll see," he finally said.

When we got to the boat, I heard Pawkie murmur to Drum that he'd listened to the forecast, too, and he said, "Some real dirty stuff's comin' through tomorrer—wind backin' to nawtheast, twenty to thirty."

"It'll be fine," Drum said. "Cask wouldn't do anythin' dumb."

We cast off at 9:00 P.M. sharp, glided out between the jetties, and steamed into the wide bight under a sky that was like a great city of lights. At first, a moderate southwest breeze gently rocked our fat-bellied *Gannet* as if she were a cradle. Then we rounded up into those mild airs and made for the open ocean. The big diesel Cat in the boat's guts hummed. I was off watch until midnight, but I stayed out on the afterdeck until we rounded Gay Head and I could know, peering out ahead over the rail, that there was nothing but the vast reach of the sea between our tiny vessel and magical faraway anchorages of my imagination: Bilbao, Lisbon, Casablanca. I felt free out beyond Gay Head and No Mans, on the wide waters of infinity, free from all the considerations ashore that tied one down—telephones, groceries, laundry, parents, the evening news, and, yes, even friends—free to exist without thinking, free to be afraid only of things that were really fearful. That last was a great gift of the sea. I filled my lungs, over and over, with air that I imagined was redolent, thanks to the great sweep of a dying fair-weather high, of the sweet flowers of Bermuda. After a while I went below and plunged into sleep in my clothes.

Caskie, who had taken the first watch to set our course solidly for our trawl lines, waked me at eight bells, and I took my turn in the pilothouse. *Gannet* steered herself, on auto, into the void. There was not much to do: check the compass now and then, take a turn on deck every half hour just to make sure that all was secure—and, well, you couldn't call the gradual emptying of my mind daydreaming: it was dark out.

The skipper had assigned our new mate the dawn watch. I went down at 3:50 A.M. and put a hand on a big round arm, which felt as solid as a great sausage, and shook it. Benson came roaring up out of sleep, looming and pugnacious, his hands fisted, as if he'd had to spend his whole life defending himself. Then he evidently realized where he was and went limp on the bunk for a minute, with his mouth open and working, drinking consciousness until he was full enough to get up. I went back to the pilothouse, and when he turned up, right on time, I showed where things were—Loran, radar, radio, switches, fuses, button for the horn, all the junk. There was a small round seat on a stanchion behind the wheel, like a tall mushroom, and Benson heaved himself up on it and perched there in a massive Buddha's calm. I still couldn't find him in his eyes, but I'd obviously been wrong: he couldn't have been drugged. He understood, he could deal with the electronics, he had handled the marlinspike when he was splicing with an old-time sailmaker's precision.

"What happened with the other mate?" he asked me. His voice was mild and rather high-pitched, as if he housed an inner person who was less assertive, less rough-cut, than the exterior one. He wanted to know how come he had lucked into this site.

"He just up and left," I said.

"I heard a rumor, some guy at Poole's," Ben said. "Somethin' about the guy was fed up with the cap'n hangin' on to lobsterin' when all the rest of 'em give up and switched over to draggin'. Said the cap'n was stubborn as a stone."

"I wouldn't know," I said.

"Said the cap'n was a peddler. Wasn't no lobsters out there."

"We've been getting a few," I said.

Ben gave a resounding snort, deep and haunting, as if he had a conch shell for a nose. I felt uncomfortable hearing such words about the captain behind his back, and I sidled out of there and went below. But I got only an hour's sleep, because Caskie had risen around five and, as usual, had steamed straight to the Loran fix of his first trawl, south of the steamer lanes in fifty fathoms of water, on the shelf about midway between Block Canyon and Atlantis Canyon. He had picked up the radar buoy on the scope in no time, and had sent Ben down to roust the rest of us out.

The wind had freshened from the southwest, and we were rolling. I pulled on my oilers and my metal-toed boots. *Gannet* had been converted from a seventy-two-foot Gulf shrimper, and her cedar planks clung to oak ribs that had been steam-bent to make a belly as round as a bait tub, unlike the deep-keeled draggers built for northern waters, so to tell the truth she wasn't too sea-kindly. She wallowed in broadside waves. Caskie had gone down to Key West fifteen years ago and bought her for The Company for $20,000; she'd be worth ten times that now. He'd had her hauled and done some work on her, and she was sound, though her white-painted topsides were grimy, chipped, and rust streaked, and her bulwarks were draped with old tires, so she looked like an aging hooker of the sea. Who cared? Inboard she was roomier than the North Atlantic draggers, and we thought we lived in style. Pawkie called her the Georgie's Bank Hilton.

In the gray half-light we were on deck trying to adjust our land legs to the argumentative gravity of the sea. Caskie came out to con the boat and run the hydraulic hauler from the auxiliary controls, abaft the deckhouse on the starboard side. He was cool. He swung the boat into the eye of the wind with his usual skill, as if it were a toy in a tub, and eased up alongside the aluminum staff of the radar buoy marking the western end of the string. We were pitching a bit in the seaway, and Ben, in his first chore as bulwarkman, missed a grab at the flag with a gaff. Pawkie was standing by with a grappling hook in case it was needed, and he made as if to toss it, but Ben waved him off and leaning out over the rail managed to catch the staff. He hoisted it aboard, Drum detached the end line and served it through a block hung from the starboard boom, Pawkie fed the line into the hydraulic lift, Caskie started the winch, and we were in business. The half-inch polypropylene rope snaked and hissed through the sheaves of the hauler and coiled itself on the deck underneath it.

When the anchor of the end line came up—a sturdy bucket full of concrete, a hundred-pound weight—Benson lifted it aboard and stowed it as easily as if it were made of Styrofoam. Finally the first pot appeared. Not a single lobster. Pawkie groaned. Benson heaved the heavy oaken trap on board with a power in the shoulders and a look of anger in the face that gave me a shiver. He detached the pot from its becket with a snort like the one I had heard from him in the night, when I'd said we were catching "a few." After that we were all herky-jerky, retrieving this first string of pots. Big Ben knew what he was doing, all right, and he had strength to burn, but Pawkie and Drum didn't know his moves, and they kept semi-interfering in efforts to ensure the continuity of rhythms that are a must in hauling pots. Each time they leaned or reached toward Benson to lend a hand, he shook them off with a guttural sound that wasn't quite speech and wasn't quite a growl, whereupon they fell back and got out of sync on what they were supposed to do next themselves.

The harvest was miserable. A good-sized but lonely lobbie now and then, and a few eels and crabs and trash fish—which we would keep and sell in New Bedford. My job was to peg, which in our case meant slipping rubber bands over the claws, and half the time I just stood around and waited. Caskie looked grim. From thirty pots in that first trawl we gleaned only twelve lobsters.

Drum served us breakfast after that trawl. Caskie stayed in the pilothouse. We ate silently. Toward the end of the string I had noticed that a human presence had finally made its appearance in Ben's eyes, and that the persona of that presence was a peckish human being who had decided to hate our captain. It struck me that the eyes had been dead until bad blood infused them with a sparkling life. Between pots those eyes threw laser beams at Caskie. Everyone knows that there is a noble tradition, among seagoing men, of hating the captain. Captain hating, even of good captains, goes very far back; the animals in the ark probably hated Noah, even though he was saving them from drowning. There were two troubles here. One was that Pawkie and Drum had learned over many years, probably not without pain, how not to hate Caskie—who would dare utter the word "love"?—and I could sense that there had been some mute emotional transactions going on out there on the deck between the three crewmen, which were as threatening as the turbulent dark clouds that had begun to loom over the landward horizon. The other was that this guy who had showed up in the hollows of Big Ben's eyes looked like a born spoiler, who didn't belong on a cockleshell of a boat out on the open sea.

The crazy thing was that when we started pulling up the next trawl, all five of us began working in perfect teamwork, with the marvelous harmonies of a string quintet playing *The Trout*. The gang meshed better than it had when Cautinho was aboard. As each pot came up, Caskie stopped the hauler; Big Ben reached out and swung the trap aboard and guided it onto the rail and untied it from its gangion; Caskie reengaged the hauler to bring up the next trap; Ben and Drum pushed the pot along the rail to the picking station; Pawkie opened it and, first off, stabbed eels that were trapped and dumped them writhing into the eel barrel; he and I dropped the lobbies, if any, in the lobster tank, the trash onto the culling table, and the crabs into the fishbox; Drum rebaited the pot; Ben slid it aft along the rail and stacked it; while Drum, standing at the culling table, threw eggers—females with roe—and shorts—sexually immature ones—overboard; I began banding; Pawkie threw the gurry into the sea and cleaned up; then we'd all be ready to receive the next trap. If anything got the slightest bit out of rhythm, perhaps after one of Pawkie's hesitations, the guys would spontaneously jump to shift jobs without anything said. It was miraculous. It was as if this disdainful muscleman had been on the boat forever, and all of us could see that the smoothness of our work originated in his skill and alacrity—and anger. Whenever a pot would come up empty, the sounds in his throat now shaped themselves as words: "Shit, not again!" or "Jesus, man," or "I can't *believe* this."

Caskie said he had decided not to reset the trawls in that lobster-forsaken area; he said he would wait and set them "inside"—in shallower water north of the ship lanes. "I should hope so," Benson muttered. But as we resumed hauling, in the third and fourth strings, as the stack of empty traps built up on the afterdeck, the catch was a bit better—seemed to be improving as we followed the sets out to the eastward. Meanwhile, the wind had indeed begun to back around, as Pawkie had said it would, and had freshened; it was out of the east at that point. We had to widen our stance on the deck to keep from staggering around. As we got into the fourth trawl, *Gannet* was pitching like a hobbyhorse, the pots swung ominously from the boom when they came up, and the many hundred-pound traps tied down in a big stack athwartships strained dangerously at their lashings.

By the time we had shipped all the traps from that trawl, the wind was snarling in from the northeast with its teeth bared, chewing the tops off eight-foot seas. There was a gale brewing. Caskie, with his long habit of consultation with his gang, said, "How about it? Shall we pack it in?"

"Jesus Cripes," Benson shouted into the wind, "just when you're catchin' a few?" His echo of my words in the night gave me the shudders. But now when I think about it, I realize that what really shook me was Benson's challenge to everything that I thought of as valuable in an orderly life. His tone of voice was a threat to the very idea of captaincy. Caskie was a mild island man of a certain age; he consulted out of courtesy but always made his decisions entirely on his own, and the serenity we had enjoyed when Cautinho was aboard, though possibly false, had rested squarely on the dependability of Caskie's gentle authority. He had always got us back safely to Menemsha basin. Now this raw Benson had come down here off Newfoundland's bitter waters to break the contract seamen invariably make, whether they like it or not, with skipperhood. You can hate a captain, but you obey him nevertheless. This wasn't a generational thing; I was far closer to Big Ben's age than to Caskie's, but I had been raised to a reasoned life, and I think I was more frightened of mutiny than I was of drowning.

Caskie, his expressionless face soaked with spray, looked at Benson for a long time. "All right," he finally said. "One more string, then we'll see." I was shocked by his yielding, and I saw Pawkie and Drum both literally step back away from Benson on the deck, as if he had raised a fist against them.

"Maybe it's just a squall," Drum stupidly said, so desirous of peace aboard *Gannet* that he lost all touch with mother wit.

You could hear, over the wind raking the rigging, that conch shell of a nose in a wild snort of derision.

Caskie had gone into the pilothouse, to steam us to the next flag. It seemed to take us forever to get there. And sure enough, after a while, he came out on the careening deck and called out to us over the wind, "Flag ain't there."

"Damn Russians!" Pawkie shouted.

Of all times for this to happen! We always blamed snagged or lost trawls on the Russians, though there were also Japanese, German, Polish, Italian—and maybe Spanish, maybe Bulgarian—and probably other—vessels out there, huge factory ships with satellite boats dragging the bottom with enormous nets, ripping up the ecology of the shelf, slaughtering all God's species with a greed and rapacity that gave no thought to times to come. And ruining puny us, sure enough. Any time we lost a whole string of forty pots—and it had happened more than once—The Company was out a couple thousand bucks, and we were that much nearer to being out of work.

Caskie shouted that he was going to steam out to look for the tide balls at the other end of the busted line: maybe some of the pots could be salvaged. He went back in the pilothouse.

Pawkie was shaking his head. "How you going to find those damn floats in this shit?"

"Caskie'll find 'em," Drum said, putting his whole heart into his hoping.

And this time Drum was right. Caskie did. The fat hull pounded and shivered and wallowed out to the eastward. I was the first to see the orange spheres playing hide-and-seek in the spume-capped waves, and I called out the bearing at the pilothouse door. Caskie eased up to them. Out on deck Pawkie picked up the grappling iron and its line, but Benson grabbed it away from him and on a single throw caught one of the tide-ball lines and pulled the rope aboard. With all the strength of his anger, Benson got the first ball on deck, and then the second. By this time Caskie was again at the auxiliary controls, and between them Pawkie and Drum fed the end line into the winch sheaves.

"Somethin's wrong," Caskie said right away. The end line was skidding and laboring in the sheaves. It came up slowly. Caskie had brought *Gannet*'s bow up into the wind, and she was bucking like a Brahman bull in a rodeo with burrs under its saddle. Each time her fat forefoot crashed down into a trough, a ton of spray flew up over the pilothouse and cascaded down on us, icy and stinging, like a deliberate and repeated rebuke of a sea scandalized by our folly.

When the last twenty feet came up, we saw that the end line had somehow become tangled and twisted with the bottom trawl line, so that the bucket of cement that had anchored the end line and one of the pots had risen together. No sooner had they cleared the waves than those two lethal objects began spinning around each other as the ropes from which they were hanging worked to untwist themselves.

Seeing the danger to his men at once, Caskie braked the lift and, depending on a friend he had worked with through many a hazard, shouted, "Pawk! Get the long gaff and try to hook the pot."

"No!"

It was not a shout, it was a roar. We all froze—or at least, as I look back, I see us immobilized in a still picture of that terrible moment of disobedience. Benson had his hands raised in a stopping gesture, as if to beat back the captain's command. Pawkie already had the gaff, with its murderous hook lifted and aimed out over the bulwarks, in his two hands. Drum was in a kind of crouch, as if to dodge some physical blow against the accepted way of doing things that he could sense but could not believe. Caskie stood with his hands on the conning controls, his face all too readable for the first time I could ever remember. I saw rage there, and I saw knowledge, and I saw defeat—the defeat of a quiet man whose calmness had its footing on a set of old, old rules of the sea, always accepted on *Gannet* until that very instant, the most important of which was that a word from the commanding officer in a tight moment is not to be questioned. The first law of the sea: The captain *is* the ship. He had yielded once, and I saw on his face that he would give in now. In the still picture that hangs on in my mind, *Gannet* herself was poised in a tremble of horror on a high crest, and the concrete weight and the lobster pot, spinning around each other, were making a dreadful blur of the reality to which the big mate had attached his defiance.

Then Ben made his move. With a lunge he snatched the gaff from Pawkie's hands and threw it away on the deck. Next, with breathtaking disregard for the danger, he leaned his body out over the rail and snatched the end line in his left hand, just above the fast-moving handle of the bucket of concrete. He was very nearly pulled overboard by the momentum of that hurtling weight, but he managed to hook himself to the rail with his right hand and a bent knee. The spinning stopped. The deck lurched on the crest of a big wave. Ben took advantage of *Gannet*'s plunge and heaved the weight over the rail and onto the deck. The lobster pot came in easily then. It had several big ones in it.

We got in four more pots, and that was all. The trawl had been cut. We headed for home.

In a marvel of balance in the galley as *Gannet* steeply lurched up each wave and then dropped in what seemed a free fall until it hit the rock bottom of the ensuing trough, then rose shuddering again on the next vicious sea, Drum fried four eggs for each of us. Pawkie was on watch. Caskie sat down to his lunch across from Big Ben. I was at the end of the table, and Drum was cleaning up. As if we were floating on a dead calm, Caskie began to speak in a quiet and respectful voice to the man who had countermanded his order and made a success of it, and my heart sank as I listened to his appeasement of Benson. Big Ben gave no answers; eating, he made grunting sounds.

"I don't think you understand," Caskie said. "The Company says, 'Keep on lobsterin',' and you've got no choice. They own you, don't you know. I told Persons, I said, 'It's all over for lobsters out there this year, we ought to go to draggin', but he says, 'We got to have lobsters, we're gettin' all the yellowtail an' fluke and scup we can handle from the other boats, we need lobsters.' If I say my gang can't make a livin', he says well, it's tough titty, he can get other skippers, he can get other guys for crews. I said I'd been on my boat for nineteen years, I didn't like that kind o' talk, and believe me, Mr. Benson, he blew up, he used language I wouldn't repeat to you. He was extremely definite, you know. Extremely."

It was horrible. The sweet sap of command had been drained right out of Caskie, and now all he had left was his impressive New England decency, which was taking the form of groveling. Benson didn't even look up at his captain. The brute had egg on his beard. I felt seasick and had to go up on deck.

I don't know what happened after that. I asked Drum, when we got ashore, but he just shook his head. We tied up in New Bedford after midnight, and Benson heaved his backpack up on the dock and climbed ashore and walked off. When we got back to Menemsha, Pawkie quit. I hated to do it after six trips, but I had to tell Caskie that I thought I wasn't going to make it at sea, I didn't have good sea legs, I thought I'd try carpentry.

Caskie said, "Good luck, son. Don't take any wooden nickels." I couldn't for the life of me tell from his face whether he was glad or sorry to have me go.

LESSONS

BY CHARLES GAINES

CANOES AND I go back. For some adolescent boys (and I was one of them), they are what horses often are for adolescent girls—things to fall violently and permanently in love with. You can spot the people this happens to, long after they are grown, at boat shows and along riverbanks, by the way they handle a canoe if it is theirs and by the way they look at one if it is not. One such person happened to be on the banks of the river a few years ago when I almost killed my wife in a canoe. He was upset about what nearly happened to my wife, but it was plain as his limp that he was more upset about what happened to the canoe.

I fell in love with canoes in Maine when I was twelve years old. For

most of a month that summer I paddled stern in a sixteen-foot
Grumman on the Allagash River. There were twelve of us, eight boys
and four men. We slept in sleeping bags inside of jungle hammocks
strung by the river at night, and paddled during the day, carrying
everything we needed packed between the center gunwales in gray
boxes called wanigans. Canoes were the entire environment; you got
to know about them whether you wanted to or not, and by the end of
the month you were certain to feel strongly toward them one way or
another.

I learned a lot of useful things about canoes on that trip—like how
to fish in the wind from one; how to swamp, then right and bail out
without touching land; how, using the "Maine Guide" stroke, to
keep an exact line across a lake without making a sound or lifting the
paddle from the water; how to pole and ferry upstream; and, in an
enforced lesson one late afternoon, how, if you are caught with a
whole lake and a gale between where you have been and where you
have to go, you either stay where you are or kneel in the bow to
paddle. But it was none of those things that has kept me in canoes
ever since. What did that was learning that there are places in certain
rivers where the water pours instead of flows, where the sound and
look of it can tighten your throat, and where it is possible to have
more fun than anywhere I had been before.

Imagine this: It is 9:00 A.M., a bright morning in early summer. You
are in the bow of an eighteen-foot open canoe. You have been on the
river for nearly an hour, talking and joking with your friend in the
stern, paddling lazily on the flat water, and guiding the bow automat-
ically through a few easy riffles. But because it is a new river you have
also watched the bank, and as you come around a bend you notice
that it has begun to drop. You stop paddling and rest the paddle across
the bow. Your friend stops, too, and as you glide around the bend the
only sound is the drip of water from the paddle blades. Then, all at
once as the river straightens, you hit the rapids. It sounds like wind at
first, then like someone running a bath in a far-off room, and then, as
you get nearer, like nothing other than rapids. A few yards up from
the head you pull in to a boulder in midstream. Your friend, whose job
it is to pick a line, stands up. You stay on the bow seat, studying the
mean, distracted rushes and noticing again how clearly you seem to
see from the head of a rapids. A goshawk circles downstream above a

dead beech. The tracks of a hunting coon leave a stand of fir, follow the bank, and disappear into a raspberry thicket . . . the sun on the whitewater below is like grated lemon peel.

This is Class IV water, dropping at about forty feet per mile and running over a thousand cubic feet per second. It is near the limit of what you and your partner can handle. Halfway down the run both of you have seen a long standing wave, called a roller, that extends diagonally midway across the river from near the left bank. It is formed by water backlashing over a rock formation, and you know it probably contains a souse hole that can carry you or your canoe down to the base of the rock and hold you there. You remember the souse hole on the French Broad near Hot Springs that held Frank Bell's canoe down for ten minutes, and hope your friend has picked a line near the right bank. Over there the only problems you can see are a piano-sized boulder at the head of the main chute, at an angle to where you'll come in making it hard to miss, and an unavoidable cluster of two- and three-foot standing waves, called haystacks, near the tail of the rapids.

Your friend sits down and you slide off the bow seat and kneel, bracing your thighs against the sides of the canoe as it slides into the first V and locks into the current with that sudden smooth assumption of momentum that the body reads immediately as unstoppable. You always have to remember to breathe while shooting whitewater, so you take two deep breaths and reach left for the first sweep, and as the confusion of the water shuts off the part of your mind that considers, you notice without thinking about them the same three things you always notice: how the water seems to fall and separate like a woman's hair, the quick cold of the mist over the churn, and the incredible noise.

You get everything right. The light is good and you find every hole in the line your friend has put you on, prying and drawing for the far ones and sweeping for the easy ones, your paddle finding the exact angle, and the thrilling sensation of controlling a fall building in you over the uproar of the water. At the big sluice above the boulder, you grab a brace high up to the right, your lower body countering just enough downstream to keep the upper gunwale from dipping. The paddle catches solidly and holds the bow while your friend punches out three quick strokes, carrying the canoe far enough across current to miss broaching on the boulder. The canoe hangs for a moment and then falls into the chute as precisely as if it were on a track.

You take on water in the haystacks as you knew you would, but not as much as you might have. Then you are through it. You sit hunched over your paddle, the canoe drifting soggily in the tail pool, and look back upstream at what you just came through. There is a thing about shooting rapids that is very sensuous, that has to do with feeling with your body through the skin of the boat the subcutaneous curves of what you're going over. It is now you feel that most. You also feel a giddy, joyous relief, and with it a sense that you have never been so alive.

The experience is better if you have it in your own boat, but it took me a long time to buy a canoe. For years I borrowed and rented them, trying to decide exactly what I wanted. Tearing the bottom out of a rented fourteen-foot wood and canvas job in a riffle on the Nantahala in North Carolina decided me against that construction, despite its beauty. I had never liked the sound or feel of a metal canoe, but they are practical and I was once very close to buying a Grumman until Roger Bourland and I swamped his on a river in Wisconsin and then found what was left of it later, downstream of a falls, looking like a big piece of crushed tinfoil.

I looked at and tried kayaks, decked canoes, and special open rapids boats, like the Blue Hole and Mad River. But whitewater was all you could do in most of these; also, they tended to be temperamental in the water, and to be made out of materials with names like Royalex or Kelvar 49. What I bought finally, the first time I saw one, was a sixteen-foot fiberglass canoe, beautifully designed to do a little of everything by a company called Old Town. It was fast on flat water, wide and stable enough to shoot ducks and flyfish from, and, fitted with a shoe keel, was a perfect wraith in rapids.

We were living in the northeastern part of Wisconsin then, a watery state where if you fish and hunt waterfowl it only makes sense to have a versatile boat. But over the next few years what started as a simple and practical pleasure in the Old Town's versatility turned into dangerous pride. What I became proud of, specifically, was the frontier virtue of nonspecialization.

One afternoon just before I left Wisconsin, Dick Wentz and I sat in my canoe in a tail pool, looking up at the rapids we had just come through, carrying four inches of water from haystacks, feeling very alive, and watching four C-2's hit nearly every rock between the head of the rapids and us. A C-2 is a whitewater boat for two people with a completely covered deck. It looks like a banana. The paddlers sit in holes, with spray skirts drawn around their waists to keep any water out. The C-2's regrouped in our pool. The people in them had on wet suits, helmets, and snappy red life jackets. They looked at us the way you might look at the remains of someone's breakfast. "You came down through Gilmore's Mistake in *that*?" said one of the C-2ers. I looked at his boat, wondering if Champlain would have put a foot in it.

"Yup," said Wentz.

"You must have shipped a hell of a lot of water," the guy said.

"Nope," said Wentz.

That was it. By the time we moved to New Hampshire, I was as ripe with pride as Oedipus—and convinced that all I knew how to say to kayakers and C-2ers was yup and nope.

The atmosphere by the river was festive and hearty. People dressed in tweeds and down vests shook martinis and spread out picnics on the bank, and waited on the action. It was a crisp day in March and the Mascoma, a tough little river even in the summer, was bank-full and raging. My wife, Patricia, and I, and a six-foot German friend named Karen, found an open place on the bank at the head of a short rapids which was followed by a little stretch of calm water and then by a long frothing Class V piece, set with slalom poles. It seemed like an excellent place for disaster. We put down a blanket, opened up the wine, and waited along with everybody else for the best canoeists in the country—in trials here for the Munich Olympic teams in slalom and wildwater—to come Eskimo-rolling by.

I had brought along my Old Town, sort of in the same way you might put your old pointer named Bob in the car to go to a field trial of five-thousand-dollar setters. From where we sat, I could look over and see it in the parking area, surrounded by a sea of kayaks and decked bananas. We drank the bottle of wine and watched racers getting into wet suits and helmets, and some others practice eddy turns and peel-offs behind a boulder upstream. I opened another bottle, noting there was still forty-five minutes to wait. I began to feel crowded. For the fifth time I examined the little piece of whitewater just below us, particularly how it tailed out into enough calm water to make the bank before the big rapids.

"You know," I told Patricia, "Karen would enjoy these races a lot more if she just had a little taste of what it feels like . . ."

It took twenty minutes to talk them into it.

The small rapids had a single chute out in mid-river, so I carried the canoe about thirty yards upstream and around a bend to give us plenty of room to make it. From there it was just a matter of paddling to the middle of the river, turning the canoe into the chute, letting it ride until it reached calm water, and paddling back in to the bank. I pointed out the simplicity; and to Patricia, who would be in the bow, that all she had to do was paddle on the left until we made the chute. Then I gave them each an old orange life preserver.

"Are three people supposed to ride in these things?" Karen asked.

"No," I said.

"It won't be, Charles," Patricia said.

"What?"

"Simple. I don't really know what I'm doing. And I don't think we're far enough upstream."

I said that I reckoned we were. "Just paddle hard on the left." The fact is that we probably *would* have been okay, except that Karen shifted mightily on the floor of the canoe just as I pushed off, dipping the gunwale and half filling the boat with forty-degree water. Up to her hips in it, she looked around at me as calmly as if she had spilled a cup of coffee, and said, "Uh oh." Back-paddling with my right hand and clutching at the bank with my left, I tried to smile. Patricia kept paddling hard on the left. We came around the bend like that, picking up speed, the foundering canoe uncontrollable, its bow pointing toward midstream, its stern just off the bank.

Without turning around, enunciating each word very clearly, Patricia shouted. "We are not going to make it, Charles." It was clear she was speaking the truth.

I have taken a lot of grief over the years about what happened next. A friend of mine still calls it the Great Tom Mix Escape. Just as the bank straightened, the canoe's stern passed beneath the branch of a big fir tree. What I did was grab it, locking my legs under the seat, in an attempt to stop the canoe. I weigh two hundred pounds and the Old Town didn't even slow down. It must have jerked though, because Karen turned around again. What she saw was me already ten yards astern, hanging from a limb, and onshore. It was a situation that seemed better than her own and she sprang for it, all at once, like a cat. She landed twenty feet from shore, and as I swam out to help her in I saw the weightless stern of the canoe swing into the rocks to the left of the chute. Patricia was still paddling gamely. She hadn't heard me shouting at her from the tree and didn't even know she was alone in the boat until it capsized.

Running full speed down the bank I got to the flat water just before she did. There was a Marine standing there, in the river up to his knees, shoving a log into the pool. I stripped off my jacket and jumped in. "You get out there over your waist, buddy, and it'll be Katy-bar-the-door. Both of you'll go over," the Marine said.

Patricia was halfway down the pool by then, about thirty feet away and back-stroking hard toward us. By the time we got the log to her she was no more than five seconds away from the lip of the big rapids.

We waded back in to the bank and I thanked the Marine. He had a bad limp and a Southern accent, and was pale and gaunt-looking in a way you knew immediately had to do with hospitals. "It's good we got it to her," he said. "There ain't nothing in that next piece of water your mama would've put in there."

On the bank I covered Patricia with my jacket and was wrapping my arms around her, trying to hug off her shivering, when she spotted the Old Town.

"Oh baby, look at our canoe," she said.

It had hung in the rapids and was just now drifting upside down into the pool. The three of us watched it float by. Most of the bottom had been knocked out and a big piece of the bow was missing.

"Shit," said the Marine, shaking his head.

When it hit the heavy water it bucked once, then rode up and began cartwheeling, turning end over end silently down the rapids. We watched until we couldn't see it anymore.

The Marine looked at me, his face pale.

"Buddy," he said, "what in this *wurll* made you think you could do what you was wanting to do in that beautiful little Old Town?"

WORSE THINGS HAPPEN AT SEA

BY ROBERT F. JONES

In the spring of 1951, at the Chancroid Hotel in Yokosuka, Culdee met a cute Japanese girl named Mariko. After a while he bought her out of the hotel and set her up in a hooch down at Kamakura. He liked the beach there, Yuigahama, and the view of the sea from the little paper house up on the hillside was like something from a Hokusai print. Every summer they held a beauty contest on the beach as part of the Kamakura Carnival. Mariko finished third in it once, she told him, the year before she went to work in the Chancroid. The *daimyō* of Kamakura Castle used to gallop the beach on horseback in the old days, practicing his archery.

There were two temples in Kamakura. The big one, Kōtokuin, had the Great Buddha called the Daibutsu. People came from all over Honshu and the out-islands to see it and pray to it. This Daibutsu was cast from bronze, was more than forty feet high, and had a huge placid face that the plaque said was nearly eight feet long. There was a three-foot span between his closed, calm eyes. His mouth, as wide as a man is tall, was curled in a proper Japanese smile, which made it smug and contemptuous. Culdee hated Japanese men but loved Japanese women. Most round-eyes felt the same. It was a holdover from World War II.

Culdee preferred the small temple up on the hill near their house. This was the Hasedera Temple, devoted to Kannon, the goddess of mercy. She was Mariko's favorite goddess. Kannon wasn't as big as Daibutsu. She was only about thirty feet high, but she had eleven faces on her head, all of them skinned over with gold leaf. Some of the faces were contorted and ugly to Culdee's eye, but Mariko couldn't see it that way. "She pretty, *ne?*" she always said. "You're prettier," Culdee said.

Mariko said this Kannon was one of a matching pair, carved from a huge camphor log ages ago, back in A.D. 720, by a priest named Tokudō Shōnin. The priest sent the first statue he carved from it up to a temple in Nara, the holy city in the mountains above Kyōto. This second Kannon he cast adrift in the Inland Sea near Ōsaka. Wherever she washed ashore, he proclaimed, Kannon herself would sanctify that place. Anyone who prayed to her there for salvation from the sea would receive her protection. "You pray, Jimmy. *Ne?*" Mariko said.

Culdee hated to admit it, but he was still pretty twitchy from Inchon. He'd been shot up as cox'n of a landing craft during MacArthur's invasion. But praying to a hunk of camphor wood? He walked out onto the flagging outside the temple and stood at the parapet. Below he could see the swayback rooftops of Kamakura, the bare treetops of approaching winter and the gritty thumbnail of beach where *shōguns* galloped and zipped their long arrows. Beyond lay the bay with its endless chain of Jimas and Shimas, dropping south across the curve of the Pacific like stepping stones. The Bonins—Iwo Jima was down there somewhere. The Marianas—Saipan and Tinian. Then Guam. Wake Island somewhere off to the east. Way, way to the south it all fanned out. Leyte. Peleliu. Buna Beach on New Guinea. Tarawa—Betio Beach. The Solomons—Guadalcanal, Savo Island, Sleepless Lagoon, Ironbottom Sound. He looked back at Mariko. She had prayer in her eyes for him. He went in to Kannon and bowed his head.

"Eternal Father, strong to save, Whose arm doth bind the restless wave, Who bids the Mighty Ocean deep its own appointed limits keep, O hear us as we cry to Thee for those in Peril on the Sea." You too, Goddess, he thought. It was the best he could muster. Mariko came over and hugged him.

He drew some leave from the Navy that fall and they took the train down along the Inland Sea, staying at Japanese inns wherever Mariko felt like stopping. The inns were cheap and the *hotsi* baths wonderful. At night behind the paper walls they made love on the sweet-smelling hardwood floors, sometimes on tatami mats and thick quilted futons, sometimes on the smooth cold wood itself. The inn shook as if from minor earthquakes. Culdee could hear Mama-sans giggling through the walls. He wrapped his Wellingtons in his pants for a pillow. The wood block alone gave him a stiff neck. In the morning a servant girl knocked on their paper door and brought in hot *cha*. For breakfast Culdee ate fried eggs over steamed rice, but pretty soon he was eating raw tuna. He liked the green *wasabe* you dipped it in, the way it burned both ways.

At Nagoya they hired a cab over to the Nagara River and caught the tail end of the cormorant fishing season. Mariko knew Culdee would enjoy it. She talked them aboard one of the fishing boats, a long, slim sampan with a four-man crew. The helmsman stood at a sweep in the stern and guided the sampan down through the rapids. The skipper was always addressed as *Ushō*. He stood in the bow in a big, funny hat, a tall, thin, very serious man, with twelve tame cormorants on strings leading from his left hand. The cormorants, awkward-looking birds with long necks and long, downcurved, spiky beaks like mergansers', had cords knotted around the roots of their throats. The cord necklaces kept the birds from swallowing any but the smallest fish. The *Ushō*'s assistant, who was called *U-zukai*, had four birds of his own in hand. He was serious but nervous. The final crewman, a husky little fellow with a big happy grin, tended the fire in the iron grate at the sampan's bow. They fished just at dark, for *ayu*—little trout as best Culdee could tell.

The boat swept down through the rapids and the *Ushō* shouted something in the guttural Japanese they use for orders. Culdee could see small fish darting up to the flare of torchlight. Sparks and smoke blew behind them like a comet's tail. It was good to be in a boat again—Culdee's first time since Inchon. The cormorants went into the water without a splash. They dove and surfaced, dove and surfaced, the boat racing down through the black water suddenly foaming white beneath the bow, guttural shouts from the *Ushō* and from five or six other fishing boats that followed close behind. When a cormorant had swallowed enough he would dart toward the boat, eyes bulging, swaying his long, thick, fish-swollen neck. The *Ushō* hiked him up into the bow and, still holding all the lines in his left hand, used the same one to milk the cormorant's neck down into the basket. A torrent of flopping silver *ayu* gushed out. Like a very ominous short-arm inspection, Culdee thought.

He'd brought a jeroboam of *Ichi-ban* sake with him—finest grade, from the Nada district near Kobe—and he took long one-handed swigs from it as they careened through the firelit night down the river. The helmsman in the boat just beside them saw him chugging, grinned thirstily, and waved Culdee aboard. Culdee leaped without thinking across the racing black water and lurched as he landed. The helmsman caught him, laughing. That sampan's *Ushō* looked back sharply and snarled. But then two of his birds came aboard and he was too busy to take disciplinary action. Culdee, the helmsman, and the fire-tender killed the bottle. He could see Mariko watching fearfully from the other sampan.

When the sampans swirled to a halt near the bridge where their cab was waiting, Culdee took one last pull from the bottle—Polish people claim there's always a hundred drops left in any empty bottle—and threw it at the bridge. The bottle caught the torchlight as it spun, end for end, like a crystal Indian club. It shattered against the stone abutments with a crash as loud as a five-inch shell. The bits went tinkling onto the smooth stones below.

Next day they walked through Ground Zero at Hiroshima. It was a little more than six years since the bomb. There were new cast-concrete benches to sit on and the earth around the ruins of the little church, the only building left standing after the flash directly overhead, looked pretty much the way it must have the morning when the dust cleared. Only the dead were missing. The earth itself was still crunchy away from the promenade where the sand had been fused to glass. A few older Japanese men glowered at Culdee when he stepped off the pavement to test it, but one man, a seedy-looking guy in a pin-striped business suit with the right sleeve pinned up, smiled at him almost gleefully. The sun shone bright but weak, the air was salty, crisp with autumn. Rosy-cheeked Japanese mothers pushed English prams full of groceries and rosy-cheeked babies along the sidewalks. How many ghosts here? A hundred thousand? Two hundred thousand? Maybe after the first ghost there is no other? No, not a one.

At Ujina, the port of Hiroshima, they boarded a ferry boat to Shikoku. Mariko wanted to visit Matsuyama. She knew Culdee would enjoy the old castle on the hill that dominated the town. It was an "Important Cultural Property," very well preserved, full of ancient lacquered-bamboo armor, strange helmets, samurai swords and spears, and the oddly shaped longbows he liked so much in the Kamakura museum. Culdee saw the one-armed man who had smiled at him at Ground Zero, coming aboard with the last of the passengers. No sooner had the deck gang—seamanlike boatswains in British-style sailor caps—cast off the mooring cables than everyone got seasick, Mariko among them. The other passengers disappeared below, to the saloon deck, where they could not see the swaying horizon. Mariko wanted to go with them. "Stay topside," Culdee told her. "The fresh air's better for you. Down there they'll all be sick, and the smell of it will make you even sicker." Mariko smiled bravely, *wasabe*-green under her cut-rate PX makeup, then looked at the horizon. It tilted radically from left to right, then sideways. Then she gulped and ran below.

Culdee studied the wind and the hundreds of little islets that dotted the Inland Sea. The one-armed Japanese came up the ladder from the saloon. He had a bottle of whiskey in his only hand and he took the ladder two steps at a time. He stuck the bottle under his stump and tried to unscrew the cap. The bottle turned against the shiny serge of his suitcoat. He tried again but almost dropped it. He caught it on his shoe and flipped it up, spinning, then caught it deftly. Finally he turned to Culdee and smiled apologetically. They were only a few steps apart.

"I say, old bean," the one-armed man warbled in a fruity British accent, "could you bear a hand with this beastly bottle? There's a good chap." Culdee almost laughed, but took the bottle and unscrewed the cap. Suntory Scotch. "Many thanks. Now hold out the cap, thusly. That's it!" He poured and whiskey splashed cold over Culdee's knuckles.

The one-armed man raised the bottle in a formal toast. He clicked his heels—the shoes were spit-shined but cracked and terribly round-heeled from wear—and bowed slightly from the waist, smiling up at Culdee all the while. He had a wicked, crooked grin.

"Cheers," he said. "*Kampai!* Here's how! That sort of thing."

Culdee tossed back the capful of whiskey. The one-armed man's throat worked twice to Culdee's once. Well, it was his bottle.

"My name's Sōbō," the one-armed man said. "Matsuo Sōbō. You're Navy, are you? Couldn't help noticing the *décor*." He gestured at the tattoos on Culdee's forearms. "So am I—was, that is. Navy, I mean. Imperial Japanese Navy. One of your hated Nipponese opponents in the late war." He hissed the word "Nipponese" and squeezed his eyes tight. He laughed. "No? Perhaps before your time. *Mo no ippai?* Another swallow of the old Scottish Wine?"

Culdee accepted the bottle and tossed back a large swallow.

"Korea then, you? Got knocked about a bit, did you? How can I tell, you ask. It's the eyes, old bean. We all look like that, after. Wears off in a while, though. Never fear, hope is near. Two years, three at the outside. *Mo no ippai?*"

They tossed back another.

"Where you from?" Culdee asked.

"Sasebo, most recently. Old home port. You know how it is. You get to know all the people—shopkeepers, women—on a cash basis. Helps later when you're strapped. We all owe one another a living, don't we just? I'm a writer now, or trying to be one. Your sailors call me Sōbō the Hobo. Doesn't bother me a bit. Water off a duck's back. All our best writers of the past were gentlemen of the road. *Mo no ippai?*"

They drank from the bottle again.

"Written anything lately?" Culdee asked.

"Funny you should ask. Little short story, more a vignette, you might say. Wrote it just after I saw you at the Peace Shrine back there in Hiroshima. Two merchants are standing outside a teahouse, exchanging the latest disaster news. You know how those chaps are, all atip with the horror of it, but delighted at the same time that it didn't happen to them. Bandits slay pilgrims enroute to Fuji-San, rape all the women. Ronin assassinate *daimyō* of Iga. Korean pirates hijack junk fleet, all hands walk plank. Earthquake at Edo, tsunami at Ōsaka—thousands feared lost. Rumors of war in northern Honshu. Certainly we live in evil times, the end of history as civilized men know it. *Mo no ippai?*"

They drank again.

"At any event, as they're talking an old sailorman comes trudging past the teahouse, dragging a mast behind him. His naked back is scarred and covered with tattoos. Pauses for a rest, listening to them. Finally he snorts a coarse laugh. The merchants gather their robes about them and stare at him with pointed disdain.

" 'Worse things happen at sea,' the old sailor says. Then he trudges on down to the harbor. Like it? *Mo no ippai?*"

Once again they took large swallows from the bottle.

Culdee walked over to the windward rail. His legs felt a bit unsteady. There was a strange crossways chop working the ferry's keel. One-armed Sōbō strode beside him, steady as a tightrope walker. They leaned on the windward rail. Sōbō stared dreamily at an islet in the bay. There were official-looking buildings on it, like the buildings of universities Culdee had seen stateside, with thick ivy on the walls. But the lawns were untended and some of the trees trailed broken branches from the storms of recent years. Maybe from the bomb itself? Two U.S. Navy minesweepers lay alongside a stone wharf that stuck out into the harbor.

"Eta Jima," Sōbō said. "The Japanese Annapolis. All our best officers went there. Closed now, of course. Japan will never fight again. We learned our lesson, that we did. You bet." He laughed again. *"Mo no ippai?"*

"Thanks, but I'll pass."

"Too strong for you then, old bean? I could *nip* below—no pun intended, ha ha—fetch us some glasses and a siphon?"

"Oh, just a short one." Culdee held out the bottlecap. It was a deep bottlecap.

"Where were you?" Culdee asked. "In the war."

"Oh, that. At sea, mostly. Cruisers in the early going. Gunnery officer. We had some good ships then, beauties, faster than your cruisers by a country mile, but no armor to speak of. That's why we were faster. Let's be honest, shall we? We had the better navy, at least when the war began. Better trained, better gear, more *esprit*. But once you woke up we stood no chance. Our only hope was to take you out swiftly. We very nearly did, too. But it was not to be. All for the best, in the long run." He sighed. *"Mo no ippai?"*

Culdee now felt committed to the whiskey and to lasting as long as the one-armed man. He tossed back another deep capful.

"Later, destroyers," Sōbō continued. "Had my own command there for a bit. Rather enjoyed that part. *Yunagi,* a sweet little vessel if

I say so myself. We did a good job one night, off Savo Island in the Solomons." He broke off and gazed out wistfully over the waves again. He hummed a few bars of a familiar American tune. *"Chicago, Chicago . . ."* A Japanese destroyer had indeed slugged it out with the crippled cruiser *Chicago* on that ruinous night, Culdee knew. Some balls, all right.

"Ah, well. Later one of your submarines hammered us. They always do, don't they? Easy come, easy go. *Mo no ippai?"*

"Arigato," said Culdee as he tossed back another. "What about later? After you lost the can?"

"Staff." Sōbō laughed bitterly. "Fate worse than death. It was beastly duty. Mind, we had some damn fine flag officers in the IJN, don't take me wrong. But I got stuck with the dimmest bulb in the whole blazing admiralty. Rear Admiral Shoji Nishimura by name. Rear Arsehole we called him. Thick as two planks."

"Never heard of him."

"Pity. You chaps should erect a statue to the twit—at the real Annapolis. *Mo no ippai?"*

Culdee was beginning to dread that phrase but refused to give in and say he'd had enough. He raised the bottlecap and drank one more time.

"Why's that?" Culdee's voice sounded hollow to him, more defiant than he'd intended. "The statue to whatshisname, I mean."

"Well, after all, Nishimura gave you the greatest surface victory in the history of naval warfare, didn't he? Handed it to you on a platter. The last great clash of battleships the world is likely to see. The battle of Surigao Strait. That was during the Leyte invasion, MacArthur's long-promised return to the Philippines. The plan was to smash your landing force while the transports were off-loading their troops and equipment, before you'd established a beachhead. One force of our force, under Admiral Ozawa, lured your Admiral Halsey and his fast carriers away from Leyte almost as far north as Formosa—the infamous 'Battle of Bull's Run.' Another element, under Admiral Kurita, came down through San Bernardino Strait and nearly wiped out your supporting force of escort carriers and destroyers—would have, actually, except for the pluck of your destroyers' slugging it out with the torpedoes and five-inch guns against our battleships. That was the 'Battle off Samar.' The third force was Nishimura's, coming up through the Sulu Sea from the southwest with two battleships, a heavy cruiser, and four destroyers to shoot the gap between Leyte and Mindanao, then turn left and wreak havoc on your amphibious force. But it was not to be. 'The Battle of Surigao Strait' intervened." Sōbō laughed wryly. *"Mo no ippai?"*

They tossed back another.

"What happened?"

"Your Admiral Oldendorf was waiting for us. With clouds of mosquito boats—what you chaps call PT's—hordes of destroyers, eight cruisers, and six battleships. Ironically, five of the six had either been sunk or badly damaged at Pearl Harbor. A fitting vengeance. Imagine Surigao Strait as the upright bar of a capital T. Oldendorf had his PT boats and destroyers waiting in the dark, against the loom of the land, as we steamed up it. The cap of the T consisted of your heavies—the cruisers and battlewagons, steaming crosswise, ready to deliver broadsides at whatever came up the Strait. From Trafalgar to Tsushima, sailors have learned to avoid having their T's crossed. But Nishi the Ninny apparently was absent the day they taught that letter of the nautical alphabet. He steamed dead ahead into the cap of Oldendorf's T. Lost six of his seven ships. *Mo no ippai?"*

"Why not?" They drank. Sōbō laughed nastily.

"It was worse than the Bight of Benin," he said.

"What's that?"

"Surely you know the old verse? 'Sailor, beware of the Bight of Benin. There's but one ship comes out for the three that go in?' Surely you've heard that, old bean?"

"Oh, that one," Culdee lied. Where the fuck was the Bight of Benin? "You seen it, did you? You were there?" He sounded aggressive. Well, fuck it.

"Bet your sea boots, sailor boy." Sōbō laughed again and this time his eyes were nasty, too. Full of contempt, like the Daibutsu. He flapped his empty sleeve. Culdee hated the sneering look on his flat face. *"Mo no ippai?"*

"Give me the fuckin' bottle," Culdee said.

"Why, of course! Sorry, old bean. Been rather greedy, haven't I?" He handed the half-empty liter to Culdee. Culdee chugged three swallows and coughed. But he kept his cookies.

"So what was it like?" Culdee's voice was rasping now. "At Surigao Point? I mean Strait?"

"Rather wicked, if you must know. Your torpedo boats hit us first, followed by destroyers on either flank. One of your fish blew the battleship *Fuso* in half. Then a night full of armor-piercing projectiles falling upon us from a great height. Fourteen-inch stuff, twelve-inch, eight-inch. All of it crashing right down through the armored decks. Old Nish plowed on, didn't even know the *Fuso'*d gone, along with most of our destroyers. *Mogami,* the cruiser, was burning. Press on regardless, what? Only toward the end there, when his own flagship, *Yamashiro,* had been pounded to a hulk, burning from stem to stern, did he have any doubts. Indeed, I'm afraid he browned his knickers, as you might say, just before *Yamashiro* turned turtle. Went down with all but 150 of her hands. Of those, only three of us lived out that sunrise."

"You written anything about it?"

"Just a haiku, I'm afraid.

"Surigao autumn:
The admiral is shitting
In a sea of fire."

He smiled shyly and his eyes were pleading. Then he laughed his dirty laugh.

"You call that a sea story?" Culdee said. "Edgar A. Guest writes better stuff than that. Our sea stories have blood in them. Splattered guts. AP shells shrieking like banshees. The groans of the maimed and dying. Sharks eating guys from the toes up. Gasoline fires. Burning fuel oil. Flooding compartments where you can't undog the escape scuttles. Chickenshit officers, brave whitehats. Madmen and heroes. They have *punch lines,* for Christ's sake!" Culdee was yelling. "What you told me's a fucking limerick, and it doesn't even rhyme!"

"That's the difference between us, then, old knob. Asians don't need that kind of romantic nonsense. Caucasians can't live without it. All of you are weaklings. Now, now—just a few home truths between messmates. Nothing personal, old son. Simple sailorman, me. You, too. Simpler still, if you get my drift."

" 'Weaklings'? Shit, we kicked your ass."

"What do I mean? Well, fat for starters. Not just physically, but in your very souls, if indeed you have any. Soft. Complacent. Fearful. Cozened by women from cradle to grave. And of course you're thick. Not *your* fault really, it's all in the blood. Born that way. Very slow at math. Barely count to ten. I take that back. Five. Can't see spatial relationships even on a sidewalk, much less inside your heads. You need maneuvering boards to keep station, slide rules, now computers. No natural seaman's eye. No sense of history, no tradition. Let's face it, old knob, you're born fags. No, no—I mean it in the English public school sense. Natural underclassmen, fit only to spit-shine the boots of your betters." Sōbō smiled complacently, as though thinking he had just turned a rather nice phrase. "I didn't mean to impugn your masculinity, though." He paused and scratched his head. "Hmmm. Then again, why not? Yes, I fear you're all instinctive cocksuckers. Especially your Navy enlisted man. Boatswains are the worst of the lot."

Culdee went for him then.

But Sōbō wasn't there. His left fist was, though. It buried itself wrist deep in Culdee's solar plexus. He folded at the middle and spewed like a Nagara River cormorant. Sōbō's shiny shoe tapped his backside and Culdee lurched forward, then skidded in his own vomit. The teak deck met him face to face. Blood and bits of tooth . . . Culdee tried to roll on his side and grab Sōbō's legs. Sōbō kicked him crisply in the right side of the belly, just under the rib cage. Culdee's world went white, then red, then blindingly white again. He couldn't breathe for the pain—it was like Inchon . . .

"That's your liver, old chum, in case you were wondering." Sōbō's voice came from the wavetops well off the starboard beam. "No, it's not jiu jitsu, nor any of that silly nonsense. Just plain old bar fighting, Imperial Navy style. Don't try to get up for a bit. Never fear, hope is near. You'll live. I've been kicked there more often than I have fingers left." He counted them—this-little-piggy fashion. Then he sat down on the clean part of the deck beside Culdee. "*Mo no ippai?* Rather not? I understand, old son. Don't mind if *I* do though, do you? That's good." Then he took four long swallows.

"By the way," he went on, "I couldn't help noticing the way you use your hands, sailorman. Bit of advice from a wise old Nip bar fighter. Never punch for the head if you can help it. Use a bottle or a chair. Get a man down one way or another and kick him to death. Knuckles are fragile, you see. Hand bones, too. You'll just bust 'em up if you insist on smacking skulls with 'em. Then where are they when you really need 'em?"

"You set me up," Culdee said finally. He could breathe again.

"Of course, old top! Don't we all?"

"Why me?" Shit, now I'm whining, he thought.

"Nothing personal," Sōbō said. "Now and then I have to let the bulldog out for a stroll. A few drinks in some nice quiet bar somewhere, then pound the pee-willy out of some obliging American sailor. Marines are even better, they last longer as a rule. Then afterward, seek out a nice, plump American *hausfrau* for a bit of the old slap and tickle. Navy wife's best of all. I don't see what you chaps find so exciting about Oriental women. Cold mutton in my book. Old chief once told me he'd rather eat fried eggs than diddle a brown-skinned wench. Yes, give me a big fat blonde from Long Beach every time. Hotter than the fires of Hades—or anyway the Surigao autumn." He chuckled and Culdee found himself joining in.

"Well, old shipmate, it's time I toddled off topside to chat up the captain. Old classmate of mine, Eta Jima, '39. Simple old sailor-man, he. Just like us, what? Nice chatting with you. Here, keep the bottle."

"Hey, not so fast. Where'd you learn to talk like that, anyway? You sound like David Fuckin' Niven."

"Junior year abroad. London School of Economics. Weekends at Portsmouth and Dartmouth. Long vacs at country houses by the sea. *Drake's Drum,* that sort of thing. Ever read Captain Maryatt? *Mr. Midshipman Easy*? Try it, old bean. You'll find me on every page. Ta-ta."

Sōbō's ragged cuffs and bright black shoes strode out of Culdee's widening cone of vision. He could hear Sōbō singing a variant on his theme song. *"Shikoku, Shikoku, that wonderful isle . . ."* His shoes tapped a quick little riff and he was gone.

By the time Matsuyama swam into view—swaying bell buoys, mossy breakwater, a grim black castle glowering like a war helmet down on the harbor—Culdee had finished the bottle. Passengers began appearing at the head of the saloon-deck ladder. They looked doubtfully around them, then spotted dry land and stepped straight-backed out on deck. Mariko was still pale but she smiled with relief that the passage was over. She smelled faintly of vomit, strongly of orange blossom perfume. Culdee kissed her full on the mouth. His liver felt fine. He slung the empty Suntory bottle into the wake. Gulls screamed and dived, pecked at it briefly, then towered and cried out angrily into the churning sea. Fathoms of ropy white chalk.

"We'll grab a cab to the very best *ryokan,*" Culdee told Mariko. "A *hotsi* bath, some solid food and a little sack time, you'll be right as rain."

Up on the bridge, Sōbō was watching them. Culdee paused at the top of the gangway once the ferry had tied up alongside the wharf.

"Permission to leave the ship, sir?" he yelled up to Sōbō.
"Granted!"
Culdee snapped him a proper salute. Sōbō flicked his own back casually, officer style. He was smiling his wicked grin. Culdee smiled back. Sailors on liberty: The brotherhood of boats.

SEA CHANGE

BY DAVID SEYBOLD

THERE HAD ALWAYS BEEN boats. Always. Skiffs, runabouts, cabin cruisers, sailboats. They were there at the small yacht club, neatly arrayed in their slips like bright spools of thread in a sewing basket. Or they were scattered over nearby harbors and bays, where sometimes they truly looked like grazing sheep. They bobbed and pulled at mooring buoys and their rigging slatted and creaked as their bows swung into the wind and tide. We saw them every day; they were as common to our lives as gulls over tidal flats. And we played and tossed about in our boats and thought for the longest time that all the world was the same.

It was on the North Shore of Long Island, in a small harbor village called Stony Brook. To grow up there twenty-five years ago meant knowing what a centerboard and lower unit were before being introduced to team sports. When Whitney Roberts and I were sailing his Snipe out of the harbor and into Long Island Sound, so that we could race other sailboats miles away in Port Jefferson, we were not yet concerned with learning to drive or how to dance.

At the end of the lane our house was on was West Meadow Creek. It was there that I learned to row and fish and observe. I was taught these things by an elderly man who knew the creek and its secrets better than anyone. He was our neighbor and lived in a small farmhouse that had no electricity or plumbing. In the summer I would wake and go to his house and sit on the porch and wait for him to come out. When he did he would look at the sky and not say anything, until finally: "Well, she's going out." And I would sort through the aromas of honeysuckle, oak, dogwood, and rhododendron until I could smell the creek and the outgoing tide. He would look at me and say, "Your mother know what you're up to?" As often as not I would lie and say, "Sure, you bet." And then I'd follow him down a shaded path to where the creek flowed and his rowboat lay above the highwater mark.

I would row while he sat in the stern and talked in his low, raspy voice. I'd hear him but be concentrating too hard on rowing as expertly as my eight-year-old arms would allow to ever know what he was saying. When an oar jumped a lock, as one often did, he would lean forward and put it back in without missing a syllable. We always rowed close to the reeds, because it was easier going and because along the fringe was where most of what we were after lived. I'd be pulling on the oars and he would suddenly say, "Pull in here, hard." And I'd pivot the boat with a deep stroke and ship the oars as we glided through reeds and cattails and into a secret channel that I'd never seen before. We'd get out and pull the boat up the narrow waterway until it rested on the bottom ooze. Then we'd trap killies or dig bloodworms for bait and spend the day fishing with hand lines for flounder or mullet or blackfish. On other days, depending on the tide, we'd net crabs or catch eels around the pilings of an old boathouse. And all the time he'd talk while I rowed and tried to listen. He'd forecast the weather and talk about the shapes of clouds and direction of the wind, and I'd try to remember what he said. He showed me where the hard clams were plentiful and where the black ducks nested at the head of the creek, in a small bay that existed as a watery cul-de-sac. One day he told me about a prized game fish that lived and spawned in the creek. No one knew the fish were there, and I promised never to tell another soul. That was over thirty years ago, and his secret is still safe.

A few years later I got my first motorboat, a six-foot pram with a three-horse Evinrude, and I abandoned the creek and meadow for the Stony Brook Yacht Club, where my friends and I kept our boats and made a career of terrorizing the yachting neighborhood.

It was a wonderful boat for about two weeks, which is how long it took me to become bored with plowing through the water instead of skimming over it. In an effort to transform my pony into a steed, one that would leap out of the water like a hydroplane, I swapped the new Evinrude for an old five-horse Johnson. Then I decked the pram with plywood and put on a racing steering wheel.

In my haste to complete the refitting, though, I wrapped the steering cable on the wheel drum backwards. And when I jumped in the pram and opened it up to race by the clubhouse, I turned to go left but went right. I missed ramming Mr. Michaelson's beautiful Richardson cabin cruiser by inches. It was a wild, inspiring experience, one which gave me an idea for some fun.

A few nights later I camped out at the town bluff and stole through the darkness to the club with wrench and screwdriver in hand. I climbed down into half a dozen runabouts and performed my particular brand of magic.

They talked about it for years—about how on a certain Saturday morning six members arrived at the club to gas up their boats for a multifamily outing. I was told it was like bumper cars, only with boats. For half an hour chaos and confusion filled the marina as boats rammed into boats, docks, and pilings. Men swore and threatened to end each other's lives. A few even took unplanned swims.

No one had to rat on me: By then it was a given that I was the culprit in any act of a nefarious nature. To make restitution for my sins, I had to clean boats, mow lawns, wash windows, and weed gardens for the six members. But it wasn't bad. Especially when it came to cleaning boats. By the middle of summer I had picked up jobs cleaning a dozen boats and was earning fifteen dollars a week.

The following summer several other members asked me to clean their boats, and it wasn't long before I had a thriving business. I cleaned Pacemakers, Chris Crafts, Richardsons, Lymans, Thompsons, Grady Whites—all kinds of beautiful cabin cruisers, inboards, and runabouts. I was imbued with the rich smell of varnish and marine paint.

One of the boats I cleaned was a sleek twenty-one-foot Century Coronado with a V-8, 238-horsepower Perkins Marine and dual exhausts. It was owned by John Gambling, who had a radio show called *Rambling with Gambling*. It was all chrome and mahogany and thick vinyl-covered seats. I had the keys, as I did with most of the boats, so that I could keep the batteries charged and run the bilge pump. I spent a lot of time on that boat because Mr. Gambling never used it. He would show up once a week to inspect the boat and pay me. Then he'd leave. In time I began to think of the boat as my own.

At first I would start it and only pretend to drive it. I would step on the chrome gas pedal and rev the motor until the entire marina reverberated with its sound. I'd keep the pedal down until every hull plank vibrated and it felt as though I were holding back a wild stallion. Then I would idle it down and listen as the dual exhausts gurgled and popped and spoke to me of power and speed.

Within weeks it was too much for me to endure, and I started to drive the boat in and out of the slip, like a teenager driving the family car up and down the driveway. Then I grew bolder and took it around the marina, being careful not to throw a wake or disturb the other boats. When members looked at me and asked if I had permission to drive the boat, I lied and said, "Sure, you bet." In time no one questioned me.

It was called *The Blessing of the Fleet*. Every year a minister would stand on the float in front of the clubhouse and say a prayer for each boat as it passed by. Members would polish their boats and fly pennants, burgees, and ensigns, and dress in nautical blazers and caps. The commodore, vice commodore, rear commodore, and all the other commodores (I was fifteen before I realized a commodore was a rank in the Navy and not just a member of the Stony Brook Yacht Club) would lead the procession in front of the clubhouse and down the channel and out into the Sound. It was a big event, one which the townspeople lined the public wharf to watch.

I asked Mr. Gambling if he was going to put his boat in the parade. But his answer was the same as always: "Not going to be around." So I got it in my head that *I* would put the boat in the parade. And on the morning of the big day I gathered my pals and told the members who asked if I had permission, "Sure, you bet." There we were, my pals and I, passing the minister and waving to the spectators as we motored down the channel. It was wonderful.

How was I to know he was lying? When an adult tells an eleven-year-old he's not going to be around, the kid is inclined to believe him.

At the end of the public wharf was the town beach, and above the beach, tucked in the shade of oak and locust trees, was Dave's Bait and Tackle Shop. And sitting on the shop's porch on the day of the *Blessing* were Dave and Mr. Gambling. They were watching the parade when Dave said, "Isn't that your boat, John?" But Mr. Gambling shook his head and said, "Couldn't be. No one can use the boat but me." Then Dave handed Mr. Gambling his binoculars. What he saw was his boat filled with kids who were climbing over the decks and seats and each other like puppies in a box.

When we returned to the marina and rounded the pier that led to Mr. Gambling's slip, I saw, to my horror, the figure of my employer standing in front of the ladder that led to his absent boat. My pals abandoned ship like rats jumping off a fumigated barge. They thrashed and swam their way to safety while I was suddenly very alone. I backed the boat into the slip, tied it up, and straightened the cushions without once looking up. When I finally did, though, I saw a set of alligator eyes staring down at me. He stood with his arms akimbo and his foot tapping the planks. Though not a large man, Mr. Gambling suddenly appeared huge and threatening. There was only one thing to do. I climbed the ladder, handed him the keys, and said, "I quit." I was halfway down the pier before he overcame the shock and began yelling at me.

When I started sailing with Whitney Roberts and my brother, I knew I would never care about motorboats again. There was something about going eight knots under sail that made going three times that speed in a runabout seem meaningless. Sailing imparted a closeness and personal involvement with wind, water, and boat that was absent from any motorboat experience I had ever had. I spent as much time as I could on Whit's Snipe and the Lightning my brother had borrowed from friends. I also started crewing on a Raven and a Tartan sloop.

But girls did not like to sail as much as ride in fast runabouts that could pull water skiers. And since I liked girls, I didn't hesitate a second when I was asked to go boating with some nonsailing friends.

"Sure, you bet," I said. I even lied when I was asked if I knew how to water-ski. "Hey, who doesn't?"

How hard could it be? I had watched plenty of skiers and it never seemed that difficult a thing to do. Heck, the boat did all the work. When it was my turn, I did exactly what the person before me had done. I put on the skis, grabbed the tow rope and, when the slack was taken up, yelled, "Hit it!" I plowed through the water, wobbling and swaying, but kept the tips up and stayed with it until I was standing and actually skiing. It was a snap. They took me around and around, and soon I was cutting outside the wake and waving to the girls and feeling as though I were ready for Cypress Gardens. Then they motioned toward a deserted beach and shouted for me to drop off when we were close to it. I had seen skiers let go and coast up to beaches before. It looked easy . . . and *cool*. No problem, I thought. When they angled the boat close to the beach, I made my cut across the wake and raced toward certain glory, and maybe a session with Wendy behind a sand dune. When I was twenty feet from the beach, I let go of the rope and threw out my chest and raised my hands in victory.

They said I screamed when I popped from the skis and went flying through the air. I wouldn't know. Things happened pretty fast after the skis and I parted company. One second I was feeling cool, the next I was airborne and heading for the side of a sand dune, where I landed in an ignominious heap of torn flesh and bruised pride. I stood right up, though. "Hey, no problem," I said. "Let's do it again." But the expressions on their faces said, "Oooh," and I assumed I wasn't a sight for the fainthearted.

It was known early on that I was perhaps a few turns shy of a tight seal. Even so, it was not my idea to go into the underwater salvage business. My only suggestion was that I be the diver. And so it was that when Whitney heard about underwater caves that were filled with treasures left by sea captains who had sailed into the harbor a hundred years before, he talked me into being his partner.

The caves were located off the town bluff, in the middle of a narrow channel, and in about twenty feet of water. Our plan was to attach two garden hoses together for a breathing device, use motorcycle goggles and a football helmet for head gear, a spear to ward off any giant eels that might be dwelling in the caves, a clam basket to load the treasure into, and a cement block to keep me on the bottom.

On the morning of the dive, we made a dry run on land, to test the gear. Everything checked out, all systems were go. It was only a matter of hours before I was filling the clam basket with gold bricks and bags of coins. Soon we would be rich and buying boats and shotguns and fishing rods.

We rowed out to where we thought the caves were and anchored. I jumped overboard and held on to the side of the boat. Whitney, who would stay topside and feed me the hose and raise the baskets of treasure, handed me the goggles. Then he pitched the clam basket overboard and lowered it to the bottom while I spit on the goggles' lenses and slid them over my eyes. Next came the helmet, which I pulled on and cinched down around my chin as tight as I could. I looked at Whitney. He looked at me. This was it. I gave him a thumbs up. In minutes I would be boldly going where no twelve-year-old had dared to go before.

"Are you ready?" Whitney said as he handed me the hose.

"Sure, you bet," I said.

I took the hose and put the end in my mouth and nodded. He handed me the spear and I treaded water while he grabbed the rope that was attached to the cement block and lifted it onto the gunwale. The combined weight of the block and Whitney made the boat tip to within inches of the water.

"Are you ready?" he said again in a strained voice.

I grabbed the rope and gave him my Marlboro man look. Was he kidding? You bet I was ready. In my heart was the belief that I had been born for this very moment. Just give me that sucker, I thought. I wanted the gold, the treasure . . . the glory.

"Are you sure? Are you sure?" I nodded my head and tried to say so with the hose in my mouth.

I watched as he leaned out with the block and saw his face turn beet-red. He was grimacing and grunting. Suddenly he slipped and the gunwale went under and the boat started to ship water. He yelped, and my pal, my blood brother, lurched back into the center of the boat while leaving me in charge of the cement block.

It was really something, to be suddenly yanked down and racing to the bottom like that. I'll bet I was going fifty. My goggles slipped up to my forehead, I dropped the spear, and the hose was ripped from my mouth. But I never let go of the block. No sir. I held on until I slammed into the bottom.

Amazingly, despite my rather dizzying descent, enough brain matter had stayed intact that I retained a will to live. The instant my helmet and upper body hit the bottom I dropped the rope and headed back up to the surface. When I broke through, I started shouting, "Holy shit, holy shit, holy shit." I climbed into the boat and looked at Whitney, who was speechless and looking at me as though I had contracted a new disease of the flesh while on my brief but wild journey down. Then my head and ears started to throb and ache and I ripped off the helmet and held my head while taking up the refrain, "Holy shit, holy shit, holy shit."

When we rowed back to shore, Whitney said, "We'll try it again. But next time we won't use a cement block. We'll make some of those diving boots, the kind that have weights in them."

"Sure, you bet," I said.

It was extraordinary luck to live in that harbor village when I did, at a time when marshes and estuaries, meadows and wooded shorelines were valued more for their natural state than as potential real estate developments. And to be granted the freedom to explore my surroundings was a great and rare gift.

But of course I had to leave. I had to because I was made that way. To live my life where the horizon was always the same seemed to contradict, even flout, the freedom bestowed upon me. Although where I lived was warm and safe, it answered no questions, sated no desires. As Herman Melville said regarding his own flight from youth, "I was not rushing to havens ahead, but from havens astern."

I went to college on the western edge of Nebraska and stayed for two pheasant seasons. As much as I favored the hunting and desolate beauty of prairie and range—the near-garish sunsets that swept over and consumed the land—I was not where I wanted to be. And since I didn't know where I wanted to be, I grabbed my flyrod, notebooks, and backpack, threw out my thumb, and headed off on a nondirectional course through the Midwest and Northwest.

I ended up in San Francisco, where I took up ohming at the Family Dog, selling my blood on Mission Street for five dollars a pint, and indulging my curiosity about various drugs. I wandered along the wharf section and walked by the marinas and only thought about boats. Somehow it was enough. But then the 1960's ran out of room and all the goodness was gone from whatever historians are wont to label that period. What was left, what I literally walked through on my way out, resembled a city street on the morning after a block party for the morally and physically deficient. I got out and was grateful to do so while I could still stand erect. Many who stayed were reduced to all fours and clapping their hands for raw fish. It was that kind of a party.

I moved back east and forgot about the Haight and free clinics. For a period that lasted nearly a year, I changed my ways. I cut my hair, retired my foil-lined smoking pipes, and went back to college. I wore Weejuns, Brooks Brothers shirts and ties, plaid Slim Guy boxer shorts. I adopted a malocclusion and prognathous jaw, so that I sounded like Thurston Howell. My friends became people of fashionable pedigree who thought lysergic acid diethylamide was what the mechanic put in their car battery. They could remember the last twenty-four hours.

When I joined them on a cruise to Newport, Rhode Island, aboard someone's family's 106-foot, gaff-rigged ketch (a bear of a boat with a white steel hull, Sitka spruce spars and oak hoops, backstays that were attached to the deck with five-foot stanchions that had to be walked fore or aft with each tack, and dark-paneled salons and staterooms), I discovered that only a few of my shipmates had any hands-on sailing experience. They were versed in the nomenclature, up on the proper attire, but winced at the suggestion of sheeting in the main or tailing a winch. It was a nautical version of lip-syncing, and my disgust was acute. But in Newport I saw sailboats that made me forget my shipmates' false love of everything but themselves. Moored at the Ida Lewis Yacht Club, and elsewhere around the harbor, were beautiful wooden sailboats designed by John Alden, L. Francis Herreshoff, William Atkins, and W. Starling Burgess. They left me speechless, and dreaming of classic wooden sailboats with sweeping sheers, shapely overhangs, gleaming brightwork, luxurious interior joinery, and polished brass fixtures. All white ducks, white bucks, and blue blazers aside, I was grateful to have been asked along. Even when the strain on my facial muscles made me quit my Thurston Howell imitation, and long after I had abandoned the Buffy and Chatsworth crowd and entered the heady world of commercial clamming, I thought of that sail to Newport and those lovely wooden sailboats.

Bullraking for clams in winter from a flat-bottom workboat that always has half an inch of water and slicks of slippery muck that unexpectedly send you crashing to your knees or slamming against the freeboards or flat on your freezing ass makes you wonder if a career in the out-of-doors is all it's cracked up to be. Even when the work took us to areas where we could partake of fine waterfowl gunning and good fishing for striped bass, mullet, blues, and sea trout, I had my mind on other temperature zones and careers. When the romance of sorting through mudders, little necks, cherrystones, and chowder clams came to a swamping halt on a brisk March afternoon, I sold out of the business, paid my debts, and took off with enough money for a one-way plane ticket from Miami to Barranquilla, Colombia, South America.

I hitched to Miami and went to the airport and located the Aero Condor terminal and its agent. We discussed my travel plans over a card table and I was informed I would need a round-trip ticket, which would cost $120—a lot more than I had in my pocket. But a friend of a friend later I was working in a boatyard on the Tamiami Canal. I lived on a houseboat that was permanently moored in a backwater that was the marine equivalent of a trailer park.

Josey Moline, an artist who eked out a living selling paintings of boatyards and would-be mariners, was my landlady, and she helped me find work on houseboats, which were, and probably still are, in various stages of completion. It was an easy life, full of colorful people from around the country who had quit mainstream living and moved there to build their boats and sleep until noon without guilt.

Of course I had thought about building my own houseboat and steaming home. I'd build a forty-footer with a V hull and big single-screw diesel. I'd have a casting and shooting platform off the stern, a few plastic flamingoes on the roof, a birdbath on the foredeck, and cute cement squirrels fixed to the corner boards. The image of showing up at the Stony Brook Yacht Club in a tidy center-chimney houseboat with double-hung Andersens became so real that Josey was inspired to make sketches of my vessel with me at the helm.

I cut, nailed, and caulked enough marine plywood to earn the money I needed. And when I grew weary of living amid everyone else's dream, I hugged Josey and went to Colombia and did things that had absolutely nothing to do with boats.

I lasted in that country of poverty, glorious wild orchids, fabulous gold museums, bland food, and beautiful women a scant four months, which was all the time it took to spend my money and sell everything of value that I had in my backpack. I returned home with my tail between my legs and went back to school, where I devoted an entire duck and pheasant season to reading and listening to Louis

Simpson, J. D. Reed, and other scholars at the local university. Then I quit and bought a 1967 Chevy Impala and drove north until I found myself in Toronto, Canada. Why I drove there and not to, say, Alabama, is anyone's guess.

On the second floor of the Brunswick House on Bloor Street, I sat among Toronto's journalists, who came for the low lights, smoky atmosphere, and jazz. One night someone mentioned he had read about a man who was looking for a crew to help sail his boat to Antigua. Everyone at the table sighed and lamented his inability to leave the cold of Toronto for the warmth of the Caribbean. I, however, called the man the next day and applied for a position on his sailboat. When he asked if I had done much ocean sailing, I said, "Sure, you bet."

A few days later I sold my car and shipped some things home. Then my new shipmates and I left Port Credit two days before Halloween and set sail across Lake Ontario, bound for the Erie Canal, Hudson River, Atlantic Ocean, and the blue Caribbean.

The sailboat, called *Rodger Dodger,* was a forty-five-foot fiberglass Sparkman & Stephens yawl with truly lovely lines. She was owned and skippered by a fifty-year-old Royal Canadian Air Force pilot who had been permanently sidelined from his career as a result of crashing his fighter jet and losing all mobility of his lower left leg. His crew was made up of a young female journalist, a young male journalist, a television director, and myself, who used the appellation "student."

Halfway across the lake we were in complete darkness and being buffeted by thirty-knot winds and seas the size of which I had never expected to encounter on a lake. Both journalists were helpless, as they couldn't stop saying goodbye to the contents of their stomachs, and the director, who weighed close to three hundred, had all he could do just to keep his bulk in one spot. The skipper was hanging on to the wheel with a look on his face that did not instill confidence in his crew. And I kept looking at the twelve-foot Zodiac we were towing. The possibility of our needing it was growing stronger by the minute.

We had developed a lee helm and were slipping downwind and putting more and more strain on the number-two genoa, which was absolutely too large a sail to have up. Unless we got the sail down we were going to jibe, shudder, and yaw. I looked at the skipper, waiting for him to say something, do something. Finally I screamed at him to head upwind so I could either drop the genoa or cut it loose. But it was too late. And for the rest of my life I will see perfectly the instant when clew and sheets separated from the genoa and it exploded forward. I remember the craziness that followed, the wind and bucking motion of the boat, the wildness of the sheets and sail whipping and beating through the air. And I vaguely remember going forward and dropping and gathering in the sails. But I see so clearly and precisely the genoa and clew parting and the white sail rocketing forward into the darkness.

I am not a tenacious navigator or shrewd tactician or accomplished helmsman. In fact, I do not consider myself a highly skilled sailor. What I am is a *competent* sailor who knows his way around most anything that has sails. I can follow orders and do what I'm told reasonably well. I also know enough to recognize incompetence in others. And when sailors with less skill take charge of my well-being, I have a tendency to rebel and do whatever is necessary to cover my ass. Which is why on the morning following our debacle at sea, the skipper and I had a heart-to-heart and came to new terms regarding each person's responsibilities during the rest of the passage.

When we entered the Erie Canal we were obliged to unstep our masts, because of low bridges and high-tension wires, and cradle them over the boat. Then we turned over the clunky Perkins diesel and vibrated our way through dozens of locks. We stepped *Rodger Dodger*'s masts in Kingston and continued on to the 79th Street Marina on Manhattan's West Side. Flotsam comprised of spent prophylactics, beer bottles, chunks of Styrofoam, produce crates, tires, and soggy pizza boxes vied with us for a berth with such tenacity that we eventually gave in and headed for Ambrose Light and the open Atlantic.

Though not particularly agile on deck, the director was a skilled navigator with many Caribbean passages to his credit, and he plotted our course for Bermuda. First, though, we took a heading due east for a hundred miles so we could avoid coastal storms and the nightmarish presence of freighters, liners, and tankers in designated shipping lanes. The journalists, who had never sailed on the ocean at night before, were told that if they saw two white lights, one on top of the other, to shout, scream, tack, or jibe, because a vessel the size of the town they were from was bearing down on us. When they looked at me with faces that were half amused, half serious, I elected to stay topside during hours of darkness for the first seventy-two hours.

The first days of the passage were cold and rough and we were banged around, like everyone is who makes that sail at that time of year. We suffered and endured the usual minor hardships: malodorous clothes and bodies, a cramped tenseness among and between certain shipmates that made the boat appear the size of a dinghy, a temperamental Radio Directional Finder, tiredness from hot-bunking, a boring diet of tuna and macaroni salad and fruit cocktail, and the occasional wave that would catch us off guard and knock us over and swamp the cockpit and put the cabin in complete disarray.

But through it all, despite the cold and crampedness, was the sailing on the open ocean, without anyone or anything on the horizon except wind, sky, and water. We quartered seven- and eight-foot seas, surfing down into foaming troughs that rose above us, and then climbed back up until the great expanse of the Atlantic was suddenly there and stretching out and all around forever. For days we sailed up and down, up and down, in a powerful, surging rhythm that I never tired of seeing or feeling. And beneath us were thousands of feet of water, an entire world of mountains and valleys, gorges and prairies, and exotic creatures. There were nights when the sea was invisible and all we knew of its presence was its black hissing sound as it slid by within arm's reach. And on nights when it was clear and shooting stars and moonlight illuminated swaths of yellow and silver ocean, the boat cradled us and we became aware of its own pulse as the angle of heel, sail trim, and hull speed made the entire boat hum as though it were alive and purring in sweet content.

A day or so south of Bermuda, which we had decided not to visit, we saw long, thin clouds on the horizon that meant we were close to engaging the easterlies. When we did, steady ten- to twelve-knot air gave us long tacks and made us feel as though we had finally gotten off a potholed dirt road and onto a freshly paved highway. We began to like each other.

Twenty-two days out of Port Credit, Ontario, we sailed into English Harbour, Antigua. We tied up, jumped off, and waited for the land to stop swaying. The skipper found a permanent mooring and waited for his girlfriend to arrive from Canada. The director and the journalists flew home. I stayed. First I went to a small inland club and got very drunk and ate sandwiches of goat meat and hot sauce. Then a very large and friendly and beautiful island woman took me to her home, where I was told I had the face of Jesus Christ and the smile of

God . . . and that she wished to share (for a fee) her personal charms with me.

Flat broke but in new-shoe spirits, I returned to the harbor a few days later and surveyed my new surroundings. Tethered to moorings were dozens of sloops and ketches and staysail, topsail, brigantine- and gaff-rigged two-masted schooners. Some were old, others near new. Many had classic lines while others looked like chunks off an iceberg. They were sixty feet, they were a hundred and thirty feet. All were for hire. And since the charter season was about to begin I decided to get a job aboard one and spend a few months sailing among the Leeward Islands.

I got a job crewing on a seventy-five-foot, two-masted schooner called *Nose Gay*. The skipper was a Norwegian named Busa, and the owner was his girlfriend, a raspy-voiced, hard-looking American woman whom everyone called Billy. Busa, who was in his late thirties, had the personality of a gored pit bull, and the crew avoided him. But Billy, who could have been forty or fifty-five, was smooth and confident and possessed a sultry charm that made everyone want to please her. The crew was made up of three men and one woman, with the other two crewmen being islanders who lived ashore until we were out on a charter.

As though they were living storybook lives, Busa and Billy had matching sea-serpent tattoos. His appeared on the inside of his left forearm, Billy's on her upper left thigh. It was impossible to look at them and not stare at their tattoos. When I wasn't polishing brass or varnishing brightwork, I was rowing Billy to and from shore, which I never minded because she would sit in such a way that I could see up her dress and glimpse the tail of the serpent. I slept in *Nose Gay*'s forecastle, on the berth above the boat's cook, a young woman from Guadeloupe who sadly thought of me as a brother and not the lover I wanted to be. The forecastle was hot, stuffy, and cramped—so much so that every night I would wake in a sweat and go topside and sleep on cushions. When it showered at dawn, which it always did, the rain was light and refreshing.

But I quit *Nose Gay* a few days after we took our first shakedown cruise, which was when I was informed I would not get paid until the end of the season.

Then I met Rusty, a spirited, red-headed Australian who skippered a fifty-seven-foot ketch called *Espuma* for a widow who had inher- ited tin mines in Bolivia. She paid Rusty to live on the boat year-round and sail her and her boys to St. John, St. Thomas, and St. Croix for the month of January. He said I could stay on *Espuma* until they arrived and work for room and board plus twenty-five dollars a week. It was a deal. By day I polished, varnished, and washed down the boat. By night I went to the Admiral's Inn and imbibed quantities of rum and ginger. Occasionally we would take *Espuma* out for a day trip. We'd sail in perfect ten- to twelve-knot air under postcard skies and laugh as though we were sharing a private joke. Other times we'd invite friends and sail around the island or out toward Nevis or Montserrat, a lovely little island that rose out of the sea like an Indian maiden's amber breast, and we'd get wild and trash the boat and spend all the next day cleaning.

My stay on *Espuma* and Antigua ended prematurely, which I've always regretted. What precipitated my departure was a simple mis-understanding, one that gave credence to the expression "two nations divided by a common language."

One night at the Admiral's Inn there appeared a few English cruise ship officers dressed in uniforms—white shorts, knee socks, shoes, shirt, and hat. The bar was crowded with tourists and sailors and I was over by the swing-a-ring post. Two of the officers came over and started to play the game, which involved taking an iron ring that was tied to a string and suspended from the ceiling and sending it forward ten feet to a spike that was nailed at an upward angle on the post. Flip the ring onto the spike and win. Simple in theory, frustrating in practice—especially after several rum and gingers.

At the time, all I knew about the English was that they possessed a penchant for understatement and pale complexions—and that they once ruled forty percent of the world's population but couldn't figure out central heating. I looked at Charles, the Biwi bartender, who smiled and took out the tally pad. Then I turned to the officers and suggested we play a match for drinks. They agreed. We played and I won and they bought the drinks. Then they won and I bought. It wasn't long before we had each of our eyes angling toward different continents. Sometime during the ensuing fuzziness one of them started talking about fags and how he'd like one even though he hadn't indulged his desire for over a year. I said I couldn't help him, but then he pointed at *me* and smiled. When he reached over for the cigarette I had in my mouth, I hauled off and pasted him. He went down and I proceeded to jump all over his bones. But his mate got me from behind and was making my head bounce off the floor like a ball bearing. In a matter of seconds the entire bar was a sea of swinging arms and legs, a stadium of shouting and screaming.

The officers were taken back to their ship and Rusty, who had thought the night a huge success, helped me back to *Espuma*. My head felt like an overripe cantaloupe and rapidly took on the appearance of an eggplant. I was told that the Englishmen were fine and had not been hurt, which caused my pain to go a little deeper, last a little longer. When I learned that "fag" was British slang for cigarette, I did not say, "Golly, how interesting."

A few days later, when the swelling went down and I no longer looked and sounded like I'd just had fourteen root canals, the girl who ran the radio shack for Nicholson and Sons Charter Service stopped by to say she had located a boat in need of a second mate. The position paid seventy-five dollars a week, which was a lot of money, and the standard room and board. Since my time with Rusty was drawing to an end, and since I was no longer a welcomed patron at the Admiral's Inn, I said, "Sure, you bet," and signed on.

Two days later I was en route to St. Thomas and a harbor called Red Hook, where my new job awaited. The only information I had about the boat was that it was an English Thames schooner with tabernacle masts that had been converted to a pleasure vessel. She was called *Rara Diva* and her owner was a wealthy Frenchman who used it sporadically, a few days here, a week or so there.

I was taken out to *Rara Diva* in a launch just in time to share a lunch of roast duck, garden salad, and Heineken beer with the crew. We dined in the main salon, a beautiful room amidships that was paneled in red oak and decorated with original oil paintings depicting seascapes and harbor scenes. Well, what the hell. Good pay, good food, a private boat with an owner who was seldom aboard. I smiled at my new associates. Things were looking up.

The crew of *Rara Diva* was comprised of a captain, engineer, first and second mate, chef, and two deck hands. The first mate, a pessimistic American from Connecticut, said he hoped I wasn't looking for adventure because none existed aboard *Rara Diva*. The deck hands, islanders from St. John, were reserved and ate quickly and left. But their glassy eyes and steady grins told me they were also stoned, which I quickly learned was their common state. The engineer was a serious German who showed himself topside only when the boat was under way and when he took his morning and evening swims. And the chef, a plump, bald-headed Frenchman in his sixties, immediately informed me that it was beneath him to be there and that he planned to return to his homeland in April.

Later that day I met the captain. His name was Peter, and he looked like an underfed Liberace in rose-colored short shorts. He wore a gold chain, pinky signet ring, white linen pullover, and leather sandals. It was obvious that the only thing straight about *Mon Capitaine* were the comb lines in his gelled platinum-colored hair. He said we would "mingle" later and then walked away like a window dresser on deadline.

I learned that our captain's title was the result of his being the brother of the owner's American wife. Peter, as it turned out, had no nautical skills whatsoever. The engineer was the working skipper, Peter the token captain. Peter's role was to stay out of the way and leave the crew alone, a rule he had apparently broken with my predecessor.

If we had sailed, I would have stayed longer than I did. The owner, however, wanted the boat to stay there until he arrived in late February. The time I spent on *Rara Diva*, which was three weeks and one day, was devoted to eating, sleeping, reading, snorkeling, and smoking a lot of dope with the deck hands. But as cushy a sinecure as my position was, I was restless by the end of the first week. I really wanted to sail. And if I couldn't sail, I might as well do something to earn the money I was being paid. Yet there was nothing for me to do. The deck hands did what I had done on other boats and they rejected, even resented, my offers to help. The first mate, who had told me on my first day there to take it easy and not let guilt get in the way of a good time, was never around except for breakfast, when he would tell the deck hands what to do. The engineer remained a gofer, the chef a frustrated professional who swore at his ovens and our pedestrian palates. And Peter, who was never up before noon, was either sunning himself on the foredeck, to look "dreamy" for that night's foray ashore, or flitting about in a state of euphoria or absolute despair as a result of the previous evening's outing.

Then life aboard *Rara Diva* became even stranger. I felt as though I had been cast as the protagonist in a remake of *The King of Hearts*. Somehow I had become the ship's spiritual leader, a father confessor to all but the deck hands. The chef, engineer, first mate, and Peter would pull me aside and tell me secrets about themselves or each other. And when one saw another confiding in me, he would seek me out in private and try to get me to reveal what I had been told. Finally I took to hiding in the sail locker and sleeping on deck. But at the end of my third week, I decided it was time to escape. One morning I took our launch ashore and boarded a rickety bus that took me across the island to the airport in Charlotte Amalie. I flew over blue water and peaceful islands and wondered how long it would be before the authorities realized the gate to *Rara Diva* was open.

Within a year of returning home from the Caribbean, I had gone back to school, quit, and moved to Stonington, Maine, first to help a friend build a house for a college professor on a small island, then to live and write in the village. I wrote a few articles for Nat Barrows, who had just purchased a weekly newspaper called Island Ad-Vantages, and lived with an elderly woman. I paid five dollars a week to sleep and write in a room that overlooked the harbor. It was an old house in need of repair, and when the wind blew from the east or southeast it shook on its granite foundation and the lights flickered. From my window I could see Crotch Island, the Thorofare that connected Stonington Harbor and Jericho Bay to East Penobscot Bay, and outer islands. I learned that even though the sun was out and the day appeared fair, if the lobster boats remained in port, foul weather was on the way.

I met a woman who was a seasonal resident and the owner of a 210 double-ended racing sloop. I crewed for her on that long and narrow machine, and I was always astonished at how her personality changed from that of a sweet sixty-five-year-old lady ashore to a ruthless Captain Bligh on the water. If I were slow on a tack, off on my sail trim, she'd snap and yell and otherwise reduce me to guppy chow.

A kindly person made me the loan of a peapod skiff, a seaworthy lapstrake rowing boat, and I used it for clamming and fishing and exploring the islands. On a row to Sheeps Island I saw my first Friendship sloop and instantly became smitten by its humble, utilitarian charm. Gaff-rigged and beamy, with a bowsprit and large cockpit, she appeared as seaworthy and comfortable as any sailboat I had seen. She looked like a boat I would be comfortable in.

I left Maine after a year and returned home and went back to college. But either Stony Brook or I had changed too much in the six years I had been traveling for me to stay. Something was wrong. Though I was where I came from, I felt a long way from home.

On a lovely spring day, a friend asked if I wanted to take an airplane ride to New Hampshire. He was flying his mother there in a Cessna 172 to look at some property and there was room for a third. I said, "Sure, you bet," and we flew over Long Island Sound and up the Connecticut River valley until we touched down in Newport, a small town in the west-central part of the state.

A real estate agent drove us to the small village of Bradford, where I stood on a one-car bridge and stared at the shallow stream running underneath. Large maples and pines bordered the stream and fractured the sunlight, so that the surface was dappled in the middle and in constant shade along the edges. I picked out the shapes of two brook trout finning in the current and suddenly, though without bells and whistles going off, realized I needed to live in such a place.

A year after I had moved to New Hampshire, which was nearly twenty years ago, I forgot about sailboats and pursued landlocked salmon and ruffed grouse. I inexplicably started to settle down. At first my transformation was subtle—a library card here, a mailbox key there—and I thought I was merely going through a phase. And when I founded a weekly newspaper and no longer did fun things like pull my pants down in bars, I thought I was in the throes of adulthood. Instead of spending my nights illegally dipping smelt or romancing coeds in the back of my Chevy Vega, I attended zoning board meetings and sixth-grade plays with a pencil and pad.

What followed was an outbreak of yuppie hypocrisy. I espoused Democratic causes while secretly voting Republican. I declared my distaste for space-age materials but couldn't wait to purchase my first graphite fly rod. I drank light beer and bought a Saab 99. I found myself joining a friendly band of lake sailors and crewing on a Star boat, a greyhound of one-design racing sloops that is the most demanding boat I have ever sailed. The owner actually had me convinced that making his boat perform at maximum efficiency was more important than world peace. For two summers I spent every weekend pulling and tugging on backstays, jib wires, jib luffs, jib sheets, barber hauls, outhauls, downhauls, cunninghams, travelers, boom vangs, mast benders, and enough other hand controls to get me a job as a puppeteer.

"*Enough*," I told myself when I realized I was looking for excuses *not* to sail. Campaigning a Star was too much like having a second career, which I didn't need. I'd also had it with a style of sailing that put me on my knees more frequently than a contrite Muslim at sundown. I graciously bowed out of that pastime and returned to one where I could create my own hours.

I went on a tear and loved and drank and played to excess. My newspaper went under and I took a job as managing editor of another. It was apparent, however, that I needed surcease from the organized world. What I required was a kinship with those who saw virtue in a life of sport and moral dissipation. I needed to know again those ruthless souls who thrived on biting the hands that fed them. I quit editing and renewed my allegiance with the sturdy, free-thinking, renegade sons and daughters of America's sporting class. And I have not yet stopped sighing with relief.

There came a day, now over fifteen years ago, when I met Bob Gurnsey. Gurns, as he's called by those who know him well, was an ocean sailor whose past included many boats in many places. But where I had stopped deepwater sailing, Gurns continued as a skipper on other people's sailboats. He rescued me from dry dock and I started crewing for him. As a skipper and shipmate, it was obvious from the beginning that he was the best I had had the pleasure to sail with.

Our last voyage was four years ago, when we sailed a thirty-six-foot Islander from Virginia to Gloucester, Massachusetts. For the most part, it was a pleasant voyage. We went offshore, made a one-night detour into Atlantic City, where I fed a generous amount of quarters into a bank of one-armed bandits without reward, and then went back offshore for a run up the coast. It was beautiful sailing until our last night out, when at 1:00 A.M. we found ourselves in Buzzards Bay being pounded by gale winds and wild seas. At one point we were doing fourteen knots under bare poles! But Gurns, who thrives under such conditions, made the right decisions and we pulled through unscathed. What I remember most about that voyage, though, what made it truly memorable was something that happened when Gurns and I were clutching the boom and furling the mainsail. While water and wind raged about us, we looked over at each other and our seriousness suddenly gave way to laughter, great big bushel-basket roars that we could barely hear above the wind. There was no denying it, the bottom line was that despite our white knuckles and genuine concern for our lives we were having a kick-ass good time.

*   *   *

I do my boating in canoes these days and paddle over ponds, beaver bogs, and lakes. The only sailboats I get close to are those I see when my wife and daughter and I are on vacation in Maine. And, to be truthful, it wasn't until two years ago that it no longer hurt to know I couldn't row out to one of the sailboats I was mooning over and weigh anchor. It used to be that whenever I looked at boats under sail or saw them bobbing on moorings with their bows into the wind and tide, I would hear the sweet music of their rigging slatting and creaking and have to turn away.

But times have changed and I now have it in mind to get back on salt water very soon, in a sailboat of my own. I even know what type of sailboat I want. While on vacation in Maine last summer, in a cottage that was only a few yards away from Eggemoggin Reach, I saw a little Friendship sloop sail by that looked just the right size for a family of three. Ashley, my nine-year-old daughter, was next to me and I watched her bright blue eyes follow the boat until it neared the bridge that connects Byard Point on the mainland to Little Deer Isle.

"What kind of a sailboat is that?" she said.

"Friendship sloop."

"Let's get one," she said matter-of-factly.

"Maybe we will, in a year or two."

"Really?"

"Sure," I said, "you bet."

THE WAIT

BY RICK BASS

WE DRIVE THROUGH THE CITY, through the rain, January: a man I've never met before, Jack, and my best friend, Kirby, still my best friend—almost twenty years. Jack and Kirby live in the city, and are almost best friends themselves now. A dentist and a real estate appraiser. I drove three days and nights to go fishing with them—not just wade fishing, not sissy-pants shore fishing, but in a boat. Jack has a boat, with a motor and everything.

I watch Jack as he drives. He looks serious, intent. He's poor, even though he's a dentist, because he's got a wife and three kids, and this is not a good time in Houston, for dentists or anyone. Jack's boat is old, and the chances are good—excellent—that something will go wrong with it today—if we even get out on the water. Kirby is not so poor, because both he and his wife work, and they have only one child, a little girl, who is also named Kirby.

We drive slowly through the thunderstorm, through the lightning, through the heart of downtown Houston, and tall buildings leap into the sky all around us with each lightning flash. We pass the building where Kirby works; we pass the building where his wife works. They all look like tall jails to me, the shutdown of a life. I feel like an outlaw, sitting in the back of the jeep with the two married men, the fathers, up front. I feel almost as if one of them *is* my father, and the other one of my father's friends, though in fact I am slightly older than either of them. It does not help that I have never been fishing from a boat before.

It has been so long since I've been around anyone—man or woman—other than my girlfriend. We're separated. We have done this before, and I think we'll come back together again, because we've been together far too long *not* to come back together.

This time, after Margie left, it was a little different—I felt alone right away, and also, I just wanted to do something new, and I did not want to be in that house alone.

It wasn't the usual list of griefs, this time—not, Why don't we get married, not, Why are you always traveling so much, not, Who was that woman who called?—those are the little things, the things that can be erased. Or if not erased, at least put aside.

This time, said Margie, she was tired. Just tired. A little frightened, but mostly tired. She went home, back to Virginia.

I did not want to be in that house alone. I just wanted something new. And after a while, that gets hard to find, sometimes.

We listen to the thunder-crackle of the local AM station, the early morning fishing report. The roads are slick, and there are other cars out, so many other cars, but none of them are pulling boats.

Kirby and Jack lean forward and watch the road and sip their coffee. The rain is coming straight down, beating against the windshield. We all try to hear what the Fish Man is saying on his talk show. He is telling us the fishing has been poor to spotty the past few days. Kirby smiles slightly, then grins, but Jack scowls and says, "Gottdamn." I don't really care one way or the other.

In Texas, young men and women are taught to believe the world can be tamed. It's a bull that can be wrestled, and with strength and courage and energy you can lift that bull over your head and spin around and throw it to the ground. In certain parts of the world, and even in certain individuals, such a thought would be ludicrous. But in Texas I have seen the myth become truth, lightning strikes, men and women burning across the prairie of their lives, living fast, living strong. I have *seen* it—my father, my mother, and others; and I feel like an imposter, not having any children to follow after me, even though I am trying to live one of those strong lives myself—fast and free, scorning weakness.

A bolt of lightning smashes down on our left, raising our hair, and Jack shouts in his fear, and Kirby laughs, leans back in his seat and rolls the window down a little. A few sprays of rain blow in on his face, and on mine in the back seat. It feels good, and I crack my window a little, too.

I mean, Margie takes care of me. Sometimes I get really wild. Sometimes I just run out of the house, and up onto the mountain behind our cabin: just *running*. I'll be gone all afternoon—lying up there on the mountain on some damn rock or something, like a dog, lying in the high mountain sun—and when I finally come back, later that day, she'll be very quiet, and we'll just sit together, and it'll all be real calm. What I'm saying is, she takes care of me. And I take care of her: I do. Just not enough, I don't think.

Not only are Jack and Kirby best friends, now, but their wives are, too.

"I dreamed you were in my garbage can last night," Kirby tells Jack matter-of-factly. "I dreamed you were a raccoon, banging around in the garbage, sorting through my trash."

"Uh, huh," says Jack, seeming amused at the thought of being mistaken for a raccoon.

There's a metal box in the back of the jeep, a strange looking box with small holes punched in the sides of it, and I keep imagining I hear grunts and clicks coming from it.

"What've you got in the box?" I ask Jack.

"A coyote," he answers, without even looking back. Eyes on the road.

"No shit," I say, happy that he trusts me enough, already, to bullshit with me. "Where'd you get it?"

Jack does not answer, and I can tell that Kirby thinks we—Jack and I—are playing some sort of joke on him, one that he refuses to pick up on, and so the subject is dropped. But I can still hear something in that box behind me, something alive, it sounds like, moving around from time to time, occasionally making what sounds like spitting noises.

Near Galveston the night ends, and the flags on buildings are snapping straight out to the northwest, toward Montana, from where I've come. There's a warm southeast wind, which is the best for fishing, and though we are still in the squall, Jack is crazed by the southeast wind, rolling his window down, despite the rain, to smell it. He believes that there is the tiniest chance it will be raining on land, but not out in the bay, that it will be wet and storming in one place, but dry and windy at that place's edge. As we start driving past the refineries, past the tidal inlets, Kirby and I begin to believe in his wild, crazy hope; we have only a few miles to go, but it's true, the rain has died to a drizzle, and we can see patches of early-pearl sky, the first openings of slow gray light, and low black clouds tearing away in tatters and wisps, strange things happening above us. The sky is breaking apart, breaking up.

"We did it," Jack says, amazed, delighted. "We fucking outran it."

There's no one else out on the bay—though soon they'll begin showing up, diluting the space with their presence—but for now it's just us, and we get out and watch as Jack backs the trailer down the boat ramp into the water. There are barnacles on the pier beneath us, a little bait shop at the end of the dock, which is not open yet because the weather has been so bad, even though it's early light, dawn, fishing time.

Towering above our launch spot is a huge billboard, with the photo of a dark-haired beautiful woman on it, perhaps the most beautiful woman we've ever seen, on one of those "Wanted—Missing Person" advertisements. She's smiling, laughing on the billboard; and way above us like that, up in that strange, windy, cloud-parting sky (whitecaps splashing out in the bay), she looks like a goddess, giving us permission to go fishing, to go out and play.

HELP FIND RENEE JACKSON, the billboard says, and I study her more carefully than I would otherwise as I try to remember if I have ever seen her before—and then I think how the name sounds familiar, and I wonder if she is someone I might have gone to school with. But that is too long ago, it is old pork, stored in salt, gaps in memory, and there is only the future. I would like to help if I could—I would like to lift that bull, too—but it's all I can do to hope that Renee is all right, to give her my earnest, best hope. And it is not a good feeling.

We're lowering the boat into the water with a winch, the click-click-click of the wire cable spooling out. Kirby's operating it. He's been on a hundred fishing trips with Jack before. I get the sack lunches that Tricia, Kirby's wife, packed for all of us, and I carry them down the dock and hand them to Jack, who is already in the boat arranging things—gauges and fuel tanks, meters and such.

"Tricia make these?" Jack calls up to Kirby, who's about to pull the jeep and trailer away, to go park.

"Yep," says Kirby.

"She's so sweet," says Jack, opening one of the sacks and slowly sorting through it.

"Would Wendy make a lunch like that for you?" Kirby asks.

"Hell," says Jack, still looking through the lunch as if it's a discovery, "she didn't even get up to say goodbye."

Kirby is beaming, as if he's gotten away with something. I don't know whether Tricia fixed those sandwiches or not.

The sign looms above us as we climb down into the boat. The first thing I notice is that there aren't any life vests, and I can't swim, but I'm not worried. I'm not going anywhere. I look up at Renee Jackson, the most beautiful woman I've ever seen, it seems, that early in the morning, having driven all through the night and rain to get here, to launch beneath her gaze. The wind is whipping at my windbreaker, and I feel my eyes beginning to blur and go to water.

"Hey, are you crying, man?" Jack asks, and I wonder if Kirby has told him about Margie and me separating. "It's okay if you are, man," he says. The engine has finally caught, and is sputtering—clouds of blue smoke floating out over the bay, and the summer-sweet smell of outboard fuel, the engine clicking and gasping—and Jack the dentist is another man now, down low in the boat, working with the throttle, the steering wheel, the engine. He's suddenly an outlaw, too, the happiest one, and I think that's how it always goes, how the longer you go without something, the happier you are when you finally get it. I think about how happy, say, Renee Jackson's parents would be, were she to show up at their front door today.

"I mean, it's all right," Jack says again, squinting at me in the gray light. The sun is an arc of bright gold, rising through red-streaked clouds across the bay. Every raggedy cloud in the sky is fleeing, burning flame-red above us as the sky begins to light up—though down here on the water, in the waves, it's still dusky and gloomy, still foggy-gray. "Kirby cried for half an hour after we lost a redfish last year," Jack says. "I don't mean lost it on a hook—I mean lost it, dead. She was a forty-five-pound female with eggs, and it took so long to land her that she wasn't any good by the time we finally got her in. We tried to let her go again, right away, but she just lay there, in the surf, gasping, and then rolled over on her side. We worked with her for two hours, before she died. For a while we thought she was going to make it," Jack says. "She was as big as a dog. Two hours. What else could we do but cry?"

I have to turn away from the picture of Renee Jackson, or I *will* cry.

"Hand me one of those Rolling Rocks," I tell Kirby.

"Running like a fine watch!" Jack shouts, revving the engine. An alarming thump shakes the back of the boat, where the motor is housed, followed by an even more alarming miscellany of piston noise and exhaust, and slowly we creep out into the bay, following the lane of driven cedar poles out to deeper water.

We run around in large circles before entering open water, just to iron out all the engine's kinks before we get too far from shore, and sure enough, the engine cuts out, just as the sun is completely up, brilliant and golden in our eyes, strong salt wind in our faces.

We sit like fools for a while, too far from shore to swim-wade back—the water is four to six feet deep all through the bay but the current is strong—and Kirby and I, out of old habit, begin to despair and open beers. But Jack is still riding the crest of being captain, and the change in him is still evident, even from the set of his jaw. He lifts the hood to the engine and spies the problem immediately—the wires leading out of one of the spark plugs are bare and wet from the thunderstorm we drove through, and have been shorting against each other. Jack has some electrical tape in his toolbox and he wraps the offending wire quickly.

I don't mean to make Jack look like such a genius. The reason he was able to go straight to the problem is that he and Kirby had taken Jack's seventy-nine-year-old father out in the boat the week before, and the old man, a perfectionist, had ranted and raved to Jack for the first thirty minutes of the trip about the condition Jack had let the boat get into. Evidently the boat had belonged to Jack's father fifteen or twenty years ago—maybe longer—and the old man's loopy old hearing had picked up on the spark plug wires shorting right away.

"He was just howling," Kirby says. "Man, is he a hardass."

Chastened by the memory, Captain Jack slouches a little lower in the seat. Something's troubling him now; his face looks as it did when he was driving through the night, through the rain.

"Dollar-bill green!" he shouts, looking down at the water we're skimming across. I'm sitting up in the high-perched bow like a mascot, smelling the sea. "When the water's this color, and the wind's out of the southeast," Jack shouts, "you'll catch fish."

Kirby moves up to the front with me, also drinking a beer, and tries to fill me in as quickly as possible about all the things I should know, all the things he and Jack have learned from fishing together for the last five or six years.

"There's dolphins out here, but you never catch them," Kirby says. "They just follow you. Sometimes they come right up to the boat and stick their head out of the water and look you in the eye. A lot of times you can tell where the speckled trout are by the way the seagulls are acting. In warm weather—the summer, usually—you can look for slicks. A slick is an oily, flat spot on the water where the fish have gotten into a feeding frenzy on the shrimp and have eaten so much they've regurgitated it, and all the oils and digestive juices make this big slick on the surface of the ocean. It smells like watermelon. You smell watermelon out at sea and you'd better be ready, 'cause you're about to start catching fish."

"We may run aground," Jack shouts from the back. "Be careful." I picture us sliding to an immediate stop, beached by a barely submerged sandbar. I picture myself *not* stopping, but being catapulted forward, a human cannonball, and I sit a little lower in the bow and grip the sides.

It all looks the same to me. I can't see the shore anymore, can't see where any sandbars might be that could cause us to run aground, though I keep watching. We bounce across the chops of waves a little longer—seemingly by whim, with no plan, no landmarks—and then Jack cuts the engine, and we're drifting.

"Start fishing," says Jack. The silence sounds wonderful. Jack is already scrambling like a child, anxious to get his lure—an artificial shrimp, blood-red ("strawberry") in color—threaded onto a quarter-ounce jig and into the water. It's a big deal, I find out, to catch the first fish.

"We bought Kirby her first pair of shoes this week," Kirby says, once he has his rod set up and is working it, casting, retrieving, casting again. There's a high anticipation among all of us—any of us could catch the first fish at any given second, even me. "Man, was she mad!" Kirby laughs, remembering. "She kicked and waved, trying to throw them off just by *kicking*." Seven months. He's been a father for seven months. Pretty soon it'll be a year.

Jack's silent, intense, almost manic. It's a lovely day. The sun is warm on our shoulders, though just off to our left, where land is, we can see the black squall line—savage thunderstorms, wicked cold streaks of lightning. And also, coming from that direction is a line of boats, raising high waves, far in the distance, coming like a posse.

"The *popdicks*," grunts Kirby.

"You got any popdicks in Montana?" Jack asks, glancing in the direction of the oncoming boats.

"Say what?" I ask.

"Popdicks," says Jack. He's watching his line again, reeling in. I don't think I've ever seen anyone as serious about anything as Jack is about catching that first fish.

"What's a popdick?" I say. I'm almost afraid to ask. Kirby and Jack howl, delighted to hear me say the word. It's some private joke between them, some word they've made up, and I feel as if I've crossed some magical boundary, as if I've been initiated, included in something. Suddenly I feel further away than ever from Margie.

"Popdicks," says Kirby, "run their boats across the water in front of you, going too fast, so that they scare all the fish away."

Just then Jack's rod bows. He's got a big one, the first saltwater fish I've ever seen caught. Only I haven't seen it yet, it is still out there in the bay, fighting to get free. But Jack's bringing it in, and Kirby clambers about the boat trying to get the landing net ready. Presently we see flashes of silver, like underwater lightning, and then Kirby has the net under the big fish, a club-length speckled trout, fierce-toothed, metallic gray with a yellow and white belly and smart eyes, a high second dorsal fin. Jack quickly unhooks the fish and slides it into the ice chest, where it thrashes and beats its tail against the sides—a sound we pretend not to hear, or rather, not to understand.

"Easy, big fella," says Jack, readjusting his strawberry shrimp; it's been half pulled off, like a woman coming out of her slip, and he slides it all the way back up on the hook. We can't cast out again, though, because by now all the popdicks have converged on us and they drift in a rough circle around us, as if surrounding us. They are casting shamelessly into the school of speckled trout that was ours, that we had found—and they're catching them and are hooting with joy and excitement, as if they've done something special.

"I'd rather be dead than be a popdick," Jack mutters, and gives the old boat its full throttle, and guns us through the center of the schooling trout—several of them leap out of the water, bright and glittering in the sun—and then we're through the ranks of the popdicks, and running again, for open sea, open bay.

Later in the afternoon, Jack finds another school, and both he and Kirby hook a trout on the same retrieve. There are a few other boats—popdicks—following roughly the same drift line as we are, but they are not close enough to see our poles, and if we're careful, we can keep the fish a secret.

"This is how you do it when the popdicks are watching," says Jack, speaking through his teeth like a ventriloquist and holding the rod down low to the water, reeling in nonchalantly, as if nothing were happening. I see that Kirby is doing the same thing. They land the fish quietly, without the net and around on the back side of the boat, so that it looks like we are getting beer out of the ice chest.

I am not getting any strikes. Jack and Kirby try to give me pointers as they fish, but it's hard to fish and teach at the same time. Like most things, it's just something that I am going to have to work out by myself. They each catch two more fish before the popdicks realize what is going on and start their motors and come racing over.

"Hey, you *popdicks!*" Kirby shouts, when he sees the secret is out. He holds the bent pole high in the air with one hand as the fish that is on the other end struggles and dives, and with his other hand he begins waving the popdicks over. "Hey, everybody—come on over *here!* I'm catching 'em! Hey, popdicks—come on!"

Jack curses, shaking his head, as if disciplining himself to say nothing—I can tell he hates scenes—but Kirby is giggling, and we leave the spot in a full spray of rooster-tail just as the first of the popdicks arrive, friendly and curious, shameless, looking for fish.

After that, we go far inland and down along the point where no one can possibly see us. In the shallower water we begin catching hook-jawed flounder and Gulf trout. Jack catches a fair-sized redfish—a big dull-looking bull-headed fish that keeps its mouth open all the time, like a slackard, and which, before being landed, and with its great strength, runs around and around the boat, circling it like a shark five or six times before tiring. Kirby has a tube of some magic fish-catching attractant that he'd wasted three dollars on at a sporting goods store in Houston. "Kawanee" is the magical name Kirby and Jack have given to it, and after several more beers, and with the ice chest beginning to fill with fish (fish for dinner, fish for the freezer, and fish for their wives) we grow slightly loopy, and Kirby insists on smearing my lure—still a strawberry shrimp, which is what is working for them—with Kawanee before each cast.

I still haven't caught a single fish.

There is the requisite talk of sex.

"You know, Jack, when your assistant leans over me in the dentist's chair, I can see her bosoms," Kirby says. "I mean, I can *really* see them—even the tips."

"No shit," says Jack, nursing a beer. It is a slack spot in the fishing, perhaps because we have all put the Kawanee on our lures. It is a waxy, greasy substance, like ChapStick, and it smells like something dead. "No shit," Jack says again, perhaps imagining it. Then he says, "Well, that's fine, but you can't look at things like that anymore. You're married. Hell, you're even a father."

"Yeah, but I'm still a wild son of a bitch," Kirby says, and he sounds almost angry.

The wind is so warm and salty out of the southeast. It is blowing us back in toward the shore, and the tide has turned and is running back in, so that the way our course is set, we can just sit there and drift all the way back in, all the way back to where we have come from.

"Wendy's mean," Jack says, picking up another bottle, "but she's a hellcat in bed. Thank goodness."

Kirby just grunts. I can tell he isn't going to get Tricia into this, and I sure am not going to bring Margie in. And I do not really want to hear about Wendy, do not want to picture her being a hellcat. Maybe someone else—maybe even Jack's dental assistant—but not his wife. I don't want to hear about that, and I don't think Kirby does, either.

We drift like that, fishing slowly and drinking beer, back in toward shore, back toward the dark purple edge of the thunderbank that looms at shore. The cloudbank, not so far in the distance, is still spitting gold streaks of lightning.

"I can't get over how upset your old man was about those spark plug wires," Kirby says. "I thought he was going to blow a clot. Do you know how happy he was to be able to really rip into you? He'll be talking about it for the rest of his life. He'll never stop."

"Ah, that's okay," Jack says, sighing. "I know he's losing his mind, but he's still my dad. I guess I can put up with it for a few more years. We'll be goofy old fuckers ourselves someday," he says.

"I hope so," says Kirby.

We are close enough to the shore that I can see the poster again, the one of Renee Jackson. We have stopped fishing and are just drifting toward her, lazily.

"She's been missing for a long time, hasn't she?" Kirby asks Jack.

"I think so," Jack says. "But I think they found her. I think that's the one whose skeleton they found over on East Beach last spring."

We have to look at her, drifting in. There is nowhere else to look but straight out at her—with her looking back at us, looking down, smiling and laughing. It is that point in the day—and always, each day, whether you are two blocks away or two continents, you feel it—where you feel too far away from your wife, your family—cut off, cast off, drifting away—and where you wish so strongly that you could see them again, reach out and hold their hands; not for any reason, just an unspecific, heart-scrabbling loneliness. We drift up to the boat launch, maneuvering in the last several yards with the motor, suddenly tired from catching so many fish. Kirby hops out and gets the jeep and trailer, lowers it into the water so we can drive the boat up on it, and we hook the cable winch up to it and reel it in. We are ready to go home.

I know what Margie meant about feeling tired. I am tired, too. But we almost have to keep going on: We almost *have* to.

It is about four-thirty in the afternoon. Jack stops along a deserted stretch of beach on the way home—wet sand, sea grasses blowing in the dark wind, splatters of rain beginning to strike our faces, another storm starting up—and he asks Kirby and me to help him carry the steel box that has been in the back of the jeep down to the dunes.

I'd forgotten about it, but as soon as we lift it, it becomes very apparent that there is something alive in the box after all, something spitting and snarling, and we set it down in the tall salt grasses and then step back.

"I trapped it in my backyard," Jack says proudly. "I really did."

The Gulf wind is stinging our faces with a fine mist of salt and blowing drops of water in from off of the waves. But it is a warm wind. The beach, at high tide, is a long narrow strip of tan; the sky is a lurid black, a horrible purple, like the bruise on the inside of a woman's thigh. We can see condominiums and high rises farther down the beach, and lightning crackles and speaks all around us.

"Let her rip," Jack says, opening the door to the metal box. A small coyote about the size of a collie shoots out without looking back and begins running down the beach, running in a straight line, as if it has not been cooped up for hours in a small place. It's running with its tail floating behind, and running—and this is the most beautiful thing—directly toward the condominiums and town houses, running north and into the wind, without looking back, as if it knows exactly where it is going.

SAILING AT AN ELBOW'S LENGTH

BY BARBARA LLOYD

HAVING GROWN UP among the sleek wooden powerboats of the 1950's, I find it difficult now to explain my fascination with sailing. I was bred to like speedboats—whether the mahogany Chris Craft tied to our dock on Lake Ontario, or the eighteen-foot runabout we used for water skiing—but whenever I could snatch the family's only sailing skiff from the hands of three brothers, I would venture out on my own. And when I did, I discovered how the lake could be an unkindly place for a teenager with a streak of adventure in her soul. More than once, I found myself sailing off too far and with too much wind barking at my heels. Those sagas were usually followed by a restful day on the water . . . *under engine*. I had always figured that the only thing that could go wrong in a speedboat was having the engine quit, which somehow seemed far better than having an unwieldy sail blow you upside down in a squall.

A few years later, time and circumstances drew me to the ocean around Newport, Rhode Island. It was a place, as I soon found out, where sailboats rule and powerboats serve. I still remember my first close-up view of an America's Cup contender. I was a journalism student at the University of Rhode Island with little on my mind other than a good story. The yacht was *Southern Cross*, a twelve-meter sailboat owned and campaigned in 1974 by Alan Bond, Australia's financial mogul. She was on a cradle at a local shipyard when I came upon her. I remember looking up at the gigantic hull, a yellow whale of a boat, and thinking it was the most incredible vessel I had ever seen.

Later, as a reporter for the *Newport Daily News*, I would come to know the decks and hulls of many kinds of sailboats, and when it was time in 1977 to assign a staff member to cover the America's Cup competition in Newport, they asked me.

That summer I had my first ride on a twelve-meter yacht. Ted Turner, the Atlanta yachtsman and television entrepreneur, was defending the America's Cup, the sporting world's oldest and most venerable trophy, from Australia. Turner was skipper of *Courageous*, a proven twelve-meter that had successfully defended the Cup in 1974.

I was invited to go along for a ride—to test the waters as it were. As a cub yachting writer, I was grateful for the chance to see firsthand what these boats were like. I was shuttled out to sea by a *Courageous* tender, a powerboat with ample room to carry gear and sails for its America's Cup charge. I clambered aboard *Courageous* and found a place to sit just behind the mast.

We were off to the sounds of a massive mainsail riding its halyard up the mast. When we took off, it was as if we were on the back of a gazelle. The boat slid through the water in a twelve-knot breeze— slicing the waves, not bouncing over them. I remember thinking how peaceful it was.

Since then, I have been around the world to report on the BOC Challenge, the global yacht race for solo sailors, and have spent five months in Australia reporting on the 1987 America's Cup races for the *New York Times*. Yet out of the hundreds of experiences that a

journalist encounters, there are certain events that keep coming back
to you.

I cannot find a logical way to equate the startling power of the Big
Boat, the 132-foot yacht that New Zealand brought to the America's
Cup scene in 1988, with the electricity of Dennis Conner's sixty-foot
catamaran, the Cup defender that year. To look aloft on a yacht that's
the size of New Zealand's Big Boat (her true name was *New Zealand*,
but she was affectionately called "Big Boat" by one and all) is like
standing at the base of the Washington Monument. The five-
thousand-square-foot mainsail has more yardage than you'd see in a
circus tent. And the crew of forty puts more men at the windward rail
than football players on a field.

On May 31, 1988, more than three months before New Zealand
was to take on Conner's catamaran, *Stars & Stripes*, in an unorthodox
race for the America's Cup, I found myself in a powerboat off the
coast of San Diego. I was being taken out to sea to board the Big Boat
on her maiden voyage in United States waters. And even though I
was fairly adept on boats, the idea of boarding the Big Boat while she
was under sail did not appeal to me.

With me were a television broadcaster and a cameraman. They
were wearing dark clothes, which did not please the New Zealand
public relations people at all. The crew on the Big Boat were dressed
in white—which was part of the spectacle of sailing the Big Boat. To
go on board, we had to be in white, too. My outfit passed the
whiteness test, but the others had to don white paper coveralls. I felt
sorry for the cameraman, an overweight man whose paper suit made
him look like a life-sized version of the Pillsbury doughboy.

We leaped from a small inflatable boat onto the Big Boat's stern
and scurried up until we were safely on deck. The crew watched
silently from the windward rail. All we could hear were the rush of
boats through surf and the hydraulics of the biggest sloop in modern
sailboat racing doing their thing. Once aboard, I uttered a quiet sigh
and looked back. Though safely aboard, the doughboy was in paper
shreds.

I had the feeling that the New Zealand crew felt it was on stage. To
a man, they were intent in their jobs, more so than you could expect
from forty guys on a day sail. But the boat was huge, the waters were

new to them, and Hollywood was not far away. Michael Fay, the New Zealand banker who owned this massive toy, was on board, too. Easygoing as he appeared, no one seemed eager for his attention. I poked around as much as I dared on deck. Computer instrumentation in a lower hatch looked impressive, but I sensed it was a forbidden place. Minutes later, the crew politely asked the cameraman to kindly direct his lens elsewhere. At that point, the team had no more desire to give the *Stars & Stripes* crew any more edge than it already had.

I stayed low and inched my way forward on the boat. I wanted to see the 150-foot mast from its foot, and I wanted to get a sense of the Big Boat's power from up forward. The crewmen were more talkative up there. It was as if I had moved out of the dugout and into the outfield.

"Lobster pot ahead," called out the man at the bow. The message was relayed past me back to the helm. The boat was too big to expect a shout to be heard from one end to the other. David Barnes, the skipper, responded with a slight turn of the wheel. The Big Boat responded like a feather in a puff of air and swung effortlessly in a new direction.

I had been allowed to steer for five minutes or so. Surprisingly, the boat handled no differently from any ocean racer. It was hard, almost impossible to see past the expanse of deck and gear, and I appreciated the fact that there were plenty of eyes and ears on the lookout for me. The experience was not unlike the first time I put my five-year-old hands on the steering wheel of the family Buick.

When the order was given to change tacks from port to starboard, the crew made ready. On any racing sailboat, the crew sits on the "high" side, the windward rail, with their legs dangling like octopus appendages over the edge. On *New Zealand*, the stance was exaggerated—twenty-five pairs of legs instead of the standard five or six straddling the high side. It was like sitting on a fiberglass cliff. The boat heeled dramatically to leeward in less than a twelve-knot breeze. I went back and joined the rail crew. It was hard to believe my weight would make any difference in holding this leviathan down.

The *Stars & Stripes* catamaran was a completely different animal. The crew was limited to nine, including the boat's skipper, Dennis Conner. A Star Class sailor most of his life, and skipper of four America's Cup campaigns, Conner had a transition to make in sailing a sixty-foot catamaran. He handpicked his crew; half had sailed with him in 1987 when he won the Cup back from Australia (after he had lost the Cup to Australia in 1983, he vowed to win it back), and the other half were multihull experts from sailing's most technologically advanced generation.

It was August 30, 1988. In a week, the great contest of monohull versus multihull—*New Zealand* against *Stars & Stripes*—would be history. Although Conner and his crew knew they had the faster boat, they were concerned about a breakdown, which was very possible. If Conner and his San Diego Yacht Club team lost the Cup to New Zealand, it would probably be due to busted gear.

I went for a ride on *Stars & Stripes* in a fifteen-knot breeze, and immediately saw that things were different on the cat. On the Big Boat, the crew rarely got wet; on *Stars & Stripes*, walking across the webbed netting that served as a deck between the two hulls was like walking through a river during spring runoff. There was also none of the scrambling associated with the Big Boat.

We left the dock in still water. Then, only minutes later, came the surprise when we headed off the wind. Because of its hard-wing sail (a gossamer network of Mylar plastic and carbon fiber), *Stars & Stripes* was always ready to go. The mainsail was never down. And the second the wind took hold, we sprinted. Sailing on *Stars & Stripes* was like riding the back of a waterbug.

The six-thousand-pound catamaran, weighing a fraction of what other boats its size weigh, was able to skip along at twenty-two to twenty-four knots in a fourteen-knot breeze. To get the maximum out of the wind and boat, to reduce friction and drag, you had to finesse the windward hull so that it hovered just inches above the water's surface. If you let the hull ride up too high, though, you risked capsizing.

I was unprepared for the soaking I would get that day. With notepad in hand—I would be writing an article about the trip as soon as I got back to shore—I bounded from side to side as we tacked. Conner, a big man who puts on and loses weight the way a chameleon changes color, was in his heavy mode. Even so, I was impressed with his ability to sprint across that undulating deck.

I had sailed on catamarans before. I had even co-owned an eighteen-foot Hobie Cat. And while their speed is exhilarating, always present is the very real worry of digging the bow of one or both hulls into a rough sea, or flipping over if the mainsheet isn't let out fast enough. On *Stars & Stripes* I felt a touch uneasy. I knew the boat could turn reckless on a dime. Steering by a tiller (there is one for each side) rather than a wheel, you have to let go of one tiller, sprint across the net, and grab the opposite tiller. Conner handed me the tiller and, although my first impulse was to say, "No thanks," I took the steering arm. I knew that the crew, a handful of highly experienced sailors, were ready to react if I got into trouble. A catamaran moves so quickly that there isn't time to miss a beat. Although I managed to coax one hull out of the water, I was constantly concerned about the occasional puff that would lift it higher and put us and the boat in possible jeopardy. We slipped by a channel marker I hadn't seen. Conner yelped. Yes, we cleared it.

Two minutes later we were heading offshore and Conner took the tiller back. I watched him closely as he played it like a violin and expertly feathered it to adjust for puffs in the wind. Despite the fact that several of the crew had far more experience on that type of boat, it was very clear that Dennis Conner knew exactly what he was doing and that he was the boss of *Stars & Stripes*.

The wind was picking up slowly. We were in a practice race with the team's other catamaran, identical to *Stars & Stripes* except for its conventional sail. Halfway through the twenty-mile course, the waves started breaking in white crests ahead of us. One of the crewmen, Cam Lewis, handed me his automatic camera and asked me to take photographs. I thought it peculiar, considering how much access the crew must have to the thousands of images professional photographers take of the crew. It was a reminder that the America's Cup is, after all, one part showbiz.

The seas were picking up and I thought we had to be hitting at least twenty knots. I asked Conner and immediately felt the eyes of the crew upon me. There was a pause, then Conner asked me if his answer was for print. I said it was. "Then I can't tell you," he said. "We don't want Michael Fay and his boys to know that." I thought it strange that Conner was still trying to keep the cat's speed a secret when many articles had already been printed about it. When I composed the article later that day, I wrote: "One could only watch the water hissing off the stern and estimate that *Stars & Stripes* was sprinting at about twenty-two knots."

The day's sail was not without its drama. The concern that Conner expressed at the start about gear failure came back at him with a loud bang. We suddenly stopped short in the water, as if someone had slammed on an imaginary brake. The boat shuddered; all eyes looked to the mast. *Stars & Stripes* had dug both its bows into the sea. Although it could have toppled the wing mast or broken a crossbeam—both serious mishaps that would have crippled the American effort in its upcoming race against New Zealand—no one said much of anything. We soon got up to speed again and had no major breakdowns during our sail. There was, however, an uneasy quiet that pervaded the atmosphere around the cat for the rest of the day.

A week later, when *Stars & Stripes* was beating New Zealand's Big Boat on the race course, I thought back to my day on the catamaran. In the second and final race of the series, Conner was being chastised for sandbagging—holding back the catamaran so his wide margin of victory wouldn't appear quite so devastating. Although I suspected some truth in the charge, it had been a moderately windy day with sloppy seas, meaning there was more going on aboard *Stars & Stripes* than anyone could imagine.

Knowing what I did about *Stars & Stripes* made me reluctant to pass judgment on Conner. In fact, it supported more than ever my belief that yachting is truly an insider's game, one where winning or losing depends on how close players hold their cards to their vests.

I still can't say which boat was better. Even though I was allowed to steer both boats and feel the surge and power of each race up through my arms, I can't make a clear determination. To be honest, I doubt anyone can. Not even the players. But that I got to sample the waters, to peek over the shoulders of the players, and see for myself what each boat and its crew was like meant everything. It reminded me that being a yachting journalist is often as challenging and rewarding an occupation as being a player in the world of modern sailing.

TAKEN BY STORM

BY JAMES KILGO

MY GRANDFATHER SPENT the last thirty years of his life in bed, victim of an assortment of chronic maladies. During my childhood, he seemed to suffer one crisis after another—the deliriums of high fever, internal bleeding, and, once, a stroke that left him tangled in the sheets at the foot of the bed. These afflictions took him and us by storm. The news would come crackling through the long-distance wire, my mother's face revealing on the phone the danger he was in. I always had trouble accepting it. Since I had never seen him in such extremity, I could not imagine him without the authority of his faculties, and the thought of him caught helpless in the throes of fever confused and frightened me, as though he had been swept out on some dire passage from which he would not return. But return he would. By summer, when we went to visit them, Doc would have recovered, keen and full of wit, ready to resume his discourse on Shakespeare, fishing, baseball, and the Bible.

But that was as well as he got. I never saw him out of bed except when he was hobbling to the bathroom supported by my grandmother, and then I was shocked to see how small and weak his body was. When I was older, I asked my mother what was wrong with him. A lot of things, she said—allergies, digestive problems, migraine headaches; Doc had never been well. I could not understand why any of those conditions would make a complete invalid of a man, but apparently they had.

Instead of complaining, Doc laughed at his infirmities, often describing himself by quoting Shakespeare's Jaques: "second childishness and mere oblivion, sans teeth, sans eyes, sans taste, sans everything." An ordained minister, he wrote what he called sermonettes for a local paper. People came from all over the state to see him.

When Doc was in his mid-seventies, he and my grandmother (whom everyone knew as Buddie) moved to a house on a hydroelectric lake outside of town, bought a boat, and, to the extent permitted by health and weather, went fishing. They did it more for his sake than for hers. Among his passions fishing was the one he had continued to insist on, and through the years of his long decline she had cheerfully contrived ways to get him on the water. But they were too old now, their children thought, too old to go out on big water in a boat by themselves.

To a child that boat was a wonder. When we visited them in the summer, we would find it tied to the dock in front of the house, the July sun bouncing water shadows all along its dark green sides. In itself it was unremarkable, a twelve-foot skiff no different from a hundred similar craft on the lake. What made it noticeable to the neighbors and irresistibly enticing to us was the way my grandmother had converted it into a floating bedroom. With energy and resourcefulness, Buddie had equipped the boat with a folding cot and a blue and yellow beach umbrella that stood in a socket bolted to the floor. The neighbors soon grew accustomed to the sight of the old couple working up and down the shoreline. When the umbrella was open, one said, they looked like the owl and the pussycat.

*   *   *

The news of Doc's adventure came long-distance from Buddie one morning in July. In its first telling it was not so much a story as a series of exclamations—self-reproach, exasperation, and relief. Later, as my mother and her sister compared versions, they pieced together a coherent narrative. It began with my aunt's calling Buddie from her home in Columbia and asking her to drive down for the day. Doc had been free of serious illness the whole spring and into the summer. So Buddie put aside her customary reservations about leaving him and arranged for Liza, a kind and gentle black woman, to stay until she got back that night.

Liza had served my grandparents as maid, cook, and nurse off and on for more than thirty years. Almost as old as Doc and no longer in good health herself, she came now only once a week, often on Saturday so she could sit with Doc and listen to the baseball game— they were both Brooklyn Dodgers fans. I had heard my mother and her sister laughing about that arrangement. "I can't imagine what Liza could do if Daddy really needed help," my mother said. "Other than call the ambulance."

The morning Buddie left for Columbia, Liza told her not to worry. Just go on and have a good time, she said, we'll be just fine.

"Just don't let him talk you into going fishing," Buddie said. "I don't want to have to worry about him all the way to Columbia and back."

Liza laughed. "I might could get him down there, but how us gonna get back up? That's what I want to know. I wouldn't be no more help to him than he would to me. And wouldn't that be a fix. You go on now. We be just fine."

From his bed Doc could see the water. He held out until early afternoon.

I can imagine Liza's attempts to dissuade him and just as easily his persistence. They were such good friends it must have been a gentle tug of war.

"And where you gonna sit? Tell me that."

"Why, I'll lie on my cot, Liza."

"Oh no you ain't. Not in that boat you ain't. Miz Lawton done said not to let you go fishing in the first place. I sho ain't gonna help you climb in no boat."

"I'll be perfectly all right, Liza. The boat is tied to the dock. It's not going anywhere."

"Why can't you lay in that long folding chair she got. I'll put that out for you and you can fish right there from the dock."

"I just like the feel of water beneath me."

With Doc behind her, gripping her frail shoulders, Liza led him down to the lake. They went even more slowly than usual because of an angry ingrown nail on his big toe. She murmured her disapproval all the way. Easing him into the boat was tricky, but they managed. She even got the umbrella up, though that turned out to be wasted effort, for soon after he was settled a dark cloud covered the sun.

While he fished she sat on the dock and shelled butterbeans. For a while they argued about who should make the All-Star team. Then Doc complained about the failure of the fish to bite and Liza worried about the cloud. Finally, she got to her feet. "We better be getting back up to the house now. It look like it fixing to bust loose any minute."

"We sure do need it all right, but you know as well as I do that it's been clouding up like this every afternoon for two weeks and we haven't had a good shower yet." When she didn't respond, Doc added, "What I really want to do is go down yonder to that little cove."

"Well you just gonna have to want to 'cause drive that boat is one thing I can't do."

"What I was thinking is that you could take the rope and pull me along the bank. It's not very far. Do you think you could do that?"

Liza untied the rope and stepped carefully from the dock to the ground. Then with the skiff in tow she picked her way along the rocky red-clay beach just above the waterline. The boat followed easily. They were about halfway to the cove when the wind hit. A stiff breeze at first, it filled the umbrella like a sail. The rope stretched taut. Liza tried to hold the boat, but it pulled her into the shallows. She set her heels in the soft bottom, but a gust hit her from behind and struck the side of the boat like a big fist. She pitched forward. Reaching to catch herself, she let go the rope. Doc yelled to her, but the wind was roaring in her ears. By the time she got to her feet and back on the bank, the boat was too far out for shouting, but she hollered anyway, "Hold on!" and waved her arms.

*   *   *

Since Doc never gave his version of the event, the story always abandoned him at this point and followed Liza back to the house, where she called everybody she could think of. But each time I heard it I stayed beside the lake, wondering how Doc managed to ride out the storm. He never said. Maybe he was too embarrassed to talk about it. But I have lived long enough now to have learned something about boats in a storm. With a surer sense of my own mortality, I find it easy to imagine that I am out there on the water with my grandfather.

Doc's first concern was Liza. His eyes were too weak to make out her features, but he could feel her distress in the way she rocked and waved. He wanted to comfort her, assure her that it was all his fault; but there was no time to fret about that. The umbrella was fluttering loudly. Bellied against the wind, it threatened to pull loose the board through which it was bolted and tear a hole in the plywood floor. Maybe he could lift it from its socket. But just as he was reaching for it, the ribs broke with a loud pop, and the blue and yellow canvas folded into a huge shriveled flower.

Instantly, he could feel the difference in the motion of the boat, but he was well offshore by then, too far out to consider paddling, even if he had had the strength. The motor was his only hope, but even Buddie sometimes had trouble getting it started; he doubted he could pull the rope hard enough. Easing his way from the cot to the seat in the stern, he noticed Liza, still on the bank. He waved her on toward the house. She waved back. He tilted the motor into the water and gave the cord a pull. No use. Liza was toiling up the hill, into the wind. He lay back against the corner of the stern, exhausted, and urged her on.

Liza made it to the house and disappeared inside. Help should be coming soon. He wondered if the sheriff had a boat.

But maybe he wouldn't need the sheriff. When he turned he saw a spit of land ahead, a bare red-clay point that reached like a tongue into the lake. It was still some distance off. For a few minutes he dared to believe he might run aground on it. Closer, he reached for the paddle at his feet and tried to rudder the boat to the left, but, shoved by the gusts, the vessel kept no steady course. Heeling first one way and then another, it missed the point by fifty feet. He could see the bottom as he crossed the underwater bar.

In the heavy chop of open water, the boat began to pitch and roll.

Whitecaps broke against the bow, spraying his face. He grasped the handle of the motor for balance and support. And felt a surge of exhilaration. He was on his own. At first he did not know whether the thrill he felt was that of joy or fear. Total dependence had become such a habit his mind was slow to realize that for the first time in thirty years he was free of the well-meaning solicitude of wife and children, the orders of doctors and nurses, the confining bed. He was beginning to enjoy this. Then he remembered: This was the way it used to feel to get up from bed after a long bout with malaria and drive an automobile again, or to enter the woods with a gun, or to decide when and where he was going fishing and for how long. Like a child behind a steering wheel, he gripped the handle harder and pretended he was really in control of speed and direction.

But his body was not up to the game. Accustomed to being on his back, he soon needed something to lean against, and, because he was lightly dressed, he wanted protection from the wind and spray. The bow of the boat was decked with plywood. The area beneath it was small, but if he could get to the front he would fit. He would have to manage on his own, of course—a tricky business with the boat rolling in the swells—and he would have to do it now, while he still had control of his arms and legs. Already his feet were growing numb from the slosh of water in the bottom, and he was beginning to shiver.

He looked toward the shore but his glasses were fogged and without them he could not distinguish between land and lake. He had no idea where he was, but he knew that rescue was unlikely now. This was the kind of storm forecasters warned against. He had heard their bulletins on the radio: small craft advised to stay off of area lakes. Maybe he was closer to the other side than he knew. In any case, he had to get to the front of the boat if he expected to be alive when he landed.

He took it slowly, stern to cot, cot to bow, more like an inchworm than a man, he thought. In the process he struck his bad toe against something hard, and for a moment he thought he might vomit, but the throbbing soon subsided to an ache he could stand. Holding on to the bent shaft of the umbrella, he lowered himself to the floor and crawled forward into the shelter. He found life jackets there and put one on. It pillowed him against the sides and provided a little warmth. Except for the pitching of the boat, which in that position made him dizzy, he might have been almost comfortable.

His toe no longer hurt. He knew why. He reached for his foot but grasped his knee and remembered the death of Falstaff. "Then I felt to his knees," the hostess said, "and so upward and upward, and all was as cold as any stone." If death came now in the wind and rain— for it had begun to rain—he would be glad at least not to die like Falstaff, in a strange bed, babbling of green fields. That was the fear he had lived with all these years—not death, but dying in a hospital, attended by strangers. He was surprised to feel so drowsy, to think that he might actually be able to sleep in such a wet, wildly rocking bed.

What woke him was the jolt and then the grating of rocks against the underside of the boat. He lay still for a long time. Now and then a small wave lifted the stern. He began to realize he was landed. He opened his eyes and concluded that the rain had stopped. After a while he looked for something to grab hold of, found it and dragged himself from his nest in the bow. Now he could reach the gunwale and pull himself up to a kneeling position. He didn't know what had happened to his glasses. He felt around on the floor and then gave up. What he saw when he looked resembled a house, white and perched on a hill above the water. If the people were at home they should be coming down to get him. Maybe it was a vacation house, unoccupied this week. He would have to get out of the boat and see for himself.

It took him almost an hour to crawl across the slick, rocky beach and up the grassy hill. Several times he had to stop and rest. By the time he made it, knees bruised and bad toe throbbing again, he knew the house was empty. So he turned and leaned back against a banister and looked out upon the lake. The calm water reflected rosy clouds and illumined the air between lake and sky. As the sun went down the colors faded. Doc drew in his legs against the chill and waited to be found.

"They found him under the steps of a house across the lake," the story always ended. "Right at dark. Somebody spotted the boat, I guess, and followed his tracks." They had him back in his own bed safe and sound by the time Buddie got home that night.

What my grandparents said to each other never got into the story.

As for Doc's silence about the experience, I doubt embarrassment had anything to do with it. I'm sure he regretted Liza's distress, but I like to think he had no regrets at all about what happened in the storm. I like to think that instead of trying to explain he just waited until Buddie calmed down and then assured her that he would be ready to try the bream again on the next full moon.

SEAS OF
SWEET WATER

BY DAN GERBER

WHEN I WAS a child, growing up on the eastern shore of Lake Michigan, the profiles of the long ships, their bridges rising over their bows like seaborne ziggurats, and later, the more conventional silhouettes of Liberian freighters, passed on the horizon nearly as little noticed as clouds. "Ore boats," my father would murmur, looking over his paper to the west, squinting against the evening sun.

In the heat of late summer, I imagined this littoral as a Pacific island. It was always the Pacific because, as on our Pacific coast, the sun set over the water. I dug foxholes in the sand and waited for the Japanese to storm the beach from their homeland somewhere on the far side of the lake. My fantasy was reinforced by the Navy

Corsairs and Hellcats flying training missions along the shore. Frequently they flew with their cockpit canopies open, so low I could see the faces of the pilots who waved to me. Of course it was only a childhood conceit, though in 1634 Jean Nicolet, the first white man to gaze across these waters, expected to find China on their western shore and even carried a damask robe embroidered with poppies and birds of paradise to be properly attired for his arrival.

On a flight from Paris to Chicago, I was seated among the members of a French film crew. As we circled over the southern end of Lake Michigan, one of the Frenchmen tugged at my sleeve and pointed to the water below. "Quelle est cette mer?"

"Lake Michigan," I replied with exaggerated enunciation.

"Lake? Qu'est-ce que lake?" He turned to one of his companions. "Lac? No. Mer. No. What sea is this?"

The film crew remained unconvinced. This apparently infinite expanse of water didn't jibe with their concept of a lake. I have also encountered a similar incredulity among ocean sailors who envision the Great Lakes as broad pastoral ponds.

Herman Melville took pains to disparage this notion, writing of the Great Lakes in *Moby-Dick*:

". . . they are swept by Borean and dismasting blasts as direful as any that lash the salted wave; they know what shipwrecks are, for out of sight of land, however inland, they have drowned full many a mid-night ship with all its shrieking crew."

And in recent times a popular song about the sinking of the *Edmund Fitzgerald* spread some awareness to our pelagic coasts that the Great Lakes could be great in devastation as well as in size. (Though the song is misleading in that it portrays Lake Superior alone as formidable, whereas Lake Michigan has claimed many more sizable ships, like the 640-foot limestone carrier *Carl D. Bradley*, which broke in two in November 1958 and went to the bottom with thirty-three of its thirty-five-man crew.) Apart from its legend in song, the sinking of the *Fitzgerald*, because of the suddenness with which it disappeared and the mysteries still surrounding it, remains the most horrifying and intriguing. A steel carrier and two saltwater ships were in contact with the *Fitzgerald*, which was reporting thirty-foot combers and some even higher. The captain's last words were, "Big sea. I've never seen anything like it." Within minutes of this last communiqué, her lights disappeared and she vanished from the radar screens; a 729-foot ship gone down without even a Mayday call.

There's a theory that she might have been raised bow and stern by monstrous waves causing her unsupported weight to collapse her amidships. One can imagine the scream of parting steel in the dark of that storm. Another theory, and the one considered more likely, is that she was simply battered, nose down, in the trough of a mountainous wave and driven, bow first, to the bottom by the sheer weight of its water. But all that's certain is that the *Fitzgerald* lies broken in two on the bottom in 530 feet of water too cold to support the life of the microorganisms that could cause the bodies of its dead to surface.

Now, from an airplane window in late January, Lake Michigan's ice floes extend lakeward as far as I can see, their ridged and slaggy surface peaked with ice volcanoes, geysers intermittently shooting from their cones in the surge of compressed waves below. The spray freezes and the cones mount in a frozen moonscape. The ice reaches a mile from land, its curved edge replicating the serpentine contours of the shore. The brash ice at its edge dissolves into the open water beyond, and its somber steely blue is crazed with whitecaps in a twenty-knot wind.

At Sturgeon Bay I join the Coast Guard cutter *Mobile Bay*, one of the new class of small icebreakers commissioned for year-round search and rescue and clearing ice in the shipping channels. The *Mobile Bay* is imprisoned in ice at the pier, and the bubbler system is engaged to free it. Compressed air is being jettisoned below the waterline to soften the ice while the weight of the water beginning to spread over its surface works to collapse it.

The twin diesel electrics are started and we begin the laborious process of rocking back and forth against the spring lines to break enough ice from around the hull so that we can clear the tugs moored off our bow and the two lake freighters in for winter layover, astern. The ice-clearing takes approximately an hour, and I'm standing on the bridge with the engineering officer. A native of Washington, he is telling me how he had underestimated the lakes when he was first transferred to them from duty on Puget Sound. "I wasn't expecting anything like this," he muses. "On the ocean you can have thirty-foot seas and the waves will come two hundred feet apart, but on the lakes the seas get just as big, only the waves come every hundred feet." It's the difference between a queasy but rhythmic ballet and a series of rock-shuddering jabs from a heavyweight. The lake waves blast you in combination while you're still reeling from the previous blow.

The *Mobile Bay* is 140 feet long with a single screw and two engines which together develop 25,000 horsepower. Horsepower-to-length ratio is perhaps the best gauge of a ship's capabilities in navigating ice. With a ratio of about 17.5, the *Mobile Bay*'s is about twice that of most freighters and about half the ratio of the 290-foot cutter *Mackinaw*. In this age of austerity, ships like the *Mobile Bay* are the wave of the future. Two ships of its class, each with a crew of seventeen men and burning two hundred gallons per hour of icebreaking operation, can do the work of a cutter of the *Mackinaw* class, which carries a crew of 127 men and burns 1,200 gallons per hour.

Finally, we've freed enough ice to back clear of the ships astern and maneuver toward the channel. As we head lakeward, the roar of fracturing ice is a continuous rumbling explosion with no diminuendo. The bow is three-inch steel at the stem and five-eighths inch along the icebreaking belt. It's coated with something called Inerta, a superslick Teflon-like paint. We are reopening the track of approximately two-foot-thick brash ice like a serrated blade through stale bread, leaving a wake of wagon-sized slabs astern. To port, the C.O. points out two gunboats under construction for Saudi Arabia and a tuna trawler to be delivered to Ecuador. Strange progeny, it seems to me, for a boatyard in northern Wisconsin.

From the bridge, I notice that freeing the ship of ice is an almost continuous activity. Crewmen are constantly heaving chunks overboard. They use aluminum baseball bats to break it free of the rails and superstructure. The C.O. recites an old winter duty proverb, "If you break ice, you make ice," which refers to the fact that the ice in your track freezes harder and gets tougher to break each time you attempt to navigate the same frozen channel. Freshwater ice is harder than saltwater ice, tougher to break, but more stable. The broken ice comes together with the fast ice peaks and forms windows along our track.

Halfway up the channel leading out to Lake Michigan, we come into open water and suddenly there is a great stillness. The discordant roar of our bow against the ice pack had become the norm, and for a moment the quiet is eerie. We are emerging into a silent sea. On the horizon I can see "Christmas trees," wave peaks which indicate rough seas, but in this twenty-knot offshore wind the waters in the immediate lee of the Wisconsin coast have only a moderate roll. We spot several icebergs, their visible tops about the size of our ship, hazards to navigation which are noted and recorded.

In the bitter wind and arctic panorama of the shoreline it is difficult to imagine that anyone will ever swim again in what the early Jesuit explorers called "these seas of sweet water," or that in a few short months, yachts with scantily clad revelers will sail out from this icebound harbor for Mackinac, Detroit, or up the St. Lawrence to the Atlantic and beyond.

By the time we have completed our tests of all the ship's navigational systems and reentered the harbor, our channel has been reclaimed by the subarctic cold, and we're forced to break our way again through the same ice we had cleared a few hours earlier. The late afternoon dark is settling over Sturgeon Bay, and the crew is at work again with their baseball bats. After we've docked and I've groped my way off the pier to the parking lot, I can still hear them breaking ice, the metallic ching of the aluminum bats against the iron rails and the clatter of the vitreous shards spraying like scattershot off the decks and cascading down into the black water below.

MY BOAT

BY RAYMOND CARVER

My boat is being made to order. Right now it's about to leave
the hands of its builders. I've reserved a special place
for it down at the marina. It's going to have plenty of room
on it for all my friends: Richard, Bill, Chuck, Toby, Jim, Hayden,
Gary, George, Harold, Don, Dick, Scott, Geoffrey, Jack,
Paul, Jay, Morris, and Alfredo. All my friends! They know who they
    are.
Tess, of course. I wouldn't go anyplace without her.
And Kristina, Merry, Catherine, Diane, Sally, Annick, Pat,
    Judith, Susie, Lynne, Annie, Jane, Mona.
Doug and Amy! They're family, but they're also my friends,

and they like a good time. There's room on my boat
for just about everyone. I'm serious about this!
There'll be a place on board for everyone's stories.
My own, but also the ones belonging to my friends.
Short stories, and the ones that go on and on. The true
and the made-up. The ones already finished, and the ones still
    being written.
Poems, too! Lyric poems, and the longer, darker narratives.
For my painter friends, paints and canvases will be on board
    my boat.
We'll have fried chicken, lunch meats, cheeses, rolls,
French bread. Every good thing that my friends and I like.
And a big basket of fruit, in case anyone wants fruit.
In case anyone wants to say he or she ate an apple,
or some grapes, on my boat. Whatever my friends want,
name it, and it'll be there. Soda pop of all kinds.
Beer and wine, sure. No one will be denied anything, on
    my boat.
We'll go out into the sunny harbor and have fun, that's the idea.
Just have a good time all around. Not thinking
about this or that or getting ahead or falling behind.
Fishing poles if anyone wants to fish. The fish are out there!
We may even go a little way down the coast, on my boat.
But nothing dangerous, nothing too serious.
The idea is simply to enjoy ourselves and not get scared.
We'll eat and drink and laugh a lot, on my boat.
I've always wanted to take at least one trip like this,
with my friends, on my boat. If we want to
we'll listen to Schumann on the CBC.
But if that doesn't work out, okay,
we'll switch to KRAB, The Who, and the Rolling Stones.
Whatever makes my friends happy! Maybe everyone
will have their own radio, on my boat. In any case,
we're going to have a big time. People are going to have fun,
and do what they want to do, on my boat.

GREENHOUSE DAYS ON THE HIGH SEAS

BY ROBERT SILVERBERG

OUT THERE in the chilly zone of the southern Pacific, somewhere between San Francisco and Hawaii, the sea was a weird goulash of currents, streams of cold stuff coming up from the Antarctic and coolish upwelling spirals out of the ocean floor and little hot rivers rolling off the sun-blasted continental shelf far to the east. Sometimes you could see steam rising in places where cold water met warm. It was a cockeyed place to be trawling for icebergs. But the albedo readings said there was a berg somewhere around there, and so the *Tonopah Maru* was there, too.

Carter sat in front of the scanner, massaging the numbers in the cramped cell that was the ship's command center. He was the trawler's captain, a lean man of around thirty, with yellow hair, brown beard, skin deeply tanned and tinged with the iridescent greenish purple of his armoring buildup, the protective layer that the infra/ultra drugs gave you. It was mid-morning. The shot of Screen he'd taken at dawn still simmered like liquid gold in his arteries. He could almost feel it as it made its slow journey outward to his capillaries and trickled into his skin, where it would carry out the daily refurbishing of the body armor that shielded him against ozone crackle and the demon eye of the sun.

This was only his second year at sea. The company liked to move people around. In the past few years he'd been a desert jockey in bleak forlorn Spokane, running odds reports for farmers betting on the month the next rainstorm would turn up, and before that a cargo dispatcher for one of the company's L-5 shuttles, and a chip-runner before that. And one of these days, if he kept his nose clean, he'd be sitting in a corner office atop the Samurai pyramid in Kyoto. Carter hated a lot of the things he'd had to do in order to play the company game. But he knew that it was the only game there was.

"We got maybe a two-thousand-kiloton mass there," he said, looking into the readout wand's ceramic-fiber cone. "Not bad, eh?"

"Not for these days, no," Hitchcock said. He was the ocean-ographer/navigator, a grizzled flat-nosed Afro-Hawaiian whose Screen-induced coloring gave his skin a startling midnight look. Hitchcock was old enough to remember when icebergs were never seen farther north than the latitude of southern Chile. "Man, these days a berg that's still that big all the way up here must have been three counties long when it broke off the fucking polar shelf. But you sure you got your numbers right, man?"

The implied challenge brought a glare to Carter's eyes, and some-thing went curling angrily through his interior, leaving a hot little trail. Hitchcock *never* thought Carter did anything right the first time. Although he often denied it—too loudly—it was pretty clear Hitch-cock had never quite gotten over his resentment at being bypassed for captain in favor of an outsider. Probably he thought it was racism. But it wasn't. Carter was managerial track; Hitchcock wasn't. That was all there was to it.

Sourly he said, "You want to check the screen yourself? Here. Here, take a look." He offered Hitchcock the wand.

Hitchcock shook his head. "Easy, man. Whatever the screen says, that's okay for me." He grinned disarmingly, showing mahogany snags. On the screen, impenetrable whorls and jiggles were dancing, black on green, green on black, the occasional dazzling bloom of bright yellow. The *Tonopah Maru*'s interrogatory beam was traveling 22,500 miles straight up to Nippon Telecom's big marine scansat, which had its glassy unblinking gaze trained on the whole eastern Pacific, looking for albedo differentials. The reflectivity of an iceberg is different from the reflectivity of the ocean surface. You pick up the differential, you confirm it with temperature read-out, you scan for mass to see if the trip's worthwhile. If it is, you bring your trawler in fast and make the grab before someone else does.

This berg was due to go to San Francisco, which was in a bad way for water just now. The whole West Coast was. There hadn't been any rain along the Pacific Seaboard in ten months. Most likely the sea around here was full of trawlers, Seattle, San Diego, L.A. The Angelenos kept more ships out than anybody. The *Tonopah Maru* had been chartered to them by Samurai Industries until last month. But the trawler was working for San Francisco this time. The lovely city by the bay, dusty now, sitting there under that hot soupy sky full of interesting-colored greenhouse gases, waiting for the rain that almost never came anymore.

Carter said, "Start getting the word around. That berg's down here, south-southwest. We get it in the grapple tomorrow, we can be in San Francisco with it by a week from Tuesday."

"If it don't melt first. This fucking heat."

"It didn't melt between Antarctica and here, it's not gonna melt between here and Frisco. Get a move on, man. We don't want L.A. coming in and hitting it first."

By mid-afternoon they were picking it up optically, first an overhead view via the Weather Department spysat, then a sea-level image bounced to them by a Navy relay buoy. The berg was a thing like a castle afloat, maybe two hundred meters long, stately and serene, all pink turrets and indigo battlements and blue-white pinnacles, rising high up above the water. Steaming curtains of fog shrouded its edges. For the last couple of million years it had been sitting on top of the South Pole, and it probably hadn't ever expected to go cruising off toward Hawaii like this. But the big climate shift had changed a lot of things for everybody, the Antarctic ice pack included.

"Jesus," Hitchcock said. "Can we do it?"

"Easy," said Nakata. He was the grapple technician, a sleek beady-eyed catlike little guy. "It'll be a four-hook job, but so what? We got the hooks for it."

The *Tonopah Maru* had hooks to spare. Most of its long, cigar-shaped hull was taken up by the immense rack-and-pinion gear that powered the grappling hooks, a vast silent mechanism capable of hurling the giant hooks far overhead and whipping them down deep into the flanks of even the biggest bergs. The deck space was given over almost entirely to the great spigots that were used to spray the bergs with a sintering of melt-retardant mirror dust. Down below was a powerful fusion-driven engine, strong enough to haul a fair-sized island halfway around the world.

Everything very elegant, except there was barely any room left over for the crew of five. Carter and the others were jammed into odd little corners here and there. For living quarters they had cubicles not much bigger than the coffin-sized sleeping capsules you got at an airport hotel, and for recreation space, they all shared one little blister dome aft and a pacing area on the foredeck. A sardine can kind of life, but the pay was good and at least you could breathe fresh air at sea, more or less, instead of the dense grayish-green murk that hovered over the habitable parts of the West Coast.

They were right at the mid-Pacific cold wall. The sea around them was blue, the sign of warm water. Just to the west, though, where the berg was, the water was a dark rich olive green with all the micro-scopic marine life that cold water fosters. The line of demarcation was plainly visible.

Carter was running triangulations to see if they'd be able to slip the berg under the Golden Gate Bridge when Rennett appeared at his elbow and said, "There's a ship, Cap'n."

"What you say?"

He wondered if he was going to have to fight for his berg. That happened at times. This was open territory, pretty much a lawless zone where old-fashioned piracy was making a terrific comeback.

Rennett was maintenance/operations, a husky, broad-shouldered little kid out of the Midwest dust bowl, no more than chest-high to him, very cocky, very tough. She kept her scalp shaved, the way a lot of them did nowadays, and she was brown as an acorn all over, with the purple glint of Screen shining brilliantly through, making her look almost fluorescent. Brown eyes as bright as marbles and twice as hard looked back at him.

"Ship," she said, clipping it out of the side of her mouth as if doing him a favor. "Right on the other side of the berg. Caskie's just picked up a message. Some sort of SOS." She handed Carter a narrow strip of yellow radio tape with just a couple of lines of bright red thermoprint typing on it. The words came up at him like a hand reaching out of the deck. He read them out loud.

"CAN YOU HELP US   TROUBLE ON SHIP   MATTER OF LIFE AND DEATH   URGENT YOU COME ABOARD SOONEST
"KOVALCIK, ACTING CAPTAIN, CALAMARI MARU"

"What the fuck," Carter said. "*Calamari Maru?* Is it a ship or a squid?"

Rennett didn't crack a smile. "We ran a check on the registry. It's owned out of Vancouver by Kyocera-Merck. The listed captain is Amiel Kohlberg, a German. Nothing about any Kovalcik."

"Doesn't sound like a berg trawler."

"It's a squid ship, Cap'n," she said, voice flat with a sharp edge of contempt on it. As if he didn't know what a squid ship was. He let it pass. It always struck him as funny, the way anybody who had two days' more experience at sea than he did treated him like a greenhorn.

He glanced at the printout again. *Urgent,* it said. *Matter of life and death.* Shit. Shit shit shit.

The idea of dropping everything to deal with the problems of some strange ship didn't sit well with him. He wasn't paid to help other captains out, especially Kyocera-Merck captains. Samurai Industries wasn't fond of K-M these days. Something about the Gobi reclamation contract, industrial espionage, some crap like that. Besides, he had a berg to deal with. He didn't need any other distractions just now.

And then, too, he felt an edgy little burst of suspicion drifting up from the basement of his soul, a tweak of wariness. Going aboard another ship out here, you were about as vulnerable as you could be. Ten years in corporate life had taught him caution.

But he also knew you could carry caution too far. It didn't feel good to him to turn his back on a ship that had said it was in trouble. Maybe the ancient laws of the sea, as well as every other vestige of what used to be common decency, were inoperative concepts here in the troubled, heat-plagued year of 2133, but he still wasn't completely beyond feeling things like guilt and shame. Besides, he thought, what goes around comes around. You ignore the other guy when he asks for help, you might just be setting yourself up for a little of the same later on.

They were all watching him: Rennett, Nakata, Hitchcock.

Hitchcock said, "What you gonna do, Cap'n? Gonna go across to 'em?" A gleam in his eye, a snaggly mischievous grin on his face.

What a pain in the ass, Carter thought.

Carter gave the older man a murderous look and said, "So you think it's legit?"

Hitchcock shrugged blandly. "Not for me to say. You the cap'n, man. All I know is, they say they in trouble, they say they need our help."

Hitchcock's gaze was steady, remote, noncommittal. His blocky shoulders seemed to reach from wall to wall. "They calling for help, Cap'n. Ship wants help, you give help, that's what I always believe, all my years at sea. Of course, maybe it different now."

Carter found himself wishing he'd never let Hitchcock come aboard. But screw it. He'd go over there and see what was what. He had no choice, never really had.

To Rennett he said, "Tell Caskie to let this Kovalcik know that we're heading for the berg to get claiming hooks into it. That'll take about an hour and a half. And after that we have to get it mirrored and skirted. While that's going on, I'll come over and find out what his problem is."

"Got it," Rennett said and went below.

New berg visuals had come in while they were talking. For the first time now Carter could see the erosion grooves at the waterline on the berg's upwind side, the undercutting, the easily fractured overhangings that were starting to form. The undercutting didn't necessarily mean the berg was going to flip over—that rarely happened, with big dry-dock bergs like this—but they'd be in for some lousy oscillations, a lot of rolling and heaving, choppy seas, a general pisser all around. The day was turning very ugly very fast.

"Jesus," Carter said, pushing the visuals across to Nakata. "Take a look at these."

"No problem. We got to put our hooks on the lee side, that's all."

"Yeah. Sounds good." Nakata made it seem simple. Carter managed a grin.

The far side of the berg was a straight high wall, a supreme white cliff as smooth as porcelain that was easily a hundred meters high, with a wicked tongue of ice jutting out about forty meters into the sea like a breakwater. That was what the *Calamari Maru* was using it for, too. The squid ship rode at anchor just inside that tongue.

Carter signaled to Nakata, who was standing way down fore, by his control console.

"Hooks away!" Carter called. "Sharp! Sharp!"

There came the groaning sound of the grapple-hatch opening, and the deep rumbling of the hook gimbals. Somewhere deep in the belly of the ship immense mechanisms were swinging around, moving into position. The berg sat motionless in the calm sea.

Then the whole ship shivered as the first hook came shooting up into view. It hovered overhead, a tremendous taloned thing filling half the sky, black against the shining brightness of the air. Nakata hit the keys again and the hook, having reached the apex of its curve, spun downward with slashing force, heading for the breast of the berg.

It hit and dug and held. The berg recoiled, quivered, rocked. A shower of loose ice came tumbling off the upper ledges. As the impact of the hooking was transmitted to the vast hidden mass of the berg undersea, the whole thing bowed forward a little farther than Carter had been expecting, making a nasty sucking noise against the water, and when it pulled back again a geyser came spuming up about twenty meters.

Down by the bow, Nakata was making his I-got-you gesture at the berg, the middle finger rising high.

A cold wind was blowing from the berg now. It was like the exhalation of some huge wounded beast, an aroma of ancient times, a fossil breath wind.

They moved on a little farther along the berg's flank.

"Hook two," Carter told him.

The berg was almost stable again now. Carter, watching from his viewing tower by the aft rail, waited for the rush of pleasure and relief that came from a successful claiming, but this time it wasn't there. All he felt was impatience, an eagerness to get all four hooks in and start chugging on back to the Golden Gate.

The second hook flew aloft, hovered, plunged, struck, bit.

A second time the berg slammed the water, and a second time the sea jumped and shook. Carter had just a moment to catch a glimpse of the other ship popping around like a floating cork, and wondered if that ice tongue they found so cozy were going to break off and sink them. It would have been smarter of the *Calamari Maru* to anchor somewhere else. But to hell with them. They'd been warned.

The third hook was easier.

"Four," Carter called. One last time, a grappling iron flew through the air, whipping off at a steep angle to catch the far side of the berg over the top, and then they had it, the entire monstrous floating island of ice snaffled and trussed.

Toward sunset, Carter left Hitchcock in charge of the trawler and went over to the *Calamari Maru* in the sleek little silvery kayak that they used as the ship's boat. He took Rennett with him.

The stink of the other ship reached his nostrils long before he went scrambling up the gleaming woven-monofilament ladder that they threw over the side for him: a bitter, acrid reek, a miasma so dense that it was almost visible. Breathing it was something like inhaling all of a clogged sewer line in a single snort. Carter wished he'd worn a facelung. But who expected to need one out at sea, where you were supposed to be able to breathe reasonably decent air?

The *Calamari Maru* didn't look too good, either. At one quick glance, he picked up a sense of general neglect and slovenliness: black stains on the deck, swirls of dust everywhere, some nasty rust-colored patches of ozone attack that needed work. The reek, though, came from the squid themselves.

The heart of the ship was a vast tank, a huge squid-peeling factory occupying the whole mid-deck. Carter had been on one once before, long ago, when he was a trainee. Samurai Industries ran dozens of them. He looked down into the tank and saw battalions of hefty squid swimming in schools, big-eyed pearly phantoms, scores of them shifting direction suddenly and simultaneously in their squiddy way. Glittering mechanical flails moved among them, seizing and slicing, cutting out the nerve tissue, flushing the edible remainder toward the meat-packing facility. The stench was astonishing. The entire thing was a tremendous processing machine. With the one-time farming heartland of North America and temperate Europe now worthless desert, and the world dependent on the thin, rocky soil of northern Canada and Siberia for its crops, harvesting the sea was essential. But the smell was awful. He fought to keep from gagging.

"You get used to it," said the woman who greeted him when he clambered aboard. "Five minutes, you won't notice."

"Let's hope so," he said. "I'm Captain Carter, and this is Rennett, maintenance/ops. Where's Kovalcik?"

"I'm Kovalcik," the woman said.

His eyes widened. She seemed to be amused by his reaction.

Kovalcik was rugged and sturdy looking, more than average height, strong cheekbones, eyes set very far apart, expression very cool and controlled, but strain evident behind the control. She was wearing a sack-like jumpsuit of some coarse gray fabric. About thirty, Carter guessed. Her hair was black and close-cropped and her skin was fair, strangely fair, hardly any trace of Screen showing. He saw signs of sun damage, signs of ozone crackle, red splotches of burn. Two members of her crew stood behind her, also women, also jump-suited, also oddly fair-skinned. Their skin didn't look so good, either.

Kovalcik said, "We are very grateful you came. There is bad trouble on this ship." Her voice was flat. She had just the trace of a European accent, hard to place.

"We'll help out if we can," Carter told her.

He became aware now that they had carved a chunk out of his berg and grappled it up onto the deck, where it was melting into three big aluminum runoff tanks. It couldn't have been a millionth of the total berg mass, not a ten millionth, but seeing it gave him a quick little stab of proprietary fury and he felt a muscle flicker in his cheek. That reaction didn't go unnoticed, either. Kovalcik said quickly, "Yes, water is one of our problems. We have had to replenish our supply this way. There have been some equipment failures lately. You will come to the captain's cabin now? We must talk of what has happened, what must now be done."

She led him down the deck, with Rennett and the two crew women following along behind.

The *Calamari Maru* was big and long and sleek, built somewhat along the lines of a squid itself, a jet-propulsion job that gobbled water into colossal compressors and squirted it out behind. That was one of the many low-fuel solutions to maritime transport problems that had been worked out for the sake of keeping CO_2 output down in these difficult times. Immense things like flying buttresses ran down the deck on both sides. These, Kovalcik explained, were squid lures, covered with bioluminescent photophores: you lowered them into the water and they gave off light that mimicked the glow of the squids' own bodies, and the slithery tentacular buggers came jetting in from vast distances, expecting a great jamboree and getting a net instead.

"Some butchering operation you got here," Carter said.

Kovalcik said, a little curtly, "Meat is not all we produce. The squid we catch here have value as food, of course, but also we strip the nerve fibers, we bring them back to the mainland, they are used in all kinds of biosensor applications. They are very large, those fibers, a hundred times as thick as ours. They are like single-cell computers. You have a thousand processors aboard your ship that use squid fiber, do you know? Follow me, please. This way."

They went down a ramp, along a narrow companionway. Carter heard thumpings and pingings in the walls. A bulkhead was dented and badly scratched. The lights down here were dimmer than they ought to be and the fixtures had an ominous hum. There was a new odor now, a tang of something chemical, sweet but not a pleasing kind of sweet, more a burnt kind of sweet than anything else, cutting sharply across the heavy squid stench the way a piccolo might cut across the boom of drums. Rennett shot him a somber glance. This ship was a mess, all right.

"Captain's cabin is here," Kovalcik said, pushing back a door hanging askew on its hinges. "We have drink first, yes?"

The size of the cabin amazed Carter, after all those weeks bottled up in his little hole on the *Tonopah Maru*. It looked as big as a gymnasium. There was a table, a desk, shelving, a comfortable bunk, a sanitary unit, even an entertainment screen, everything nicely spread out with actual floor space you could move around in. The screen had been kicked in. Kovalcik took a flask of Peruvian brandy from a cabinet and Carter nodded, and she poured three stiff ones. They drank in silence. The squid odor wasn't so bad in here, or else he was getting used to it, just as she'd said. But the air was rank and close despite the spaciousness of the cabin, thick soupy stuff that was a struggle to breathe. Something's wrong with the ventilating system, too, Carter thought.

"You see the trouble we have," said Kovalcik.

"I see there's been trouble, yes."

"You don't see half. You should see command room, too. Here, have more brandy, then I take you there."

"Never mind the brandy," Carter said. "How about telling me what the hell's been going on aboard this ship?"

"First come see command room," Kovalcik said.

The command room was one level down from the captain's cabin. It was an absolute wreck.

The place was all but burned out. There were laser scars on every surface and gaping wounds in the structural fabric of the ceiling. Glittering strings of program cores were hanging out of data cabinets like broken necklaces, like spilled guts. Everywhere there were signs of some terrible struggle, some monstrous, insane civil war that had raged through the most delicate regions of the ship's mind centers.

"It is all ruined," Kovalcik said. "Nothing works anymore except the squid-processing programs, and as you see, those work magnificently, going on and on, the nets and flails and cutters and so forth. But everything else is damaged. Our water synthesizer, the ventilators, our navigational equipment, much more. We are making repairs, but it is very slow."

"I can imagine it would be. You had yourselves one hell of a party here, huh?"

"There was a great struggle. From deck to deck, from cabin to cabin. It became necessary to place Captain Kohlberg under restraint and he and some of the other officers resisted."

Carter blinked and caught his breath up short at that. "What the fuck are you saying? That you had a *mutiny* aboard this ship?"

For a moment the charged word hung between them like a whirling sword.

Then Kovalcik said, voice flat as ever, "When we had been at sea for a while, the captain became like a crazy man. It was the heat that got to him, the sun, maybe the air. He began to ask impossible things. He would not listen to reason. And so he had to be removed from command for the safety of all. There was a meeting and he was put under restraint. Some of his officers objected and they had to be put under restraint, too."

Son of a bitch, Carter thought, feeling a little sick. What have I walked into here?

"Sounds just like mutiny to me," Rennett said.

Carter shushed her. This had to be handled delicately. To Kovalcik he said, "They're still alive, the captain, the officers?"

"Yes. I can show them to you."

"That would be a good idea. But first maybe you ought to tell me some more about these grievances you had."

"That doesn't matter now, does it?"

"To me it does. I need to know what you think justifies removing a captain."

She began to look a little annoyed. "There were many things, some big, some small. Work schedules, crew pairings, the food allotment. Everything worse and worse for us each week. Like a tyrant, he was. A Caesar. Not at first, but gradually, the change in him. It was sun poisoning he had, the craziness that comes from too much heat on the brain. He was afraid to use very much Screen, you see, afraid that we would run out before the end of the voyage, so he rationed it very tightly, for himself, for us, too. That was one of our biggest troubles, the Screen." Kovalcik touched her cheeks, her forearms, her wrists, where the skin was pink and raw. "You see how I look? We are all like that. Kohlberg cut us to half ration, then half that. The sun began to eat us. The ozone. We had no protection, do you see? He was so frightened there would be no Screen later on that he let us use only a small amount every day, and we suffered, and so did he, and he got crazier as the sun worked on him, and there was less Screen all the time. He had it hidden, I think. We have not found it yet. We are still on quarter ration."

Carter tried to imagine what that was like, sailing around under the ferocious sky without body armor. The daily injections withheld, the unshielded skin of these people exposed to the full fury of the greenhouse climate. Could Kohlberg really have been so stupid, or so loony? But there was no getting around the raw pink patches on Kovalcik's skin.

"You'd like us to let you have a supply of Screen, is that it?" he asked uneasily.

"No. We would not expect that of you. Sooner or later, we will find where Kohlberg has hidden it."

"Then what is it you *do* want?"

"Come," Kovalcik said. "Now I show you the officers."

* * *

The mutineers had stashed their prisoners in the ship's infirmary, a stark, humid room far belowdecks with three double rows of bunks along the wall and some nonfunctioning medical mechs between them. Each of the bunks but one held a sweat-shiny man with a week's growth of beard. They were conscious, but not very. Their wrists were tied.

"It is very disagreeable for us, keeping them like this," Kovalcik said. "But what can we do? This is Captain Kohlberg." He was heavyset, Teutonic-looking, groggy-eyed. "He is calm now, but only because we sedate him. We sedate all of them, fifty c.c.'s of omnipax. But it is a threat to their health, the constant sedation. And in any case, the drugs are running short. Another few days and then we will have none, and it will be harder to keep them restrained, and if they break free there will be war on this ship again."

"I'm not sure if we have any omnipax on board," Carter said. "Certainly not enough to do you much good for long."

"That is not what we are asking, either," said Kovalcik.

"What *are* you asking, then?"

"These five men, they threaten everybody's safety. They have forfeited the right to command. This I could show, with playbacks of the time of struggle on this ship. Take them."

"What?"

"Take them onto your ship. They must not stay here. These are crazy men. We must rid ourselves of them. We must be left to repair our ship in peace and do the work we are paid to do. It is a humanitarian thing, taking them. You are going back to San Francisco with the iceberg? Take them, these troublemakers. They will be no danger to you. They will be grateful for being rescued. But here they are like bombs that must sooner or later go off."

Carter looked at her as if she were a bomb that had *already* gone off. Rennett had simply turned away, covering what sounded like a burst of hysterical laughter by forcing a coughing fit.

That was all he needed, making himself an accomplice in this thing, obligingly picking up a bunch of officers pushed off their ship by mutineers. Kyocera-Merck men at that. Aid and succor to the great corporate enemy? The Samurai Industries agent in Frisco would really love it when he came steaming into port with five K-M men on board. He'd especially want to hear that Carter had done it for humanitarian reasons.

Besides, where the fuck were these men going to sleep? On deck between the spigots? Should he pitch a tent on the iceberg, maybe? What about feeding them, for Christ's sake? What about Screen? Everything was calibrated down to the last molecule.

"I don't think you understand our situation," Carter said carefully. "Aside from the legalities of the thing, we've got no space for extra personnel. We barely have enough for us."

"It would be just for a short while, no? A week or two?"

"I tell you we've got every millimeter allotted. If God Himself wanted to come on board as a passenger, we'd have a tough time figuring out where to put Him. You want technical help patching your ship back together, we can try to do that. We can even let you have some supplies. But taking five men aboard—"

Kovalcik's eyes began to look a little wild. She was breathing very hard now. "You must do this for us! You must! Otherwise . . ."

"Otherwise?" Carter prompted.

All he got from her was a bleak stare, no friendlier than the green-streaked ozone-crisp sky.

"*Hilfe,*" Kohlberg muttered just then, stirring unexpectedly in his bunk.

"What was that?"

"It is delirium," said Kovalcik.

"*Hilfe. Hilfe. In Gottes Namen, hilfe!*" And then, in thickly accented English, the words painfully framed: "Help. She will kill us all."

"Delirium?" Carter said.

Kovalcik's eyes grew even chillier. Drawing an ultrasonic syringe from a cabinet in the wall, she slapped it against Kohlberg's arm. There was a small buzzing sound. Kohlberg subsided into sleep. Snuffling snores rose from his bunk. Kovalcik smiled. She seemed to be recovering her self-control. "He is a madman. You see what my skin is like. What his madness has done to me, has done to every one of us. If he got loose, if he put the voyage in jeopardy—yes, yes, we would kill him. We would kill them all. It would be only self-defense, you understand me? But it must not come to that." Her voice was icy. You could air-condition an entire city with that voice. "You were not here during the trouble. You do not know what we went through. We will not go through it again. Take these men from us, Captain."

She stepped back, folding her arms across her chest. The room was very quiet, suddenly, except for the pingings and thumpings from the ship's interior, and an occasional snore out of Kohlberg. Kovalcik was completely calm again, the ferocity and iciness no longer visible. As though she were simply telling him: This is the situation, the ball is now in your court, Captain Carter.

What a stinking, squalid mess, Carter thought.

But he was startled to find, when he looked behind the irritation he felt at having been dragged into this, a curious sadness where he would have expected anger to be. Despite everything, he found himself flooded with surprising compassion for Kovalcik, for Kohlberg, for all of them, for the whole fucking poisoned heat-blighted world. Who had asked for any of this—the heavy green sky, the fiery air, the daily need for Screen, the million frantic improvisations that made continued life on earth possible? Not us. Our great-great-grandparents had, maybe, but not us. Only they're not here to know what it's like, and we are.

Then the moment passed. What the hell could he do? Did Kovalcik think he was Jesus Christ? He had no room for these people. He had no extra Screen or food. In any case, this was none of his business. And San Francisco was waiting for its iceberg. It was time to move along. Tell her anything, just get out of here.

"All right," he said. "I see your problem. I'm not entirely sure I can help out, but I'll do what I can. I'll check our supplies and let you know what we're able to do. Okay?"

Hitchcock said, "What I think, Cap'n, we ought to just take hold of them. Nakata can put a couple of his spare hooks into them, and we'll tow them into Frisco along with the berg."

"Hold on," Carter said. "Are you out of your mind? I'm no fucking pirate."

"Who's talking about piracy? It's our obligation. We got to turn them in, man, is how I see it. They're mutineers."

"I'm not a a policeman, either," Carter retorted. "They want to have a mutiny, let them goddamn go and mutiny. I have a job to do. I just want to get that berg moving east. Without hauling a shipload of crazies along. Don't even think I'm going to make some kind of civil arrest of them. Don't even consider it for an instant, Hitchcock."

Mildly, Hitchcock said, "You know, we used to take this sort of thing seriously, once upon a time. You know what I mean, man? We wouldn't just look the other way."

"You don't understand," Carter said. Hitchcock gave him a sharp, scornful look. "No. Listen to me," Carter snapped. "That ship's nothing but trouble. The woman that runs it, she's something you don't want to be very close to. We'd have to put her in chains if we tried to take her in, and taking her isn't as easy as you seem to think, either. There's five of us and I don't know how many of them. And that's a Kyocera-Merck ship there. Samurai isn't paying us to pull K-M's chestnuts out of the fire."

It was late morning now. The sun was getting close to noon height, and the sky was brighter than ever, fiercely hot, with some swirls of lavender and green far overhead, vagrant wisps of greenhouse garbage that must have drifted west from the noxious high-pressure air mass that sat perpetually over the mid-section of the United States. Carter imagined he could detect a whiff of methane in the breeze. Just across the way was the berg, shining like polished marble, shedding water hour by hour as the mounting heat worked it over. Back in San Francisco, they were brushing the dust out of the empty reservoirs. Time to be moving along, yes. Kovalcik and Kohlberg would have to work out their problems without him. He didn't feel good about that, but there were a lot of things he didn't feel good about, and he wasn't able to fix those, either.

"You said she's going to kill those five guys," Caskie said. The communications operator was small and slight, glossy black hair and lots of it, no bare scalp for her. "Does she mean it?"

Carter shrugged. "A bluff, most likely. She looks tough, but I'm not sure she's that tough."

"I don't agree," Rennett said. "She wants to get rid of those men in the worst way."

"You think?"

"I think that what they were doing anchored by the berg was getting ready to maroon them on it. Only we came along, and we're going to tow the berg away, and that screwed up the plan. So now she wants to give them to us instead. We don't take them, she'll just dump them over the side soon as we're gone."

"Even though we know the score?"

"She'll say they broke loose and jumped into the ship's boat and escaped, and she doesn't know where the hell they went. Who's to say otherwise?"

Carter stared gloomily. Yes, he thought, who's to say otherwise.

"The berg's melting while we screw around," Hitchcock said.

"What'll it be, Cap'n? We sit here and discuss some more? Or we pull up and head for Frisco?"

"My vote's for taking them on board," said Nakata.

"I don't remember calling for a vote," Carter said. "We've got no room for five more hands. Not for anybody. We're packed as tight as we can possibly get. Living on this ship is like living in a rowboat, as it is." He was starting to feel rage beginning to rise in him. This business was getting too tangled: legal issues, humanitarian issues; but the simple reality underneath it all was that he couldn't take on passengers, no matter what.

And Hitchcock was right. The berg was losing water every minute. Even from here, bare eyes alone, he could see erosion going on, the dripping, the calving. The oscillations were picking up, the big icy thing rocking gently back and forth as its stability at the waterline got nibbled away. Later on, the oscillations wouldn't be so gentle. They had to get that berg sprayed with mirror dust and wrapped with a plastic skirt at the waterline to slow down wave erosion and start moving. San Francisco was paying him to bring home an iceberg, not a handful of slush.

"Cap'n," Rennett called. She had wandered up into the observation rack above them and was shading her eyes, looking across the water. "They've put out a boat, Cap'n."

"No," he said. "Son of a bitch!"

He grabbed for his six-by-thirty spyglass. A boat, sure enough, a hydrofoil dinghy. It looked full: three, four, five. He hit the switch for biosensor boost and the squid fiber in the spyglass went to work for him. The image blossomed, high resolution. Five men. He recognized Kohlberg sitting slumped in front.

"Shit," he said. "She's sending them over to us. Just dumping them on us."

"If we doubled up somehow—" Nakata began, smiling hopefully.

"One more word out of you and I'll double *you* up," said Carter. He turned to Hitchcock, who had one hand clamped meditatively over the lower half of his face, pushing his nose back and forth and scratching around in his thick white stubble. "Break out some lasers," Carter said. "Defensive use only. Just in case. Hitchcock, you and Rennett get out there in the kayak and escort those men back to the squid ship. If they aren't conscious, tow them over to it. If they are, and they don't want to go back, invite them very firmly to go back, and if they don't like the invitation, put a couple of holes through the side of their boat and get the hell back here fast. You understand me?"

Hitchcock nodded stonily. "Sure, man. Sure."

Carter watched the whole thing from the blister dome at the stern, wondering whether he was going to have a mutiny of his own on his hands now, too. But no. No. Hitchcock and Rennett kayaked out along the edge of the berg until they came up beside the dinghy from the *Calamari Maru,* and there was a brief discussion, very brief, Hitchcock doing the talking and Rennett holding a laser rifle in a casual but businesslike way. The five castoffs from the squid ship seemed more or less awake. They pointed and gestured and threw up their arms in despair. But Hitchcock kept talking and Rennett kept stroking the laser, casual but businesslike, and the men in the dinghy looked more and more dejected by the moment. Then the discussion broke up and the kayak headed back toward the *Tonopah Maru,* and the men in the dinghy sat where they were, no doubt trying to figure out their next move.

Hitchcock said, coming on board, "This is bad business, man. That captain, he say the woman just took the ship away from him, on account of she wanted him to let them all have extra shots of Screen and he didn't give it. There wasn't enough to let her have so much, is what he said. I feel real bad, man."

"So do I," said Carter. "Believe me."

"I learn a long time ago," Hitchcock said, "when a man say 'Believe me,' that's the one thing I shouldn't do."

"Fuck you," Carter said. "You think I *wanted* to strand them? But we have no choice. Let them go back to their own ship. She won't kill them. All they have to do is let her do what she wants to do and they'll come out of it okay. She can put them off on some island somewhere, Hawaii, maybe. But if they come with us, we'll be in deep shit all the way back to Frisco."

Hitchcock nodded. "Yeah. We may be in deep shit already."

"What you say?"

"Look at the berg," Hitchcock said. "At waterline. It's getting real carved up."

Carter scooped up his glass and kicked in the biosensor boost, He scanned the berg. It didn't look good. The heat was working it over very diligently.

This was the hottest day since they'd entered these waters. The sun seemed to be getting bigger every minute. There was a nasty magnetic crackling coming out of the sky, as if the atmosphere itself was getting ionized as it baked. And the berg was starting to wobble. Carter saw the oscillations plainly, those horizontal grooves filling with water, the sea not so calm now as sky/ocean heat differentials began to build up and conflicting currents came slicing in.

"Son of a bitch," Carter said. "That settles it. We got to get moving right now."

There was still plenty to do. Carter gave the word and the mirror-dust spigots went into operation, cannoning shining clouds of powdered metal over the exposed surface of the berg, and probably all over the squid ship and the dinghy, too. It took half an hour to do the job. The squid ship was still sitting at anchor by the ice tongue, and it looked like some kind of negotiation was going on between the men in the dinghy and the people on board. The sea was still roughening, the berg was lalloping around in a mean way. But Carter knew there was a gigantic base down there out of sight, enough to hold it steady until they could get under way, he hoped.

"Let's get the skirt on it now," he said.

A tricky procedure, nozzles at the ship's waterline extruding a thermoplastic spray that would coat the berg just where it was most vulnerable to wave erosion. The hard part came in managing the extensions of the cables linking the hooks to the ship, so they could maneuver around the berg. But Nakata was an ace at that. They pulled up anchor and started around the far side. The mirror-dusted berg was dazzling, a tremendous mountain of white light.

"I don't like that wobble," Hitchcock kept saying.

"Won't matter a damn once we're under way," said Carter.

The heat was like a hammer now, pounding the dark cool surface of the water, mixing up the thermal layers, stirring up the currents, getting everything churned around. They had waited just a little too long to get started. The berg, badly undercut, was doing a big sway to windward, bowing like one of those round-bottomed Japanese dolls, then swaying back again. God only knew what kind of sea action the squid ship was getting, but Carter couldn't see them from this side of the berg. He kept on moving, circling the berg to the full extension of the hook cables, then circling back the way he'd come.

When they got around to leeward again, he saw what kind of sea action the squid ship had been getting. It was swamped. The ice tongue they'd been anchored next to had come rising up out of the sea and kicked them like a giant foot.

"Jesus Christ," Hitchcock murmured, standing beside him. "Will you look at that. The damn fools just sat there all the time."

The *Calamari Maru* was shipping water like crazy and starting to go down. The sea was boiling with an armada of newly liberated squid, swiftly propelling themselves in all directions, heading anywhere else at top speed. Three dinghies were bobbing around in the water in the shadow of the berg.

"Will you look at that," Hitchcock said again.

"Start the engines," Carter told him. "Let's get the fuck out of here."

Hitchcock stared at him, disbelievingly.

"You mean that, Cap'n? You really mean that?"

"I goddamn well do."

"You actually going to leave three boats from a sinking ship sitting out there in the water full of people?"

"Yeah. You got it. Now start the engines."

"That's too much," Hitchcock said softly, shaking his head in a big slow swing. "Too goddamn much."

He made a sound like a wounded buffalo and took two or three shambling steps toward Carter, his arms dangling loosely, his hands half cupped. Hitchcock's eyes were slitted and his face looked oddly puffy. He loomed above Carter, wheezing and muttering, a dark massive slab of a man. Half as big as the iceberg out there was how he looked just then.

Oh, shit, Carter thought. Here it comes. My very own mutiny, right now.

Hitchcock rumbled and muttered and closed his hands into fists. Exasperation tinged with fear swept through Carter and he brought his arm up without even stopping to think, hitting Hitchcock hard, a short fast jab in the mouth that rocked the older man's head back sharply and sent him reeling against the rail. Hitchcock slammed into it and bounced. For a moment it looked as if he'd fall, but he managed to steady himself. A kind of sobbing sound, but not quite a sob, more of a grunt, came from him. A bright dribble of blood sprouted on his white-stubbled chin.

For a moment, Hitchcock seemed dazed. Then his eyes came back into focus and he looked at Carter in amazement.

"I wasn't going to hit you, Cap'n," he said, blinking hard. There was a soft stunned quality to his voice. "Nobody ever hits a cap'n, not ever. Not *ever*. You know that, Cap'n."

"I told you to start the engines."

"You hit me, Cap'n. What the hell you hit me for?"

"You started to come at me, didn't you?" Carter said.

Hitchcock's shining bloodshot eyes were immense in his Screen-blackened face. "You think I was *coming* at you? Oh, Cap'n! Oh, Jesus, Cap'n. Jesus!" He shook his head and wiped at the blood. Carter saw that he was bleeding, too, at the knuckle, where he'd hit a tooth. Hitchcock continued to stare at him, the way you might stare at a dinosaur that had just stepped out of the forest. Then his look of astonishment softened into something else, sadness, maybe. Or was it pity? Pity would be even worse, Carter thought. A whole lot worse.

"Cap'n—" Hitchcock began, his voice hoarse and thick.

"Don't say it. Just go and get the engines started."

"Yeah," he said. "Yeah, man."

He went slouching off, rubbing at his lip.

"Caskie's picking up an autobuoy SOS," Rennett called from somewhere updeck.

"Nix," Carter yelled back furiously. "We can't do it."

"What?"

"There's no fucking room for them," Carter said. His voice was as sharp as an icicle. "Nix. Nix."

He lifted his spyglass again and took another look toward the on-coming dinghies. Chugging along hard, they were, but having heavy weather of it in the turbulent water. He looked quickly away, before he could make out faces. The berg, shining like fire, was still oscillating. He thought of the hot winds sweeping across the continent to the east, sweeping all around the belly of the world, the dry, rainless winds that forever sucked up what little moisture could still be found. It was almost a shame to have to go back there. Like returning to hell after a little holiday at sea, is how it felt. It was worst in the middle latitudes, the temperate zone, once so fertile. Rain almost never fell at all there now. The dying forests, the new grasslands taking over, deserts where even the grass couldn't make it, the polar icepacks crumbling, the low-lands drowning everywhere, dead buildings sticking up out of the sea, vines sprouting on freeways, the alligators moving northward. This berg here, this oversized ice cube, how many days' water supply would that be for San Francisco? Ten? Fifteen?

He turned. They were staring at him, Nakata, Rennett, Caskie, everybody but Hitchcock, who was on the bridge setting up the engine combinations.

"This never happened," Carter told them. "None of this. We never saw anybody else out here. Not anybody. You got that? *This never happened.*"

They nodded, one by one.

There was a quick shiver down below as the tiny sun in the engine room, the little fusion sphere, came to full power. With a groan the engine kicked in at high. The ship started to move away, out of the zone of dark water, toward the bluer sea just ahead. Off they went, pulling eastward as fast as they could, trying to make time ahead of the melt rate. It was afternoon now. Behind them the other sun, the real one, lit up the sky with screaming fury as it headed off into the west. That was good, to have the sun going one way as you were going the other.

Carter didn't look back. What for? So you can beat yourself up about something you couldn't help?

His knuckle was stinging where he had split it punching Hitchcock. He rubbed it in a distant, detached way, as if it were someone else's hand. Think east, he told himself. You're towing two thousand kilotons of million-year-old frozen water to thirsty San Francisco. Think good thoughts. Think about your bonus. Think about your next promotion. No sense looking back. You look back, all you do is hurt your eyes.

LAYOVER

BY TIM CAHILL

THE CLOCK STARTED RUNNING when we left Tierra del Fuego, at the tip of South America, and it would stop when we reached Prudhoe Bay, Alaska, the farthest place north a man could conceivably drive in North America. We were going for a record: the fastest drive ever on the Pan American Highway, the longest road in the world.

Except . . . well, there's always an obstacle. Ours was the Darién Gap: eighty miles of roadless area in that narrow strip of land connecting Colombia with Panama. The editors of the *Guinness Book of Records* told us that we could choose to drive the gap overland—a task that would take months and a corps of engineers the size of an army—or we could take a boat from Cartagena, Colombia, to Panama.

And so, on the eighth day of our trip, we arrived in Cartagena, and there had been only seven or eight times that teenaged soldiers held automatic rifles to our necks. We figured we had gotten off easy. My partner, Garry Sowerby, the professional endurance driver, was feeling good. Not much could go wrong now.

I cannot give a list, an orderly list, of the things that a person must do to load a one-ton four-wheel-drive pickup on a containerized cargo ship out of Cartagena. Let us just say that the paperwork is a staggering ground blizzard of documents, of stamps and signatures and initialing that produces a file, which, if dropped from table height, could kill a cat. The ship was leaving in twenty-four hours. We felt that obtaining the proper forms in a half dozen different offices scattered around a strange city was one of the more unlikely challenges of our Pan American enterprise. If we failed the paper chase— if we couldn't compress a week's worth of formalities into eight business hours—we'd likely have at least a two-week wait for another ship.

The challenge was certainly daunting, though the consequences may not seem to be of any great import. Getting a truck on a boat so we could continue what was essentially a lark—with the idea that we could get our names in a book along with a bunch of people who eat enormous quantities of baked beans with cocktail sticks or who do cartwheels across the state of Nebraska—is not the noble substance of epic.

People find the drive easier to understand if I say that there was money involved. We had several important sponsors, not the least of which was the manufacturer of the one-ton pickup. Garry supports his wife and children making these records. We were motivated by ambition, a titch of avarice, and the hunger of the Sowerby children.

Now contrast our nervous situation with any number of Colombian officials, who were, on Friday, October 9, 1987, facing a three-day weekend. Monday was Discovery of America Day, a national holiday. Colombians are little different from anyone else in such a situation: Not a whole lot of work is accomplished on Friday afternoon. People were looking forward to family outings, parties, binges at the disco. What they got was a couple of twitchy gringos on a quest.

*   *   *

The shipping agent took our money, told us that our ship was called the *Stella Lykes,* and that we'd have to come back to his downtown office later with certain official forms obtainable at the port. We arrived at the port early that Friday morning and parked the truck beside a small car driven by Colombian friends we had seduced into helping us on our mission. There were a lot of people standing around the port parking lot, and a tall black man with a crutch and a withered left leg told us he'd watch the car for us. The front of his pants was wet and he smelled bad. His upper arms were huge. He said his name was Danny and that he had been in twenty-seven countries and did we want to buy cocaine. We gave Danny five dollars, ostensibly to watch the car. In point of fact, we had all noticed that the crutch would be useful for breaking windshields and generally wreaking havoc upon automobiles owned by penny-pinchers.

We gave our passports to an officer in a windowed office at the gate to the port, explained our situation, were issued red name tags, and allowed to drive the truck into the port area. We couldn't put the truck into the metal cargo container until a customs officer saw it. The customs office was not at the port but several blocks away. We took our Colombian friends' car. The customs office was a modern building, like something you might see at a junior college in Bakersfield.

A man who looked like the late comedian Andy Kaufman came out to look at the truck. He was wearing muted green slacks and a green shirt. He said he didn't want to actually examine the truck because it was raining. Did we have umbrellas? No? This is true? He found it difficult to believe that we had driven the entire length of South America without umbrellas.

A compromise was reached. Kaufman would ride down to the port, a soldier could examine the truck, report to him, and he'd sign the proper documents. Danny got another five dollars at the port parking lot.

A tall soldier in a crisply creased uniform opened the camper shell, and looked in at the mess of sodden camping gear. There was an overwhelming smell of diesel emanating from the shell, the residue of ninety gallons of fuel that had leaked from our ruptured alternate tank. Laid over the greasy diesel was a crusty skim of sour milk that we had poured over our gear in an effort to discourage lengthy searches. Sour milk, left to deteriorate inside a metal camper shell that's baking under a tropical sun produces a kind of sweet putrescence, and this odor, combined with the overwhelming fumes of the spilled diesel, produces a remarkable reek. Customs officers had been mercifully cursory in their inspections.

The fastidious soldier at the Cartagena port fingered an extra pair of shoes I had, took a clean handkerchief from his pocket, wiped his hands and went back to a large hangar where Andy Kaufman was standing. The sun was shining now but the customs agent didn't want to stand out there because, he said, the sun might fade his green shirt. Were these his disco clothes? He signed one document.

We drove the agent back to the customs office, and were taken into another, larger office. A man sitting behind a desk there wore a big gold chain around his neck. He had a bony angular face and he was doing absolutely nothing. He looked at the carnet (our transit pass for the vehicle), stamped it, signed it, and gave it back to us. We walked about fifty feet farther and were taken into another office where a large lady in a red skirt and tightly curled black hair signed something and, bang, put a stamp on it. In another office, another official wrote something in a big book. Another office: another book, another set of initials. Another stamp.

It seemed the last of the formalities. We had a sheaf of stamps and signatures and initials. But a tall, thin black man, one of our invaluable friends, ran out into the lobby in a kind of awful frenzy. "Please," and motioned us urgently back to the offices. So we trudged back through a maze of corridors to a large corner office where Andy Kaufman sat. He appeared to be very sad indeed.

His desk was a big one, with plate glass over the top, and under the glass was a portrait of Jesus, His Sacred Heart glowing in His chest. The carnet was in French, but it was pretty straightforward except for item twelve. They wanted Garry, who speaks some French, to translate. Garry can curse heartily in French, but official documents are beyond him. He had no idea what it said. People were standing around in confusion. Garry looked down at the Sacred Heart of Jesus and lied like a bandit.

"It's your badge number," Garry Sowerby said with all the authority he could muster.

Andy Kaufman got out his badge, filled out the number, tore off his section of the tripartite document, and we were gone. But not out of Colombia.

Back at the port—"Cocaine?" "No, Danny, here's five, watch the car"—they needed to conduct another search. Then Garry took off the side mirrors and backed our twenty-one-foot truck into a forty-foot container. It was tight, and Garry had to crawl out the window and over the hood.

It was noon. The longshoremen were going on their lunch break. They would be back at two. Indeed, every office in the city was closed from noon until two, and we felt that the hours between two and five would be difficult ones. We drove to the shipping lines, and were delayed by a parade for a beauty contest. There were attractive women in abbreviated black dresses doing hoochie-coo dances in the back seats of old Chevy convertibles while we muttered crude maledictions.

So we waited there, under the walls of an ancient fort. Cartagena had been one of the ports the Spanish used to siphon gold, silver, and other treasures out of South America. Officials in the old country had a sense that functionaries in South America were skimming them blind and began requiring great masses of paperwork that could be used in tracing treasures. Records were abundantly redundant, and the tradition persists. South America is the most paper-intensive continent on the face of the earth.

Back at the shipping agency, we obtained a needed receipt for our payment after demonstrating that we had customs clearance. But the man who could give us our bill of lading was not yet back from lunch. Come back later. We drove to the department of immigration, which was in an old church. The man we were directed to was in a large room, and his desk was in the back, by a window. There was a palm tree outside, and as I got closer I could see that the tree was in a courtyard that was ankle deep in litter. Still the ceiling was twenty-five-feet high, the walls were dark burnished wood, and there was another portrait of Jesus and His Sacred Heart hanging on the wall.

The man had a pack of Marlboros on his desk, an ashtray, a small cup of coffee, and nothing else. He handed us a couple of forms to fill out. A woman came in, took the forms to a small desk near the door, made some notations, and gave them to the man behind the desk who stamped them. He never said a word to us.

This set of papers was now in order, and we drove to the shipping agency—it was 4:55 when we got there—picked up the bill of lading and then drove to the port. We gave Danny five more dollars for good luck and old times' sake.

Nothing, we felt, could go wrong now.

The *Stella Lykes* was a Constellation class cargo carrier, registered in the U.S., 665 feet long, with a seventy-five-foot beam. A steam turbine engine generated fifteen thousand horsepower from a single four-bladed screw. There were accommodations for eight passengers in four double cabins. Passengers on board for the duration paid $3,300 per person for a voyage of approximately thirty-five days, with the usual ports being Cartagena, Balboa, Buena Ventura: working ports. There were two Panama Canal transits.

Our stateroom was set amidships and might have been a room at a clean economy class motel. There were four such staterooms, but we were the only passengers. Across a hall was a large lounge with three couches, two card tables, a coffee table, a television, VCR, a bookshelf, and a small galley.

We went down four flights of stairs, to the officers' mess. Outside there were compressed air tanks against a wall, very tightly secured, and above them was a big sign informing passersby that such tanks can fall over and that compressed air can escape through a hole the size of a pencil, which would cause the heavy tanks to rocket around and ricochet off the walls and kill people.

We had a good diner-quality American meal; our waiter was a man who looked like the entire front line of the Washington Redskins. We mustered the courage to ask him if there was any liquor available.

The front line of the Redskins approached another gentleman, a tall black fellow who had a way of standing that suggested his bones had a great deal of elasticity to them. The front line said: "These boys haven't had a taste in some time."

The rubber man—his name was Frank—told us to go up to our stateroom and that he'd arrive sometime later with a half gallon of vodka and a bucket of ice. We gave him twenty dollars. And he did.

Several drinks later, Captain Juergin Steinebach, the head of the Stevedorian Company, stopped in for a visit. He was a burly man who had been around the world and done some rally driving himself and knew why we were concerned about our vehicle. It was now after midnight. The longshoremen were supposed to stop working at 1:30 A.M. The captain took us for a stroll down the pier. We walked past a ship called *Encouragement,* and Captain Steinebach said that there was more to a cargo ship than one that will carry a lot of weight at a good speed. He was most interested in the loading gear: "A cargo ship," he said, "becomes obsolete not because of its hull or engines but because of its capacity to load and unload quickly."

The night was hot, the air heavy with humidity, and the pier was still wet with the morning's rain. Light from working ships fell across damp pavement in sheets and patches. All else was darkness, and it occurred to me that here, in a major Colombian port, there was a possibility that persons currently pursuing a career in international crime might be hard at work and that such individuals could resent an accidental intrusion. It was no place to be, half drunk at one in the morning.

Still, we needed to be sure that the truck was loaded onto the *Stella Lykes.* In the utter darkness behind warehouse number seven was a large rust-colored container that was carrying our truck. It was loaded at 1:30 A.M., exactly, the last container to go on the ship. The longshoremen brought it on the back of a towing trailer, hooked the *Stella Lykes*'s crane into it with a spreader device (most of the other containers were twenty-footers), and loaded it atop four other forty-foot containers on the port bow.

The *Stella Lykes* was set to sail in the morning. Nothing could go wrong now.

There were some books in the lounge. One was about a man who killed people and kept a diary detailing his foul deeds. His wife found the diary. There was a confrontation and the wife was in jeopardy for some time but the bad guy got his in the end. I read the novel in about two hours, lying in the sun on a lawn chair on the gray metal deck in a deep canyon formed by towering stacks of rusty orange containers.

It was a clear day, the water was a brilliant deep-water blue, and there wasn't a whitecap in sight. It was a 260-mile voyage through the Panama Canal to the port at Panama City. To the west I could see a bit of jungle: the Darién Gap we weren't going to drive. There was a momentary shadow, a patter of rain, then it was clear again. The sun touched the clouds on the western horizon and they burst into flame, burned out spectacularly, then darkened down into the color of a deep bruise. Below these damaged clouds, there was the occasional flash and streak of lightning. Then it was dark.

About two the next afternoon we were in Gatún Lake, the huge man-made lake in the center of Panama, eighty-five feet above sea level. We had passed through the first set of locks, and risen into the lake at two in the morning. The water was greenish and there were strange circular islands, tufts of tangled emerald jungle that dotted the lake. The islands generated a slight misting fog that rose out of the greenery in drifting, silver pillars.

The large freighter was hugging a meandering curve of red buoys, carving a wide sinuous wake around the jewel-like islands.

The *Stella Lykes* passed close to the southern shore and I could see areas where the waters of the lake had eroded the banks. The land there was the deep red of jungle clay. Creeks that emptied into the lake flowed red—the color of diluted blood: an astonishing color against the impossible greenery of the jungle and the more muted palette of the lake.

The channel winds twenty-four miles through Gatún Lake before it enters the Gaillard Cut, an eight-mile channel blasted through the rock of the continental divide. In places the freighter steamed a stone's throw from the shore, and the land looked vaguely prehistoric: ferny grasses, large leafy plants. Frank, the rubber man, said that before the cut was widened, about twenty-five years ago, a man on the deck of a passing boat had to duck overhanging branches.

"Snakes on those branches," Frank said.

The jungle seemed to close in on the ship, and the odor of the land, rather than the sea, freshened the air. Bird calls burst out of the jungle with increasing urgency just at dusk, the whistles and melodic songs of jungle life and not the shriek of seabirds.

The last set of locks—Pedro Miguel, a thirty-one-foot step-down, and Miraflores, a fifty-four-foot two-step-down—dropped us back to sea level. The boat was pulled through the locks by four small locomotive engines called mules.

"They used to really use mules," Frank said.

Beside us, a large cargo ship, painted bright yellow, was rising in the adjacent lock as we sank. The lights of the lock complex, set on

high poles, were blinding, and the night seemed exceptionally dark
behind them.

"Ought to be tying up in Panama City in a couple of hours," Frank
said.

At nine that evening, the *Stella Lykes* was in port. Longshoremen
began working immediately, and we waited for them to off-load the
boat. Frank, who hadn't been around for some time, emerged from
the crew's quarters wearing an iridescent gold suit, gold boots, and a
wide gold-brimmed hat. He carried a polished wooden walking stick
with an ornate gold handle. On board, Frank was a man who wore
T-shirts and faded jeans.

"You boys ought to come along," Frank said.

"We're going to be sure they off-load the truck," I said.

"Be a shame to miss the flatback factory here," Frank said.

"Next time."

Several hours later they unloaded the truck. Garry and I stood on
the pier, shaking hands and assuring ourselves that nothing could go
wrong now. We could clear customs in a couple of hours, head
north, and have the record in our pocket inside of two weeks. About
that time, Frank appeared out of the darkness, flanked by two Pan-
amanian policemen.

"Forgot my shore pass," he explained mildly. We followed him
onto the *Stella Lykes*. "Maybe you boys want to go to the lounge,
have a drink," he said. "I don't think you're going to like what I have
to tell you."

"What's that?" I asked.

"See, you should have come with me. I met this girl, she was a
master of tongue fu."

"Frank."

"She could . . ."

"Frank."

"Seems that, uh, tomorrow is this, well, it's a national holiday.
National Revolution Day. They tell me ain't nobody works on National Revolution Day. Customs don't work for sure."

I stared down at the locked container carrying our truck. "This girl
I met, she says they'll be working down at the flatback factory,"
Frank said. He thought that might make us happy.

BULL GATOR

BY RIP TORN,
WITH J.T. GLISSON

WHEN I WAS A BOY I spent summers with my mother's parents in Granger, Texas. It was and still is a Czech farming community. Although my grandparents rarely spoke Czech at home, they did converse fluently with their neighbors and relatives.

My grandfather, Arnold Adolph Spacek, was mayor of this small town in the middle of the blackland prairie. My grandmother, Marie Cervenka Spacek, was called Mary. She called my grandfather Arnold. His legion of friends called him Double A, but his sons and grandchildren called him Pops. He was a small man, very strong, handsome and well formed. Besides Czech, he spoke German and English and Spanish. His everyday English was cultivated, with no

Texas accent, but with hints of a Southern or Delta flavor. He didn't pronounce, for example, the final R in hammer; it was, "Hand me a hammuh." He was jolly and warm, with a fierce temper that exploded quickly, but just as quickly blew over, and whoever he cussed one day was likely his friend the next. My grandmother was a beautiful woman, but shy. Her home and garden was her domain. She could read the clouds and foretell the weather. I worshiped my grandparents. Their old-country culture seems, in memory, more human and civil than today's. Their Thanksgiving tables were always overflowing with wild turkey, venison, quail, fried chicken, squirrel, rabbit, poppy seed rolls, four or five different cakes and pies—so much food, warmth, and love.

My grandfather took me on hunting and fishing parties when I was five. He had a changing array of setters and pointers for hunting quail, but he was never satisfied with these animals and claimed that, "Sonny here is my best bird dog." I guess my grandmother thought so, too. When my grandfather, who always bought the groceries, failed to appear on time to start supper, she sent Sonny afield to fetch him home. There weren't too many places to look: the ice house, the cotton gin, Jerry's Garage, the post office, cousin Arnold's swap shop, the butcher shop and grocery. Although I never looked there first, the trail generally led to an old beer hall. You could smell it coming up the one main street that crossed the railroad and highway. I never remember the ten or twelve men inside as drunk; it was the old building that was besotted, soaked with those ancient ferments. I circled in the gloom and there he'd be, the groceries perched on one leg behind a row of dominoes, the other leg hiked up on the rung of his chair, blue eyes complete concentration through his "specs," hat perched back of head—an ever present cigarette in the corner of the mouth, sending wreaths to join those of the other players and kibitzers.

With a grin, without taking his eyes off the table, my grandfather cried, "What took you so long, Sonny boy? Here, take these groceries home before your grandmother gets mad at you." The men laughed.

I replied, "She told me not to come home without you." The men laughed again.

Pops put the dominoes down, and in a hurried, hushed conference—pushing me out the door—he announced he was moments and a few moves away from being the new domino champ of Granger, and it was evident this meant more to him than being mayor.

I hung at the door, watching through the blue haze while he won. However, his victory was challenged by the ex-champ. My appearance at the crucial moment was criticized as a design to break concentration, and the conversation and exchange of the grocery bag might have involved another exchange affecting the game.

"By Jogas," exploded my grandfather, "that's enough to fight over," and down in Texas lives have been lost for less.

I ran home and told my grandmother, and she put on a bonnet and hurried to throw her childlike voice into the dark and dank tavern. "Arnold, I've got to feed this boy, and you've got to meet with Parmelee about the sewer line." More laughter and my grandfather's fierce laugh with the oaths, "By Jogas, we'll settle this later." The red-faced mayor and former dominoes champ exited his meeting hall, his spectacles clouded with heat. He picked up the sack of groceries left at the door and thrust them into my arms. "Here, Sonny—catch." He whistled out the door, up the gravel street to the Mexican-tiled two-story house he designed and built himself. Pops did a fierce dance and shook his fist in the air and turned back to my grandmother with glee. "Oh, Mary, I did it. I beat old man McIntosh. I'm the dominoes champ!"

And he gave a curious whistle, like a pintail. Then he said, "Sonny, there goes our boat." My grandfather, you see, had sold his boat to old man McIntosh, the ex-champ, although he had retained a friend's use of it. But now, after this round of dominoes, my grandfather would never request its use again.

After dinner my grandfather savored his cigarette and coffee, and the brandy my grandmother would pour for him. Then he pulled out the drawer of the white-enameled table and with pencil and paper began to sketch. "Sonny," he'd say, "let's build a boat that will be ours to use whenever we want it. This is the kind of boat the Cajuns in Louisiana used on Caddo Lake and on the rivers in East Texas where you live. A pirogue or bateau, they call it. But we want it stable enough to stand in. We need cypress boards about fourteen inches wide and three-quarters of an inch thick, but we'll use pine and plywood and put tin under the bow, so we can pull it up on the gravel banks."

So we built ourselves a boat, me holding the boards while he nailed and screwed it tight with a seat fore and aft and a storage space in the middle. Then we pitched it and painted it black. We fished the San Gabriel and a natural wide place above a falls called Katy Lake, where Berry's Creek entered the river. In my youth the rivers and creeks of Central Texas were unlike the tea-stained creeks, bayous, and cypress swamps of East Texas. The water was clear and blue over white limestone ledges and golden gravel. Now there are condominiums where I fished, and the blue water is milky. But in those days the creeks and rivers and springs were rich with watercress and schools of spotted bass, bluegills, channel cats, sea-run gaspergou. We'd wade with fly rods for bass and bream, and in the evening seined red-horse minnows to bait our catfish lines.

When my grandfather died, the little boat was given away.

After I got out of the Army, I spent many years in the theater in New York, mostly with Geraldine Page as companion and wife. As an actress, Gerry was meticulous about design and application of makeup, about the detail and cut and authenticity of period costume and shoes, and about the objects one uses on stage: the steps, doors, windows, lights, hand objects—be it a telephone, scissors, fan, or the right book. These tools, called properties, are maintained by a property master who sets them on stage. That is his job, but it is the responsibility of the actor to check them. This attention to detail, which I shared with Gerry, often caused conflicts when I "hired out" into the world of cinema.

Since the writer, producer, director, cameraman, designer, lighting director, sound man, prop man, and makeup personnel have been with the project longer than you, the actor, diplomacy is needed to get your own ideas a hearing. And it was knowing this that helped me get a very special little boat into a film I was working on.

A few years ago I got hired for the film *Cross Creek* by my friend, producer Robert Radnitz, and director Martin Ritt. The cast—Mary Steenburgen, Peter Coyote, Dana Hill, Alfre Woodard, and myself— were flown to Ocala, Florida, to undergo a couple of weeks of rehearsals. The film was about novelist Marjorie Kinnan Rawlings's relationship with the community of country people, called Crackers, who farmed, fished, and hunted in the scrub and waterways of northern Florida in the 1930's. I played the part of Marsh Turner, a Cracker who cares for his large family by farming, raising cattle, hogs, and horses. He also runs fish traps and makes moonshine.

I was satisfied with my costume, wool suit and hat with an osprey feather found below a fish hawk's aerie. After looking at a number of mounts, I finally chose a wonderful black quarter horse with a walking-horse gait that gave a sense of foreboding when I came into town to commit the violence that ended with my death. I was happy with my shotgun, bought from a local antique shop. But my boat was all wrong: It was big and clunky and had an outboard. How was I to run a moonshine still and fish traps and hide from the revenuers and the warden using a boat you could hear a mile away?

I tried diplomacy with my director and producer. They were sympathetic but we didn't communicate when I explained we needed a small "sneak" boat that was paddled and not a putt-putt. The idea, after all, was to reach a still hidden in the shallow reaches of a cypress swamp as quietly as possible. "What if I bring the boat in to show you?" I asked. "Fair enough," said the director, "but don't count on our using it."

I had rented a tenant's house on the lake in the orange grove where our set was built—one of the inducements made by Bob Radnitz when I was hired. "I'm not paying you what you usually get, but you can live on the lake and fish." The rest of the cast and crew lived thirty miles away in Ocala, in air-conditioning, while my house was in the swamp, with a fan. I was, however, exactly where I wanted to be.

I asked Leo North, foreman of Horace Drew's grove, about the kind of boat I had in mind for the film, and he replied, "I know what you mean, Rip, but I haven't seen one of those little boats around for a long time. If anyone would know about them, though, it would be J.T. Glisson. His folks lived across the road from Marge Rawlings when she wrote those books. Get the park ranger to introduce you to him."

At dinner in the Rawlings's house I met J. T. Glisson and his wife, Pat. J.T., an inventor, pilot, and artist, was a man of quick wit and great energy. Over catfish, hush puppies, collards, and purple hull peas, which we washed down with big glasses of iced tea, J.T. confirmed what I'd already heard—that he wouldn't have anything to do with the film. He had endured years of rude tourists and publicity people coming to the Creek to rediscover Marge Rawlings. He was sick and tired of it.

We talked about fishing and hunting in Florida and in Texas, our families, and ambled through what is more or less a Southern ritual for getting acquainted with a stranger. My answers were not as important as the vocabulary I used. J.T. nodded and laughed and I knew I was home. "Well," J.T. finally said with a grin, "you may live in New York, but you know country ways. I like ya despite your association with Hollywood."

Even though J.T. and his beautiful wife, Pat, had lived and worked all over the world, they preferred to live near the Creek, and it was the Cracker in him that was coolly observing me. What won him over, though, as he later told me, was my straightforwardness in answering his questions.

"So, what's your problem?" he said, which was his way of accepting me.

I told him my concern about the boat. "No matter how good the acting is, if the props are phony, everything goes down the drain." Then I borrowed a tablet and pencil from him and sketched the little boat that my grandfather and I had built long ago. J.T. seized the tablet, studied it, and began to talk as he sketched another boat. "Your hull was different," he said, "and I bet you put tin under the bow so you could pull it up on gravel banks." I smiled and nodded.

"We used to hunt frogs and alligators in the marshes and swamps," J.T. said as he sketched. "Trapping and seining fish was illegal, but the Crackers reasoned that if Jesus helped Peter pull a seine and caused it to run over with fish, why should some politicians at the state capitol in Tallahassee interfere with us doing it? Your boat's bow was trimmed up to slide up on the gravel banks, but we trimmed the sides of ours down off the top toward the front, so the bow would extend about an inch below the water."

When I asked why, he grinned and finished his sketch.

"It was necessary for the bow of the boat to part the lily pad bonnets and water weeds rather than ride up on them, which would stop all forward progress in the heavy growth of these lakes. The other reason was whenever you spotted the wardens, all you had to do was take a couple of paddle strokes and you were in the bonnets—where you could lean forward and become invisible. Many a time my dad and I hid in the bonnets, so close to the wardens you could smell their citronella and hear what they thought of you."

Handing me the sketch, he continued: "These boats were designed to paddle from the front, so you could maneuver in the bonnet patches and put in traps. You could pole from the rear when you hunted frogs or gators. The sides were kept as low as possible to make it easier to paddle in the wind and to hide from the wardens."

I marveled at the sketch and observed, "When you think about it, to suit the kind of water it's used in, the refinements were passed down from one generation to the next. This is a damn sophisticated little rig."

"Yes it is," J.T. said. "That simple little homemade boat may look like a fiddle, but it performs like a Stradivarius."

It was getting late, and on the way out I asked my new friend if he would drive over to the movie set the following day. "No thanks," he replied. "I don't want to get aggravated. Most of them just want me to give this project my blessing, not my critique."

I felt that I had lost my chance, but I tried again. "We'll go after five in the afternoon, after the work crew has left." He agreed.

The next afternoon we walked around Kane Hammock, the point on Orange Lake chosen by Bob Radnitz to build the run-down house Marge Rawlings comes to buy. To J.T. the transformation of the Hammock was unbelievable. "Damn. Look, a 'new' worn-out road built through the hammock parallel to the water. A *new*, run-down dilapidated house. Look here, dirt dauber nests, spider webs, a rusted-out roof—and here the road ends. This is really something. This house looks fifty years old!"

"Look here," I pointed, and J.T. laughed. A *new* run-down decayed dock supplied by Hollywood.

"And this is your boat?" J.T. said. I nodded sadly. "It ain't a Cross Creek boat, that's for sure, Rip, ol' friend. I can't find a single thing about this boat that resembles the ones we used during that time on the Creek. It's made of plywood. We didn't have plywood back then. Transom is cut for an outboard motor, and we didn't have kickers until after World War II. It's got a V-bottom and high sides—you won't be able to go in the marshes or cypress swamps."

"Look, maybe it'll work out," I interrupted. "Anyway, where could you find one of the boats like you built with your dad?" I felt dizzy from anxiety, as if I was strangling in my words. He shook his head.

"You can't," he said. "They were made of cypress hearts, which were sacred in those days, used only for boats or coffins. After plywood and outboards came in, the old boats were bought by cattlemen and used in their pastures as feed troughs."

I pressed on: "If you had to have a boat, *had to have it,* what would you do?"

J.T. gave a little smile, then said, "I'm gonna have to think on that." He looked like he had bit a green persimmon with a bad tooth.

J.T. walked around, examining the old house as if he had forgotten my question. But his enthusiasm grew as he inspected the kitchen and barn. Then he suddenly wheeled around and fixed me with a fierce look that gave way to a big grin. "I would have to build it, because all the old Cracker boat builders from around here are dead, and because the state won't allow anybody to cut cypress anymore. We would have to go to Eureka, down in the Big Scrub, to a little sawmill that has been snaking logs off the bottom of the Oklawaha River to get cypress boat lumber." He paused. "The problem is that the lumber would be too wet because cypress should have, at the least, a year to dry."

I asked, "If you had to use wet lumber, what would you do?"

"That would be tricky," he said, "because if I bucked the bottom boards tight when I nailed them on, they'd probably split when they dried and shrank."

I had not lost my determination. "Then the boat would not leak for a few weeks," I said carefully, "and the worst thing would be you might have to replace the bottom boards." He agreed. "When can we see this man about the lumber?" I asked.

He answered with a shake of his head. "I doubt the man would agree to cut it in less than a month." I let out a hoot that stirred the owls in the live oaks. "Well, he won't blame us for asking?"

As we climbed in the car, J.T. said, "I'm catching boat fever. It's been over thirty years since I built one of these boats. Whether Hollywood has the sense to use it or not ain't the point—not now anyway. I'd just like to paddle one again."

The next morning, before the sun was high enough to dry the dew, found us on the way to the Big Scrub to get cypress boards to build a boat unlike anything seen for over thirty years. J.T. was in great spirits and as eager as I was to build what would probably be the last of the boats that once had been so necessary for survival on Cross Creek.

"Rip, we should be prepared to spend a considerable amount of time convincing the sawmill man to saw the lumber, since they normally collect orders for weeks in advance to make it worth the trouble necessary to crank up the mill."

There was no one at the mill. The local folks in Eureka said the owner was a Mr. Joe Harrison, who lived back in the crossroads part of Fort McCoy. So we doubled back and after stopping at several houses found Mr. Harrison's place.

The introduction was slow and informal. He was a medium-built man, about forty, clearly used to hard work. We told him we wanted to build a cypress boat and not some flimsy plywood rig. Our intentions seemed to meet with his approval, but he said he only ran his mill when he had enough orders to run it for several days. J.T. tried not to hear that. We changed the subject back to boats and J.T. told him how when he was a boy he had helped his dad to build boats for use on Orange Lake. Then Mr. Harrison talked about his dad and living in the scrub country.

The sun rose halfway into the morning sky before we decided to go to the sawmill and look at the logs Mr. Harrison had recently hauled from the river. I considered that real progress: we'd at least be nearer the actual wood.

We followed him to the mill with only one stop to buy chewing tobacco and boiled peanuts. The mill was what they call a backwoods push-hard mill, meaning that everyone is compelled to contribute as much labor as the machinery and help with the cussing when it stops.

Old cypress logs were strewn over a wide area around the makeshift sawmill. We walked around the area following Joe Harrison on what was a guided tour without any commentary as to what we were seeing. Finally we hunkered down in the shade of a pine tree and looked at the logs that contained the precious boards J.T. and I were determined to get. To say the logs were unusual is an understatement. The sap had all rotted away, leaving only the hearts, and they were still three or four feet in diameter. Some were more than twenty feet in length.

I asked Joe where he had gotten the logs.

"They were cut in the 1880's from a virgin forest, a huge swamp that bordered the Oklawaha River, just east of here," he explained. "Them loggers tried to float the logs when they were still too green, and some sank to the bottom and stayed there for about a hundred years. All of them were way more than a hundred years old when they were cut. Some maybe a thousand."

It was a hot April afternoon, probably too hot for most people, but a pleasant time for storytelling, and J.T. told a lot of them. Gradually the subject drifted to big snakes and mean gators and then back to boats. My stomach was beginning to growl. Finally, at about three o'clock, Joe said, "Looks like you fellers ain't planning on leaving until you get that boat lumber."

J.T. replied, "I got plenty more stories to tell."

Joe said, "All right, if you'll help me get this thing to running, I'll cut your cypress." For the next two hours we cranked stubborn motors, rolled logs, piled slabs, and loaded boards.

We left the sawmill with just enough time to drive back to the Creek without a taillight on J.T.'s overloaded trailer. We had our custom-cut boat lumber, for which Joe charged only a modest sum.

After supper we cleared everything out of J.T.'s garage, then set up two makeshift sawhorses and started to build the boat. Before beginning, J.T. recited a poem: " 'Build you a boat/ and set it afloat/ Then paddle your own canoe.' "

We began by attaching the sides to the transom, which was made from a single piece of two-inch-thick cypress. The transom was flared at the top and tapering up as a rest for a push pole. The side boards were attached flush with the top on the two ends of the transom, with the excess extending down below the bottom, to be trimmed off later, allowing the bottom to rake up along the back third of the boat. Amazingly, J.T. worked without plans, only memory and sight.

When the sides were securely nailed to the transom, we set the back side of the fish-well—made from a single board—which established the two-foot four-inch beam. The angle on the ends would determine the flare of the sides and was critical to the final shape of the boat. J.T. visualized the stern and decided what was proper.

"I think the people who know the names of such things call that board a bulkhead," he said. "However, no one at the Creek ever had the opportunity to learn such things."

The front side of the fish-well was slightly shorter and had less flare, which allowed the sides to taper in toward the bow. The two sides were spaced parallel, about fifteen inches forward of the back wall. J.T. remembered asking his dad why he did not space it farther back, to make room for more fish, and how one of the fishermen watching answered, "Fer that width boat it's so that it'll hold two hun'erd pounds, an' if a feller gets more than that, he orta stop and sack 'em an' set some in the rear to balance his boat." J.T. said the old fisherman paused and laughed. "Besides, if the game warden comes, two hun'erd pounds is all he could scoop overboard."

I left at about midnight to study the script and went promptly to bed. Building the boat was a relaxing experience, but buying the lumber earlier in the day had been hard work.

The next morning, J.T. asked a neighbor's boy, Lee Deadrick, to help in order to speed up the process, because we had to have the boat ready when the director scheduled shooting the scenes that would include it.

With the stern and the fish-well set, the sides were ready to be brought together, forming the bow. J.T. said that forming the bow was the part he liked best. Using a rope, he made a loop around the sides, halfway from the fish-well to the point where the sides would join. Then, using a stick, we twisted the rope, forcing the side boards to bend inward until they came together and were secured to the bow stem. When the bow was secured, what had looked like a sixteen-foot box suddenly looked like a boat. And a graceful boat at that.

We curved the sides upward along the back third to a point that would suspend the rear above the water and counterbalance the weight of the fisherman in the front. The sides leading to the bow were shaped to cause it to extend an inch below the water.

Neighbors stopped by. "They always do," said J.T., "when someone has a special project going on at their houses." The project turned into a festive occasion.

On the second morning we finished applying the bottom and were in the process of installing the keel when Pat called J.T. to the phone. After a spell he came out of the house with a cold, determined look. He walked toward me with a pistol in his hand, looked at me for a moment, and then at an eighty-foot pine that, blasted dead by lightning, still stood in his pasture. On the tip-top was perched a starling. J.T. brought the pistol up and fired, and the bird dropped like the proverbial stone. He handed me the pistol. "Try that pinecone next to the perch." I shot and J.T. said, "I've never been able to clip it either."

Then he told me the phone call was from someone with the movie company. J.T. had asked if they wanted to speak to Rip. They had replied, "No. You give him the message. We won't be using your boat in the film." Actually, it was of little importance to J.T. whether they used it or not; what he *didn't* appreciate was receiving a call ordering him to be a messenger boy.

"I thought only a fool would refuse something for free without seeing it first," J.T. said. "I had intended to give them the use of it, and I am sure that would have been okay with you." We agreed to build our boat anyway, and use it to fish from when I finished the film.

Since the boat was a mutually owned asset, J.T. suggested we form a company, which did not require any paperwork in Florida. I agreed, and we drank to it. Then, after more deliberations, we named the boat and the company *Bull Gator*. Male alligators slip around quietly all year and then beller and raise hell in the spring. It seemed an appropriate name.

That afternoon, a sinister-looking van with black-shaded windows coasted into the driveway. A tall, thin individual, who could have been an F.B.I. type, emerged and surveyed the area as if he were clearing the way for the President of the United States. I said, "He's the producer's driver." J.T. chose to ignore whoever he was.

The driver said, "Nice boat. I'll be back." He returned in an hour with Bob Radnitz. J.T., who had lived in the village of Evinston for twenty years, said Mr. Radnitz was the first visitor he could remember who arrived in his yard wearing white tennis shorts, white Nikes, dark sunglasses, and a red bandanna.

I liked Bob and introduced him to J.T. They have a custom in this area that dictates you extend reasonable hospitality to anyone up to the point you ask them to leave. In light of the phone call J.T. had received only a few hours earlier, he found himself dangling on the proverbial horns of a dilemma. Bob looked at the boat, was obviously surprised at its class and lines, then made some low-key compliments and asked to use J.T.'s phone. We didn't notice when he left.

We finished *Bull Gator* about suppertime, and a proud moment it was. J.T. and I walked around it, congratulating one another, running our hands over the soft, smooth wood and backing off occasionally to study it from different perspectives. We savored the sweet smell of the cypress, which J.T. associated with the years he had shared with his dad, and which made me recall the years I had spent fishing and hunting with my grandfather.

We finally leased the little boat to the company for seven hundred dollars and gave Lee a hundred dollars for his help.

If you ever see the film *Cross Creek*, my appearance is in that little boat, *Bull Gator*. I'm paddling in front with my daughter in back. We move swiftly across the water, land, and in a continuous sweep move onto the porch. That boat helped create an electric entrance for us.

I also believe *Bull Gator* helped me get an Academy Award nomination. I didn't win the Oscar, but that doesn't matter; for me, the greatest prize is that J.T. and I still fish with *Bull Gator,* and that quite a few descendants of the Crackers who live at Cross Creek have told J.T.: "I liked that Rip Torn fellow. He was convincing. Kinda reminded me of my dad."

I'd say that's award enough for any man.

LOOSE ENDS

BY SUZANNE KEHDE

I FIRST SAW MILLER on a Sunday. I knew it was Sunday because the tourists were late to S.F.'s famous wharf. I'd been up all night and was headed toward a bed when I saw him standing on the deck of the fishing boat. It looked like he was staring at his feet. He was barefoot, and it was cold. I knew my feet were and I had shoes, although I'd left my socks somewhere. I'd really just stopped to watch him because I was tired. Of course I didn't know then what his name was. He was just this big black guy in baggy pants and a plaid shirt buttoned unevenly. I remember that because it made him look like I felt, a little off balance.

A delivery truck went by behind me and I looked over my shoulder. When I looked back the man had come about and was staring my way. I grinned.

"Hey," I said.

He looked at me straight on with his hairy brown face. He had this stubble on his head, woolly I think it was traditionally called, but it was really more like a patch of moss that became thicker as it worked its way into sideburns then grew out over his neck, up over his chin to his cheeks. The space that was left was just enough for his nose and eyes and a thin-lipped mouth that always looked best when he spread it into a smile. He did that then, smiled back at me.

"Have you ever been in the mountains?"

I hadn't expected the voice, too high for such a big man.

"The mountains?"

He nodded.

"Well, yeah, sure. I've been to the mountains. I was in Yosemite just a couple of months ago."

He nodded again.

"It was far out," I said.

He smiled at my slang. I reddened.

"Far out," I said again. "Groovy. Out of sight."

"I found it unnaturally terrifying," he said succinctly.

"Terrifying. Why?"

"Listen."

I did and heard the city getting up. I heard gulls, a car door slam, a general hum of sound that was always there, more intense at night, but so constant I was rarely aware of it.

"So?" I said.

He smiled.

"You're fucked, dude."

He laughed and a flock of seagulls exploded from the sidewalk.

"Good," he said. "Good."

Crazy, I kept thinking. This guy is crazy. But I couldn't leave. I didn't want to. I was mad though because he'd made me feel foolish, and I didn't know why.

"What the hell's so good about it?"

He scratched his head and did a movement that looked very much like a shuffle to the edge of his boat. But his movements and appearance were always denying the tone and content of his words.

"I'll be serving brunch in an hour." His teeth were disturbingly even. "Would you care to join me?"

I looked from his mouth to his eyes.

"That is, of course, unless you've already eaten."

That made me laugh, reminded me of the anger I'd felt a few minutes before because every two steps I'd taken I'd had to yank up my jeans.

"Brunch, huh?" It was the kind of word my parents used. They always had brunch at the club on Sunday after church, a ritual I was dragged along to until I'd had enough of their rituals and the life they were so neatly plotting out for me. I'd become accomplished at least at one thing though, running away. I took some pride in that.

The sun was heating the decks of the boats and the surface of the water, increasing the smell of fish blood and diesel. I looked at his boat, at him, wondering what his angle was, whether I'd have to fuck him, whether the food would be enough to warrant the effort.

"You can come aboard now, if you'd like to wait. Perhaps even help."

I liked boats. Besides what could he do to me so close to so much increasing activity? Anything he wanted to, I knew, but I was tired.

"Your boat have a name?"

It was the first boat I'd ever seen that didn't have a name. He didn't ask for mine nor did I ask for his. I heard it later from others. He never called me by name so I don't know if he ever knew mine, even though I'm certain he knew a great deal about me.

The boat had looked steady enough from the sidewalk, but once I was down beside it on the wharf, I could see its movement, the rocking he stood so solidly atop.

"Permission to come aboard?" I was well educated in many forms of etiquette by years of watching films.

"Permission granted," he said. There was no laughing at my expense in his voice, at my determination to do a few things according to form.

I went up the stepladder and down over the side, immediately thrown off balance by the roll of the boat. I clung with one hand to the warped rail, my legs spread ridiculously wide, just waiting for him to laugh at me or make some comment about my seaworthiness so I could become enraged with self-righteous indignation and storm away—he was scary in the way he kept watching me. I'd never been looked at by anyone in quite that way, a searching of sorts, his eyes squinting slightly under sparse brows.

A car backfired, and he turned and ducked down the hatch faster than I would have dreamed him capable of. I looked at the dimness below, then over to the street, the tourists, the cars, all of the movement having a ceaseless quality that made the hold the old man had scooted into very desirable.

I reluctantly released the railing and wobbled to the hatch, getting to the bottom of the ladder and staying with my back to it, letting my eyes adjust, readying for a quick exit. As my sight returned, though, I became more and more fascinated. Before me was a kitchen—living room combination. I could see a bed in the room beyond, the double bunk and the bare mattresses. I wondered why he didn't have a blanket. Of course maybe he didn't sleep; I could understand that, although if I'd had my own bed, I might have kept regular hours. I laughed.

"What do you find so amusing?" Miller asked. I'd almost forgotten him. He was standing very still in the far corner, watching me again. He wasn't fixing breakfast so I got busy calculating how quickly I could get up the ladder, but I answered him anyway, spontaneously I guess, since all this happened in a second, my observation and thoughts, the second right after my laugh.

Miller often talked about the length of a second. He pointed their length out to me and how if you had to write down what happened in just a few of them, about all the mind is capable of taking in and processing and analyzing, it would take pages to contain it all. He did it once, or tried it anyway, that I know of. I came on him writing like a madman: page after page he ripped from a notepad and let off to the side of his fury, great flakes, Miller shedding these as he often did other things, clothes, jobs, friends.

"What do you find so amusing?"

"Thinking about being regular. Doing things routinely, on schedule." I laughed again. I was still a little high. He stayed quiet, then moved from the wall, making me back up one step on the ladder. But he stopped his advance suddenly and squatted to open the door of a small refrigerator. I looked around the cabin again. It seemed I'd already become accustomed to it. It was insulated with hundreds of old *Life* magazines. They were stacked everywhere. A yellowing one by my feet claimed a victory in Korea and had photos of soldiers who couldn't seem to make their smiles of victory reach their eyes. Besides the *Life* magazines there was some fishing gear and a tennis shoe, no knick-knacks, no pictures on the walls, not even any empties or dirty ashtrays filled with butts to explain the yellowness of those even teeth, just hundreds and hundreds of the oversized magazines filled with color and black and white photos.

Miller was deftly cracking eggs into a bowl with one hand. He put the shells back in the carton. I hoped he wasn't one of those people who thought coffee was better with shattered egg shells in the grounds. It only made the grounds look more like garbage. He was liable to be though. He had so many affectations, or at least that was what I attributed all his behavior to in the beginning. The guy had made himself a character. Maybe he was even as well known as Coit Tower or that ridiculous glass elevator I found myself watching more often than I liked, all those well-dressed people floating skyward to what I imagined was a dim warmth above.

That was what Miller was doing, watching me perched on the first step of his ladder. He'd put the eggs in a pan. Butter first, a smell I'm fond of, butter frying up before anything else goes in.

"So," I said, because of the way he was studying me. "Can I do something to help? Maybe take some of this trash out for you?"

He blinked, then smiled as he looked from the magazines back to me. I smiled as hard as I could at him to show him I was more than aware he'd never get rid of any of the magazines, that they'd continue to pile up until the weight of them sank him.

"You could go pick up a loaf for us."

I frowned.

"Any kind of bread you like. I have butter and there's coffee and a nice marmalade."

He was too big for the cabin.

"Oh, and if you like there's peanut butter."

I laughed. "To go with the marmalade?"

"Crunchy," he said, then turned to attend to the omelet. This was my cue I guessed to go and get the bread which I had no money for and he wasn't offering any for, so I ended up stealing a loaf and the newest *Life* magazine on the stand by the door. The rolled magazine in the back of my pants kept my jeans up. It wasn't that I wanted to please him, at least not right away. I was just grateful that he hadn't wanted to screw me before breakfast.

He didn't want to after either. He had the magazine and was staring at a picture of a soldier in fatigues, one of the grunts trying to police Vietnam. I was taking advantage of his trance by finishing up the loaf of sourdough, getting as much butter and peanut butter and orange marmalade on as I could and washing it down with what

Miller called coffee but which was only tolerable if I put five or six tablespoons of sugar in and a little from the silver creamer. That was the only silver. We ate with plastic knives and forks and spoons. He'd eaten out of a bowl. My omelet had been slid ceremoniously onto the only plate. He'd given me more. I was still expecting to pay for it in some way, but it had been pretty good.

I managed to swallow the last of an enormous wad of peanut butter by washing it down with the last of my coffee and realized I was full. The guy had let me sit there for a half an hour and eat everything in sight and still hadn't laid a hand on me. Well, it was strange, fine, but I did have to get going, and I did owe him. He was still looking at the same picture, moving his lips and following the text under it with his finger.

"So, what does it say?" I was getting impatient and not too happy about the idea of the big old guy coming down on my full stomach. He looked up very slowly. He'd left his finger on the words as if he might lose his place.

"It says that this young man is a proud servant of his country."

"Bull," I said.

"You think not, then?" He turned the magazine around so I could see the grunt, see the cocky smile and the M16 held so casually with one hand, the stock resting on his shoulder.

"He holds it like a ball bat."

Miller blinked. "Why yes, he does." His pleasure in my observation made his voice even higher. It made me wince. "He does. Just exactly that."

He turned the magazine back in front of him, his hand coming down on the page and touching the kid and the gun, nodding and saying yes over and over. What I had said hadn't seemed all that wonderful to me, but he kept going on about it, bobbing his head and squeezing out little yeses.

"Hey," I finally said. "What can I do to work off this meal? I mean, what do I owe you?"

His hand stopped moving as did he. He just stopped. He didn't look at me or answer. The boat swayed sharply as another went by. The seat under me was too hard and the street noise too far away, and I was suddenly so heavy with food that I knew if he came for me I'd never make it to the ladder.

"I mean," I whispered, then cleared my throat to speak louder because it's always a bad idea to sound like you're scared. "I mean," I said again, "I could run some errands for you or clean up."

The guy still wouldn't move. If he hadn't kept blinking, I would have thought he'd gone with a heart attack like my grandfather did. He had just put the stock market page of the Sunday paper down on his lap and died, no sound, nothing. I was right beside him. I was looking at the color pictures of the comics. He had been seventy-seven and I had been eight and still unable to read but good at pretending. Grandfather couldn't read either without his glasses, and thus we'd had a strong affinity for each other. He smoked cigars and I Pall Malls, and we often did together in the garage by his gutted Nash.

But Miller wasn't dead. He told me later he was just trying to think of a way to make me stay. That pleased me although I didn't tell him. I'm not sorry I didn't. Anyway, he knew. I rarely had to tell him things since he often seemed to know what I was going to say before I'd even gotten a sentence formulated and practiced and delivered.

"You may come out with me this afternoon on a run," he finally looked up and said.

"Fishing boats only make runs in the morning."

"I run when I please." His hand closed into a loose fist. He stood up and so did I, but then he simply opened his hand and picked up the bowl he'd been using, reaching for my plate, turning to put them on the counter.

"I thought I'd just run out for an hour or two, get a few for our supper."

"Our dinner?"

He came back around. "You'll stay, won't you?"

I didn't know whether to flip him off and run or just run, or if I'd had too much dope the night before, or if I should do what my compulsion dictated and say as I did, "Yeah, sure, why not. Yeah, I can stay."

I don't remember much of that trip. I had no time to be frightened of my host's intentions or worry about the way the boat ran with such a list or the fact that it seemed to get dark in three minutes and the waves turned from a choppy gray to molten walls of green. I had no time for anything but throwing up over the side, holding on to that slippery rail to keep from falling over.

I did go over once but that was a month later. By then I could bait the lines and not get sick every time I had to cut the hooks from the

flexing mouths of dying fish. And by then I knew Miller could find
the wharf in the fog and the blackness and keep the pump going so
that the boat didn't simply lean over into the water and give it all up.
I was no longer afraid of Miller; I can't say I was crazy about him, but
I was still with him. If anyone had suggested it was a safe haven, I
would have told them they were fucked. But there was really nobody
who cared to ask, and it wasn't like I had anywhere I had to be. That
first night Miller pointed at the empty bunk, and I was so sick, I
didn't care about his motives. He knew better than to ask me to stay. I
just kept saying I'd hang around a little longer because I owed him
for the food and bed. As a matter of fact I only left the boat to get
supplies and sell a few fish or go to the bar with him and of course
take care of my needs, dope and stuff. I'd given up screwing for a
while because I liked to sleep on the boat, and the guys I usually slept
with slept all day, and there really wasn't anyone I wanted to be with
except Miller. He didn't seem to care if I listened when he talked, but
he always listened when I did. Even if his back was turned, he held it
so I knew he was.

I'd been telling him about this freak I'd known in Michigan, and
that was when I went over. I'd been cutting up some bait sitting
nonchalantly, stupidly, on the rail yelling up to Miller about this guy
and next thing I knew I was in the water. I went under and I couldn't
see; then I was up and spitting, sinking again from the weight of my
clothes, not scared really, amazed, I was amazed at how far away the
boat was, how it had traveled to the point of being almost out of
sight. Then I couldn't see the boat at all, and how he managed to
circle back and find me half submerged as I was is still amazing to me.
It wasn't luck although I believe in it, the bad kind anyway. Miller
simply knew where to look, for a lot of things.

I had so little with him, six months in all but almost all of that time
he was teaching me even if I was too stubborn to acknowledge it. He
was never stubborn. There were things he wouldn't do, wasn't doing
anymore, but he'd thought about them and his reasons were never
from stubbornness but from a logic he'd developed that had kept him
alive up to the point I'd met him.

"It's time to do this," he'd say, and he was always right. There
were simple things like it's time to get beer or other than simple
things like it's time to turn on the pump or it's time to stop going into
the city and getting dope. I balked at that of course.

"You don't run my life, old man."

"No one is running your life."

"Shit," I said. "It's mine and I do. So fuck off."

It was incredibly foggy that afternoon. We'd raced the big cloud for about an hour, but it had the wind and we had only an engine with a lot of its horsepower missing. So it caught us. I knew he'd get us home. That didn't bother me. I was first bothered by the smallness of our catch, and then by the damn gulls that kept breaking out of the fog and diving in and stealing the fish I'd just managed to clear from the lines.

Miller liked the gulls. I thought they were garbage eaters, which they were. Miller said we all were. I gave him that point. But when a gull miscalculated and crashed into the glass on the bridge, I was delighted and watched it flop around on the deck bleeding from its beak; then its struggle to live or die more quickly made me throw it overboard. The incident had interrupted the argument we were having. Miller was warm and dry up in the bridge, and I was already soaked from the chop and the mist, and my hands were so numb I kept getting the hooks caught in my fingers, and then that old man was telling me how to run my life.

"Fuck you," I shouted again. "Fuck you and all your generation." But he didn't really belong to the one my compatriots and I so willingly blamed everything on. Actually I liked the way he looked up in the light. I liked it when he was steering his boat because he didn't look so bothered then. He had on one of his two plaid shirts. One hand was on the wheel and the other on the throttle, and he'd opened his window so he could hear what never seemed distorted to him, the bells and warning horns and me. His beard was longer, though not much. He told me the hair on his head had stopped growing when his children had passed their puberty. Only the beard inched out, but I wondered if it wasn't stopping, too. He'd taken to pulling at it as if he wasn't ready for everything to cease.

"Who is it that gets so blind every time we have money for beer? It sure ain't me," I yelled. "That's you, old man. So who are you to tell me about abuses?" I stopped at the last word. I even let a gull come down and bank away with one of our fish. Just at that point Miller blew the warning horn, and I saw the prow of a freighter emerge suddenly from the thickness in all its deadly ponderousness and bear down on us as Miller spun the wheel. The waves from the massive movement through the water almost dumped us and threw me into the cabin.

It knocked me out. I woke up below with Miller sitting beside me looking at the newest issue of *Life* I'd just bought him.

"Did you know that if you sit long enough and quietly enough you can hear the panting of your own heart?"

"Hearts pump," I said.

"But their exhaustion must be immense." He turned a page. I wanted to see what he was looking at because he leaned forward to get a better view but my head hurt too much.

"What's on the page?"

He didn't answer. I'd lost him. So I went to sleep. It could have been anything on that page. He was fascinated with almost anything, indiscriminate things, an advertisement; I once found him studying a hairpin, standing as he did so often, amusing the tourists.

What they didn't know was how aware he was of them and how, when I thought he'd been deep in contemplation, he would see in detail a couple who stopped to take his picture and would later make some comment about them, one only someone who understood watching could appreciate.

The longest I ever saw Miller stare at any one person was in a bar one night. I was smoking from a pack he'd bought me as we'd come in. He seemed to be in a good mood even before he'd gotten any beer down. The lightness of his attitude made me watch him closely. He was behaving expansively, not talking but leaning back in his chair and letting his arms dangle down by his sides. He was looking at the bar. I looked, too, realizing that he was staring at a woman at the end of the counter who was cupped around her shot glass like she thought any moment someone might take it away from her. She looked old from where I was standing, old from my youthful perspective, although she was probably only about forty. She had a drinker's face. Her features were pressed into a swelling like the buttons on an old couch. Miller let his chair down, and it looked like he was going to get up, and he still had his eyes on the woman. Bobby pins, *Life* magazines, but he didn't overtly give people this kind of attention. I could just make out his eyes in his dark face and they were wide and interested and smiling.

She noticed him then. She put her hand on her glass and squinted at Miller and hunched a little more.

"See something you like?" she asked.

"Rarely," Miller said.

I was uneasy. I wanted Miller to stay in his chair, and he did, but he wasn't done looking at the woman.

"I want you to meet my friend."

Well, I was the only friend he had, and I knew suddenly just what he was doing even though the woman and I looked nothing alike. I was furious with him. I'd never liked object lessons. People had always said "see," to me, "see what will happen if . . ." I hadn't expected it from Miller. And I was too angry then to think about how much he'd been changing in the last month, how he'd been talking to me more and seemed to watch me more, how he'd gotten me one more blanket from the Mission because I was always cold under one of the two I'd liberated.

"You should recognize everyone here, kid," he said.

The heavy motionless smoke did make it like a dream, a nightmare. But I felt he had no right, and I told him so.

"Where the hell do you get off, you asshole. Shit, I don't even plan to live that long."

"What'd she say?" the woman asked.

Miller smiled at her.

Her glasses filled with yellow light as she turned. "This guy bothering you, honey?"

I didn't like the change in Miller. I didn't want that kind of lesson. Besides it seemed so simpleminded, too plain to be coming from the marvelous pieces of his mind. It was like grabbing me by the scruff of my neck and pointing at some mess of humanity on some sidewalk somewhere and saying, "See, if you don't get your shit together you'll end up like that." I didn't want it. It wasn't fair of him to turn on me like that. I left and stayed away from the boat for the whole of two days. I thought I could punish him.

"We need peanut butter," was all he deigned to say about my absence. He went back into his magazines and the study of that middle distance, and we went about our business of getting drunk and getting loaded and sleeping and feeling our way back to the berth through the chop and the fog. I wasn't happy, though, or as indifferent as I had been. I wanted to pound things, and I took to ripping the hooks out of the dying fish until one day I saw him watching me and I looked down at the bleeding, gasping mouth and was sick over the side for the first time in months.

I'd known him for four months then, and I took to watching him back because I had a feeling he needed watching, too. I pressed him to talk more, more about himself. I told him I was just curious, that I was tired of talking about myself. It was like trying to catch one of those thieving gulls with your bare hands, nearly impossible unless the bird had been damaged somehow or you caught it at a bad moment.

Miller's moments, his days, all seemed pretty much the same to me. I always knew where he was, on the boat or in the bar or somewhere in between. Occasionally I'd try to get him to come downtown with me or even just down the docks to look at the freighters, but he'd either just not respond or he'd say it wasn't time.

"When will it be?" I asked one day, furious again at something; my tone was sharp with him because I wasn't very good at dumping my anger in the appropriate place or on the right people. "Just when the hell will it be?" I yelled.

He put his hand on my shoulder then. He hadn't ever touched me before, at least not when I was conscious. I wanted to step out from under the incredible weight but something was wrong with his face, and I stayed.

"My beard," he said in his suffering voice, "has stopped growing."

"Shit," I said, wanting to lighten the weight on me, the weight on his mind that had pressed his sketchy brows into an expression of pain. I had an urge to touch him. "Hey, old man," I said. My hands relaxed from the fists they'd formed. "Hey, your beard looks just fine." His hand was so heavy it made me lose my balance, something I thought I'd been mastering so well. "Listen," I said. "Forget about the ships. Hey, a beer would be good."

His face was still concentrating on the pain.

"Don't you think a beer would be nice?" I was terrified he'd cry. I didn't know what I'd do if he did, get angry maybe or just stand there as helpless and lopsided as I was until he was done and then hope we could go back to being normal. I swore to myself I'd never ask him to go anywhere or do anything again that wasn't within the pacings of the routine he'd so diligently laid out.

He didn't cry, but he didn't move either. We stood on the deck as the tourists passed, Miller with his hand on my shoulder, me trying to keep straight enough to have something for that hand to rest on.

Finally I had to lift it from my shoulder. It took both my hands because he wasn't up to helping, and I let it down gently to his side and left mine holding the limpness for a second or two longer to try and make him understand that I was sorry and I wouldn't push and that I thought he was an all right guy and that I loved him. I did in an odd reserved kind of way. I didn't know enough about him or myself to love him as I have since come to love a friend, but it was love. I didn't feel sorry for him or pity him. I knew even then that pity for anyone, particularly oneself, was a waste. So I let go of the hand and stepped back and gave him a gauging look.

"You know," I said. "If we trim that sucker, I bet it will grow out faster."

He looked up at me very slowly and let his brow relax then arched one speculatively.

"No, really. I've heard that if you trim stuff, hair, you know, then it grows faster." I nodded at him for agreement.

"Seems illogical," he said. But he let me trim it. We got drunk and made it back to the boat and he collapsed on his bunk flipping his hand out at me from under his chin and beard as if he were daring me. I've always taken dares.

He in effect dared me to bring the boat in several nights after that by passing out below, not beer, just going to sleep and refusing to come to. Of course I didn't have a lot of choice. And I did get the boat in with a lot of the luck I don't believe in and with an ear and sense of place that I hadn't realized I'd developed. I knew with the fog coming in we'd be an easy target for all the murderous freighters that would only give way if so disposed and if they were given advance notice. I'd come to hate the freighters because they seemed to think that size was a guarantee of an immediate right-of-way, like so many men I'd known. And they were right to a point, right in reference to immediacy anyway. But they should always remember to watch their backs, to watch out for the damaged survivors.

Soon after I got involved with a man I almost didn't survive. I was restless and Miller didn't want to go to the bar. He hadn't for days. So I left and went down to an apartment off Market hoping to make a score. It wasn't what I'd started out to do. I was just going to walk, but then the fog came in, and it was cold and damp, and it's hard to get off the street if you don't have money enough to look like you qualify to be warm. And this made me angry and getting angry made me give up the idea of seeing if I could please Miller by staying away from dope. It made me angry with him for interfering, for pretending that he cared about what happened to me, for making me care. So I ended up heading for Eddy's.

It was early yet but foggy enough to be wary of the entryways. I was in a mood not to care, though, and didn't look first before stepping into the narrow hall that led off the street back to the apartment. It smelled like dog shit, and there was no light. I put my hand out to find the wall, and I realized the instant I touched him and saw the instant he moved the bigness of the man who'd been pressed to the wall so motionless that he'd blended with the darkness. He slammed me back into the opposite wall, getting a hand on my mouth before I could get my breath back, hitting me so hard on the side of the head I almost lost consciousness. He was huge and frighteningly strong, and he hit me again. All I could think about though was the smell. I didn't want to be raped lying in a pile of shit.

But that thug, that filthy son of a bitch hadn't been watching his back, didn't remember to watch out for other damaged survivors. Miller hit him so hard that when he struck the floor I heard his skull crack. I knew it was Miller the second he took my hand, then picked me up because my legs wouldn't work. I made him put me down outside. I knew we wouldn't get far if a patrol car saw a black man carrying away a female Caucasian. If we were picked up and if the man in the hall were dead, I would get sent home to Michigan, but far worse, Miller would go to prison. I thought all that, as the blood ran out of my ear and as my knees kept giving, because he suddenly was my charge.

When I woke the next day, we were moving. I didn't feel like getting up. All I really wanted to do was sleep, so I did. The next time I woke, the boat was no longer running. I'd slept twenty-four hours, and when I finally made it up on deck, I saw that he'd moved us from the berth to the sheltered waters east of Sausalito and had anchored there. Miller had supplied us, and we fished some and never touched land.

I didn't try to find out about the man in the hall. I hope he's dead; I hope he slowly bled to death in the darkness and the stink. Miller wouldn't talk about what had happened or why he'd followed me.

"It's not time," he said.

And I didn't press him. Time was running out, though. We'd been together almost five months. We went back to the berth when we ran out of beer. It was two days before my eighteenth birthday.

I spent those next two days cleaning fish for the Ghetto Restaurant. We were broke. One day would have been enough for our needs, but I wanted to get Miller something for my birthday. And with it coming and if such a thing were possible, I would have said that he was acting positively festive. That meant that on at least half a dozen occasions the night before the fifteenth of October, he smiled at me. He seemed quite pleased with himself, as I was with myself. We each had a secret, apparently. I knew what mine was. I was feeling a sense of elation for other reasons, too. I'd soon be eighteen, a legal adult, no longer a runaway and something subject to the whims of two people who only set the police on me when they tired of making each other miserable. I was delighted with the sensation. I was huge. I had a friend, a place to stay. I thought the accumulation of a total of eighteen years would transform me into somebody and my life into something valuable.

Since Miller no longer liked going to the bar, I went and got some beer for an early celebration. I kept reminding myself of how easy it was for him to lose track of things and how I wasn't going to be disappointed if the next day he simply stood on the deck and thought. It would be all right. Anyway most of my excitement was coming from my anticipation of giving him his gift.

But he remembered. I knew how hard focusing was for him, but when I got up sometime after noon, hung over, he was waiting for me in the cabin.

"Happy Birthday, kid," he said; then he fixed me toast and put out the butter and peanut butter and the marmalade and even managed to make coffee that was drinkable without sugar. The water heater was full of hot water for the shower in the tiny head. I couldn't believe it. Life was going to be all right. Miller would start feeling better, and maybe we could start making runs in the morning like the other fishermen and make a little money and fix up the boat.

He gave me the best gift he could have, his full attention, and I gave him what I'd sent away for. I had to write down what it was on a piece of paper because it was going to take a while to arrive. He took the folded slip in his hand. I was impatient, but I managed not to push him that time.

"It's not my birthday," he said.

"So?"

"I didn't get you anything." He looked at me then. His eyes were wet, and I panicked.

"Shit, old man. If I want to give you something, I can do it any damn time I please. It ain't no big deal."

He smiled at me.

"Oh, fuck it. Just open the thing, will you."

He did, smiling again.

There were just five words on it. He moved his lips as he read them, put his swollen finger on them and read them again aloud as if he needed to check out the content with me.

"One year's subscription to *Life*." He looked up at me. A tear had already left his eye.

"The magazine," I yelled at him, terrified even then at how prophetic it sounded. "I just forgot to put magazine."

He nodded. The sun hit the tear.

"It's just a crummy subscription, old man." I was ready to hit something if he loosed even one more. I got up because I didn't know what else to do and turned my back on him and walked out of the wheelhouse.

"Let's make a run," I said and didn't even wait for the captain's permission to kick the old engine into life and throw off the lines and take the wheel even as he sat a few feet away from me with the paper still in his hand. He didn't move the whole run. From that moment on what movement he did make seemed to tighten down to a point where he finally had no place else to turn. That was one month later almost to the day, the sixth month, the last month, the last day.

It was a day that had no right to be as beautiful as it was. We'd never gotten into morning runs or fixing up the boat although I talked a lot about it, and he seemed still to be listening to me but had pulled way back from the few other things he'd once opened himself to. The first subscription issue had come in the mail and sat where I'd put it at his place at the table, unopened. I was too busy being angry to see. No, that's not quite right. I saw; but I was too angry to try and help except with menial things, just keeping us going, making all the moves while Miller was slowly drowning inches away. I can make excuses. I was young. I'd had a shitty life. I was pissed at everyone, myself mostly, and there was that old man dying in front of me, and all I could think of was that I was doing all the chores and he hadn't touched the gift I'd gotten him and I was tired of doing without sex and dope and why the hell should I care about him anyway? He wasn't anything to me, just some old dude getting a shit load of labor from some asshole kid who was all talk and very little action. So I was furious.

He made me furious that morning. It was beautiful. I wasn't hung over. I was up early, the sun just coming up, and I thought that would be the day we started on all my grand plans, changed our lives, got ourselves together. I was determined that would be the day, and I went below to tell him so. I wanted him to come up and see what the sun was doing to the sky. There was no fog, and the rain from the day before had beaten down the smog. I even thought the gulls looked nice pinned against the sky. The city was docile and quiet. Miller and I could take it all if we moved fast enough, didn't question, just acted for once.

"Hey, old man," I yelled as I grabbed the hatch and swung into the small room. I was flushed; life was wonderful; poor starts be damned, even an old black man and an eighteen-year-old kid had rights.

"Get your butt up, old man."

He was awake. He had that scratchy blanket under his head, but he also had his hands cupping the big skull, the fingers not laced behind it but spread on either side as if he were trying to hold it together. He didn't look at me.

"It's beautiful out," I said.

He didn't move. His beard looked sparse. I looked at his chest to see if he was breathing.

"It's a beautiful day," I said softly because of how quiet it was, he was. He didn't answer again and I felt an unease. I was scared suddenly as if I understood the physical pressure he was exerting was the only thing keeping the head from coming apart.

"It's a goddamn beautiful day," I whispered.

He shifted, letting go of the head. I almost cried out in warning, but then he brought his arms up and held his head again as he turned on his side and pulled his knees up.

"Fuck you," I said but still didn't move. I could see the knots of his spine through his shirt. "A fucking beautiful day, old man." I knew I was about to cry. And I didn't allow that kind of behavior, particularly in myself. So I got mad. He was ruining our lives; he was giving up just when he could have made it. "Where the hell do you get off?" I shoved my hands in my pockets to stop myself from reaching out to touch him. I had to get out. Nobody was going to make me cry, nobody. Then he was crying. I took one step toward him and did something I'd never done, used his name.

"Miller?"

He sobbed.

I didn't know what to do. I was furious because he didn't even have the decency to cry softly.

"Fuck it, fuck you." I'd show him; I'd take us out, get things going for us, make the money, fix the boat. I didn't need him. And then if he wanted to come around, well then that would be fine, too. I was on the deck, and I could still hear his sobs, and I was afraid even the sound of the engine wouldn't smother them. I had to move, and I was off the boat and running down the street thinking the sound I heard was his sobbing still, but I realized after a block that it was my own. I swore I'd show him, show him I could take care of things and him, but he'd have to promise not to cry anymore, crying wasn't fair. How the hell was I supposed to deal with him; how the hell was I going to take that huge man in my arms?

I was going to stay away all day, but after a few hours I headed back to the boat. I'd pretend none of it had happened, and we could just get on with things. I stopped at a corner market and got some beer; then when I got to the boat I sat down on the sidewalk and smoked a cigarette. I'd forgotten about the tilt of the boat. I'd gotten used to it. I'd even altered the way I walked, listing to one side to accommodate what had become so much a part of my life. I liked that boat. I liked it the way it was. I even liked my life on the boat, or really what it was was I liked Miller. I liked my life with him. I did, I really had been happier with him than I could ever remember. I wanted to see him desperately at that moment. He'd made a differ- ence to me. He'd given me a sense of myself, a positive sense, even if he did piss me off from time to time. That didn't matter. It didn't matter that he was messed up. So was I. Nothing mattered but that he was and he liked me and we had a life together. Everything could stay the same, should stay the same. I'd open one of the cold cans of beer and take it to him and tell him I was sorry I had gotten so angry, and I was halfway down the ladder; I could just see the table and Miller's legs, his bare feet planted squarely on the floor in front of the chair he was sitting in. I was about to duck my head down so I could see all of him, glad he was up and might be ready to talk, and I had one hand on the open hatch, the beer tucked under my free arm when I heard the click. I shouldn't have been able to, but I did. I

heard it above the street noise and the gulls and the roar of the motor
launch cruising by. I heard the click of the old Colt that he'd shown
me once, the one with the rust and the stubborn hammer that took
two hands to cock. The image of the gun and Miller's strong thumbs
on it clicked into my mind as the cylinder rolled the bullet into place,
and he was turning the gun as I ducked to call out and saw the barrel
slide between his parted lips and the thumb slide into the stirrup of
the trigger, and the delicate fabric of his large head disintegrate all in
one of those terrible seconds we'd talked so much about, and then in
the next there was the sound, but it came too late.

It seems like the sound should be first, a warning somehow, an
eruption signaling the outrage, the disgust, the horror of one second
seeing someone living, whole, and then suddenly, God so suddenly,
transformed into a grotesque thing flying back in a chair, hands paw-
ing the air as the balance goes, legs thrown up, the walls and piles of
magazines speckled with gore and the body flopping behind the table,
refusing to lie still. I'd dropped the beer. I had my hand out as if I
wanted to wave the thing quiet, but then I was shaking the hand
wildly because some of that gore was on me, some of him, and I was
trying to shake it off. There was blood on my hand, and I felt a wetness
on my face and wiped at it and looked at my palm and saw the red and
there was a gray slime and part of a thin knotted vein and below a
brilliant white piece of bone on my pant leg. I picked it off. It was so
clean. I couldn't understand how it had managed to stay so clean. I
was going to ask, but the movement behind the table had stopped. The
sound was still in my ears, though. It had hurt my ears. He'd hurt my
ears. He'd made a mess. I wasn't going to clean it up. He'd made it.
He'd done it. I wasn't going to hang around and help him clean it up. I
was sick. I couldn't help it. I'd have to go up top and be sick over the
side because that was appropriate, that was the right thing to do.

I kept falling down, losing my balance and falling down, and had
to crawl the last foot to the railing. I couldn't unplug my ears, and my
mutterings were trapped in my head, never seeming to find an exit
but collecting, jamming together until I was able to pull myself high
enough to vomit it out over the side.

How do you remember things like that? What details? In what
context? Everything else is so clear to me. This comes in flashes and
will never be as real as the time he touched me or the way he held his
back when I knew he was listening. I do remember the weight of his
eyes, the sense he imparted that what I said was important, that he

was interested in the working of my mind. I remember being on the bridge later that day, the Golden Gate, and looking back down toward the Wharf.

"Fuck you, old man," I remember saying. Then I moved off the bridge, hitching up my pants after every other step, the action proba- bly making my walk look comically lopsided to passersby. I thumbed up the coast and stayed on the beach four days then decided I was hungry and before leaving to find food bummed a piece of fishing line from a man and tied it around my waist as Miller had taught me to do to keep my jeans secured.

RAPIDLY DOWN THE ST. JOHN

BY JOHN SKOW

CASTING OFF from any shore, on any sort of craft from a floating log to the Block Island ferry, is a quickening moment. The mooring lines of responsibility fall away. Any dry land chore left undone, from an unpaid phone bill to a proposal of marriage, will stay undone till the journey is over. Concentration sharpens to the requirements of the voyage, even if all that is required is that the voyager stand at the rail and watch seagulls. There is no better feeling.

In the old days wilderness was real and an enemy. Five minutes after the primal forest was defeated, however—surveyed, sold, locked in

267

courthouse ledgers—wilderness became, by some powerful instinctive process, the focus of an intense national hankering. In the northeastern part of the U.S., this is a very old story. Henry David Thoreau was our champion hankerer, and he died in 1862. Hankerers persist to this day, our thoughts not so resonant as Thoreau's but our deep wistfulness just as strong. A good place to find us in late May or early June is the St. John River, in the far north of Maine.

The St. John is described by its defenders as the last free-flowing major river in the Northeast, and in its unregulated upper reaches this is true. Defenders have been needed over the last couple of decades, because the Army Corps of Engineers has lobbied hard for a huge and ill-considered hydro project at the towns of Dickey and Lincoln on the upper St. John. This boondoggle would have thrown a dam larger than Egypt's Aswan across a watershed so small that it could fill only once a year, during the spring runoff, and produce electricity for only three hours a day. The scheme now lacks enthusiasts. But dam or not, the forest through which the St. John flows is an illusion, owned by paper companies and logged to within one hundred yards of its banks. The big woods here is a patchwork of big wood lots, and the sentimental seeker after wilderness must narrow his attention as carefully as if he were contemplating the raked gravel of a Japanese garden.

Get up at four in the morning and drive eight or ten hours, north of north, to Greenville, at the lower end of Moosehead Lake. This is a rough old logging town, now smoothed somewhat for the benefit of sports, as tourists are called here. Stop at the general store, buy as much beer as you want to lift and whatever cossets—M & Ms, jerky, sunburn goo—are likely to seem indispensable in the next five days. Now drive to the seaplane dock.

Everything that will fit in, or on, a VW Rabbit will fit in, or on, a Cessna 185 float plane. Your canoe is tied to the right-hand float supports, and its drag, which slows the plane from 125 knots to about ninety, will compensate for the tendency of the engine's torque to turn the ship left. (Part of the enjoyable ritual of flying from Greenville is that the sport, who knows nothing about planes, gets to ask the pilot a lot of questions.)

To start the St. John River trip at its proper beginning, a purist might tell the pilot to touch down on Fourth or Fifth St. John Pond. But even in late May, when melted snow is still draining from shaded hillsides and bogs, the Baker Branch that threads these small lakes to the main course of the watershed can be a bony stream, and traveling it can be a dreary matter of walking down the middle in soggy sneakers, dragging your canoe. A more prudent choice is to put in at the downstream, or northern, end of what might have been called Sixth St. John Pond, the sixth bead on the string of the Baker Branch, except that somebody named it Baker Lake. Here we land, and step off the float to the grassy shore without wetting our feet. We unload the plane and give the float a shove. The pilot wiggles the float rudders till the plane is pointing upwind and flies off, back to the late twentieth century.

We camp where our duffel is piled, and cook a steak for dinner the first night: a tradition. Though I have done the St. John trip only once before, twice around anything makes a tradition these days. At this same spot on Baker Lake, on my earlier trip, I had met a dozen out-of-shape businessmen from someplace in Massachusetts who were trying to drink up a week's supply of beer in one evening. This was because their feet hurt. They had just spent three days dragging their canoes and six-packs along the bony and barely damp riverbed from Fourth St. John Pond. By the time they had reached Baker Lake, they had run out of boyish enthusiasm and decided to give up their 132-mile north woods river expedition after twenty-six miles. So they had called Greenville from the ranger station, and the next day the flying service was coming to pick them up, and they didn't want to have all that heavy beer to load on the plane. We were feeling comfortably contemptuous of flatlanders, until one of our party unrolled his tent, clearly for the first time in a decade. It had rotted, and something had been eating it. When you took hold of the cloth, it broke. So we walked over to the noisy disorganization of the businessmen's camp, and talked humbly. "A tent?" said one of these friendly fellows. "Sure. In the morning. Take two. Take a canoe . . ."

All gone, now, ten years later. We had Baker Lake to ourselves. No businessmen, no noise, no 1979. "Alex," I say to my grown son, who is my partner this trip, "did I ever tell you . . ." After supper, as dusk gathers, I do what I have come four hundred miles to do: sit and watch the river flow past. The current tugs at my mind. I remember, in general, what is around the first bend—spruce trees, water, nothing special—but I am beginning to feel the edge of the journey. I want to be on the water.

Alex is prepared to put up with the journeying for the sake of the fish that may also be making the trip. Casting from the shore, he catches a small brook trout, barely a keeper. He releases it. Then he catches several dace, trash fish that he flings back into the St. John, and some perch. The perch look like breakfast to me, but back they go. Trout fishermen are idealists, and their families go hungry.

Morning light nags through the green walls of our tent, advising me that great events, urgently requiring my participation, are occurring outside. It is a lie. Nothing is happening outside, except that mist is rising off Baker Lake. Since I am up, however, I light my tiny Svea gasoline stove and set water to boil for coffee. Alex rolls out of his sleeping bag, mumbles something, and, not yet wearing pants, flips a few casts into the Baker to get the day started. We eat without saying much.

The canoe, as we pack it, is dew slicked and cold. Past the ranger station, then under the International Paper bridge, and we are on our way. A brisk riffle of whitewater clears the mind: quick choices, no time to brood and rewrite, a faint scrape of gravel against the nearly indestructible belly of our loaded canoe, and we are through. I notice that we have only about one and a half inches of freeboard, an inch less than when my wife paddles bow instead of our very tall son. "Pretty close," he says. "Yeah, well," I tell him. We could use a bigger canoe, or less baggage, no doubt about it. However, we are launched. The river here is about fifty yards wide, and very shallow, and its downstream dip is pronounced enough so that it is easy to see the slant. The current sings along gently at five or six miles an hour. We have something like 110 miles to paddle.

For much of this first morning I daydream, as arms and back work into the rhythm of paddling, and hot sun dries the night's dampness. Any sort of boat is good for mental drifting, but a canoe is best. Larger and more complicated craft are good only if you yourself don't own them or serve as crew. I have prosperous friends who have spent enormous sums on oceangoing sailboats, and who then have taken impressive risks and endured hideous discomfort sailing them. (*"Change!"* yells Alex from the bow, and I shift my paddle and my weariness from port to starboard.) Divorce is almost a given for serious yachtsmen, and being sunk by a grouchy whale or a super-tanker running on autopilot is entirely likely. I like hearing the stories told by my big-boat friends who still survive, and I am grateful to them for taking my own fantasies along on mighty voyages. But for actual travel by water, and for easy companionship with one's own thoughts, nothing beats a sixteen-foot, ABS Old Town.

Easy living: camp in mid-afternoon, stretch out dinner for two hours, laze through the long evening with talk. Four amiable gents from Virginia share our campsite one evening. Like everyone else, they have brought an amazing pile of hi-tech gear. In addition they have a considerable wine cellar—plastic bladders of ordinaire—and ample whiskey and beer. This is nothing; later we meet a party of eight, four sets of husbands and wives, who are equipped with three beer kegs, a city of nylon pavilions that would impress a Saudi prince, and a large, store-bought birthday cake. These folks are friendly enough, but they are also noisy, and the next afternoon we decide we have had enough of overpopulated, authorized campsites. We scout an island, find a grassy hollow out of sight of the river, hide our canoe, and set up a splendid guerrilla camp.

Now the problem is whether to start a campfire, or make do with my midget gasoline stove. Will the rangers employed by Seven Islands, the consortium of paper companies that owns this entire region, spot the smoke and kick us out just when we are easing into our second Sierra cupful of bourbon and river water? Knowing that most of northern Maine is a preserve of big business is aggravating enough to turn George Will into a socialist, but that isn't the issue here. We are trespassing, breaking the rules, sneaking a serene tenting ground where no foolishness is to be heard except our own. Shame on us. But the truth is that if you want peace and quiet in the New England outback, on private land or in a national forest, you become a guerrilla camper. This is antisocial, or perhaps anti-anthill, but very satisfying.

We light a nearly smokeless campfire, using dry wood. By nightfall it is clear that the forest fuzz is not going to catch us. Villainy has triumphed again.

Being on the river is worth a little guilt, and quite a lot of soreness through the shoulders. Coyotes howl at night. Whitetail deer drink from a gravel bank. A couple of muskrats chase each other. Hawks wheel in the thermals. No moose present themselves, though moose are a traffic hazard elsewhere in Maine. I saw a dozen or more on my earlier St. John trip, but now they are convening somewhere else. For long stretches on the river we drift, alone and self-contained, thinking long thoughts or no thoughts at all. No thoughts are required. The St. John, like all rivers, is a great metaphor of changelessness and change, and needs no assistance at being profound. It gets none from us.

Above Big Rapids, a two-mile rouser at the trip's end that is the toughest stretch of whitewater on the St. John, we brood about our low freeboard problem. The current *Appalachian Mountain Club River Guide* lists Big Rapids as Class III ("waves numerous, high, irregular; rocks; eddies; rapids with passages that are clear though narrow, requiring expertise in maneuver . . . spraydeck needed"). An earlier edition had called this stretch Class IV ("waves powerful, irregular; dangerous rocks; boiling eddies"). We had no spraydecks, and one and a half inches of canoe sticking out of the water is not enough in a protracted jumble of standing waves.

By the time my wife and I had reached this same spot, we had become reasonably adequate whitewater canoeists. The St. John is arranged to educate the paddler, and each day's lesson is a bit harder. Since it works best for the lighter partner to take the bow, and since it is the bow paddler who sees problems first and must make the decisions in quick water, part of my education had been to trust my wife, without traditional male harrumphing. Once or twice early in the trip I had countermanded an order, leaving us firmly aground in midstream, teetering on the ledge of a mossy, barely submerged male stereotype. But we had popped through Big Rapids without disaster, and without need of a marriage counselor.

Alex and I are handling the canoe well enough by now, taking turns at bow and stern. Our problem is simply that we weigh too much. He says that we could portage along the jeep road that runs just out of sight along the left bank. I am feeling too lazy and old for a two-mile carry, and I tell him that I can take the canoe through the rapids alone. "No problem," I say, lying. The truth is that I have never paddled alone in whitewater. Alex may suspect this, but he gets out, looking worried, and starts walking.

I turn the canoe around, stern first, and brace myself against the bow seat, knees splayed against the rippling floor of the hull. My weight is just to the rear of the canoe's center. Off I go, caught immediately by the current, choosing, or being chosen by, a deep-water V between rocks forty inches apart, choosing again too fast to think, swiveling down hills and through gullies of bright, fast water, riding the river's splendid hydraulics.

Oddly, everything works just right. Rocks and snags slide by harmlessly. The canoe ships no more than half a cupful of water from wave slap, though I take on at least that much adrenaline in my bloodstream. As I wait for Alex in calm water below Big Rapids, thinking well of myself, I am humbled by the sight of another lone canoeist who comes through a few minutes behind me. He is standing straight up, as if he were aboard the Block Island ferry, changing course with an occasional shove of a long setting pole against the river bottom, and—yup, I thought so—eating what I take to be peanuts from a bag perched on the duffel in front of him.

The beguiling illusion of wilderness ends here, though our trip goes on for a few more miles. Just below Big Rapids the buildings of Allagash pop into sight. We beach the canoe below a sign that says PIZZA. A phone call to Greenville brings a promise that the seaplane will meet us at St. Francis. We float on, out of the great forest that exists mostly in our minds, gnawing on a large pepperoni and sausage, with extra cheese.

A DECENT NIGHT'S SLEEP

BY DAVID EWING DUNCAN

Ah, yes, ah yes, that was what the freighter's engines sounded like, a steady, if feeble pulse. John Breslow leaned his back against the dirty steel wall, sweat gathering under his side, shallow puddles where his body sagged the bunk. *Ah yes,* calming, the machine sound was familiar, from his own century, though just barely.

He was shaking again. It was less than two days since he had last faced the man with the paisley tie. The bruises above his waist ached, reminding him how toward the end Paisley had concentrated on his kidneys. John longed for sleep, but the air was steamy and viscous. The cabin reeked of human occupation, things rotting, decades of sweat layered upon the ghosts of things rotting on this ancient, ghostly vessel.

275

John could hear the slip-slide of the water parting and rushing alongside the freighter's hull, water the color of a suburban swimming pool, stained a faint shade of umber by the soil and murk of Africa. This was Tanganyika, the Dagger Lake, named for its long, jagged shape, a liquid blade 450 miles long, cutting into Africa's heart. It was twice as big as Lake Erie and nearly a mile deep, its shores an endless progression of undulating hills, rounded and covered with sallow grasses burned brittle by the sun.

John had spent hours standing on the passenger promenade, the air blowing back his blond hair, the desolate beauty of the lake intensifying an already dangerous, sullen mood. He could hardly imagine a more remote spot. In an entire day they had passed only one small fishing village, a scattered camp of thatched roofs and mud daub walls huddled under a clump of palms. As the ship approached, the village suddenly had burst into life. Tiny figures began racing toward the water, waving their arms and manning a ragged flotilla of dugout canoes. At first, John thought the ship would pass them by, struggling at their paddles, taking short, powerful cuts into the rolling waves. But the engines finally slowed, idling with a low rumble as the villagers approached, a dozen small vessels swarming against the hull, the people waiting, anxious, as the crew lowered thick hemp ladders.

They scrambled aboard carrying fresh vegetables and salted fish to trade for wire, knives, and other products of the outside world. A dozen or so passengers, mostly city Africans, stood above them on the promenade, looking bored and worldly, silently watching as the ragged people haggled with traders on the forward cargo deck. John watched two small children, a brother and a sister, hoisted up on deck, dressed in tattered shorts, shoeless, dusty, enraptured. The freighter, to them, must have seemed like Disneyland.

John turned from his side onto his back, rearranging each bruise and lesion, trying to minimize the pain. Paisley had known exactly what to do, how to strike the same spot repeatedly, pausing each time to ask the same question, until John's skin turned pink, then red, then blue, then bloody. He had tried, at first, to reason with Paisley, to convince him that the charges were ridiculous, a case of mistaken identity. He was just a traveler, he kept saying, passing through this little town. But that was before the beatings began, when things still made sense, when he was himself, confident, firm with his inquisitors, locked in the absurdity that he was an American, white, untouchable; fundamental assumptions shattered by the first session in Paisley's cell.

"You are not cooperating," Paisley said one morning, as John was being led across the small, British-built police compound and into a special room. Once inside, Paisley told him to remove his shirt.

"What do you mean?" said John, not understanding the order. His eyes were still adjusting to the gloom after the intense sunshine outside. Someone in the corner—a guard—was smoking. The smoke burned his throat and made him cough.

"Your shirt," the man repeated. John could tell that Paisley was in no mood for arguments, that he was growing frustrated, that they didn't know what to do with him. They had been interrogating him for almost three weeks and had gotten nowhere. He had stuck by his story and had refused to sign their confession, a fantastic piece of fiction blaming him for every sort of evil: last month's poisoned well, several robberies, an explosion that had destroyed a store almost a decade earlier.

John slowly pulled off his shirt. He knew what was coming. For three weeks, he had heard screams and moans coming from this room. He had seen the victims, their faces pummeled, their bodies swollen and bloody. But he still clung to the belief that this could not happen to him, that it was only an attempt at intimidation.

"Once more, I ask you," said Paisley, taking a short, thick baton from one of the guards. "You blew up the bridge, did you not?"

"I have told you," he said defiantly, though he hardly felt defiant, "I had nothing to do with that bridge. I have never *seen* that bridge."

"Liar!" He shouted in a monotone that echoed in the concrete chamber. He struck John hard just below his shoulder blade.

"Hey!" John flinched and jumped to one side, astonished by the blow, indignant. "What the fuck are you doing?"

"You blew up the bridge, did you not?"

"I told you," he said, teeth clenched in rage, thinking how he had tried all these weeks to keep his anger in check, to argue logically in the face of almost comical accusations. But this was too much. "Listen to me. I had nothing to do with that idiotic bridge. Do you understand me? I demand to be released. I demand that you contact the American Embassy."

Paisley struck again. The club landed on the same spot with a much greater force, nearly knocking him down. He stumbled in the direction of the door, which was open. For a moment he thought wildly of escape, but the guard grabbed him by the neck and forced him to stumble back to the middle of the room, where Paisley held up the baton again, his eyes empty.

"You blew up the bridge, did you not?"

When John did not answer, Paisley struck again. The blow pulsed in waves through his back and his belly ached and he suddenly had to piss. He couldn't stop it, the pain was overwhelming. John closed his eyes, feeling wet and warm between his legs. One of the guards laughed, a low rumble. Soon all of them had joined in, except Paisley, who never even smiled.

"Why are you doing this? Why?" John asked them every day, his voice unsteady as they stripped him down to his boxers and then locked his wrists into cuffs dangling from the ceiling. There were always several guards in attendance. Their faces, after that first round of laughter, remained impassive, betraying nothing. Sometimes a woman, pregnant and dour, attended the sessions. Paisley said she was a local politician, a "party representative" interested in his case. She watched him intently, parroting everything Paisley said. "Liar!" he would say. "Liar!" she would repeat. The humiliation of his helplessness, of the woman's glaring, of the guards' laughter, had been nearly as sharp as the pain.

The memory made him squeeze his eyelids tight as he lay absolutely still on the bunk. *Ah yes, ah yes,* the freighter throbbed gently as he fought to stop thinking, to stop remembering. Nothing seemed the same. Even his own face looked different. He had seen it for the first time in weeks in the cabin's mirror and, to his horror, his skin had turned a yellow-gray. His eyes were dark and hollow. He looked old, as if he had aged half a lifetime in just six weeks. "Get a grip," he muttered to himself. "Listen to the engines. Focus on the sound." *Ah yes,* like a lullaby, he was a child again, unable to comprehend.

He had been arrested, they said, because a bridge had been blown up north of town. As the only white passing through the area, they had assumed John was the saboteur, a South African commando posing as an American traveler. They had it all figured out. Item 1: He had a South African visa in his passport, the exit stamp dated one week before the bridge was blown. Item 2: He was wearing olive-drab trousers, a similar type and color worn by the South African Defense Forces, though the Bloomingdale's tag inside confused them. Item 3: John was carrying a camouflaged pencil embossed with *Orvis*, "some sort of code word," concluded Paisley. Item 4: John had tucked inside his wallet several letters from his girlfriend, though his inquisitors decided the notes were really coded messages, that this "girlfriend" was his commander. And so it went, the list getting longer every day as they went through his belongings and minutely analyzed his every utterance.

They had picked him up in the sprawling city market, a smoky, dusty confusion of makeshift plank and canvas stalls where hawkers sold everything from maize and goats to black market soda pop. John had been waiting for a bus, standing under the plank awning of the Lionel Ritchie Cafe, a food stall decorated with crude cartoons of Lionel singing, Lionel dancing, and Lionel with his arm around a girl. John had just stepped out from under the awning when a plain-clothes policeman, dressed in an oversized gray jacket and red paisley tie, tapped him on the shoulder. "Come with me," he said, drawing out a pistol and placing the muzzle against John's ribs.

They released him six weeks later, when a policeman in a nearby town arrested a more likely saboteur. "I have such very good news," Paisley said one morning. "You are free to go," adding in a deadpan voice that he hoped John felt no ill will toward him, that these things happened, that he only had been doing his job. "It is the same in your country," he said somberly, "I am sure."

Within an hour, John found himself walking unsteadily out of the compound gate, escorted by four guards carrying Kalashnikov assault rifles. They took him to the market where he had been arrested and waited with him until he boarded the next bus out of town. A silent, hostile crowd, mostly ragged children, stood glaring at him. Paisley had insisted on the guards, saying he feared for John's safety. "The local people," he said, "they would like to kill you. They have been told you are a spy for the racists. It is difficult to make them understand. They are so ignorant."

The bus, a ragged Fiat, had been donated years earlier as part of a development package from Italy. These days there was glass in only half the windows, and the electrical system didn't work. It took eight or ten men to push and jump start the engine. But the old bus managed to carry John Breslow a hundred miles, to the southern tip of Tanganyika. There he was deposited in the faded, one-street port of Mpulungu, a town of enervating heat, thirsty palms, and three or four rust-stained bungalows.

John was anxious to board the freighter. It flew the flag of a nation to the north, which meant the moment he boarded, he would be free of Paisley's immediate influence. The freighter, however, hardly looked promising. It was perhaps sixty meters long, squat and old-fashioned. John guessed it was several decades old, and so caked in rust that he could make out only one letter on the stern, an L.

A shipping agent stopped him at the gate, telling him it would be several hours before the freighter would be ready for passengers. "We are waiting for a load of bananas," he said, his voice flat and laconic, as if nothing mattered in that heat. He suggested John pass the time in a tavern up the street, though he warned him about the prostitutes. "They are dirty there," he said. "They have diseases."

The Red Lion Disco was once a British planter's pub, though the colonialists had left long ago. Outside, two stone lions, no longer red, stood guard on either side of the door, the ferocious countenance of empire slowly eroding into pulp. Inside, the African proprietors had lathered the walls with turquoise paint, obliterating anything British about this tavern. Afro-pop boomed out of two blown-out speakers. The happy, bouncy tunes irritated John, turning his mood even grimmer, their cheerful lyrics out of sync with this dying town.

John celebrated his release from jail by getting drunk on the bitter local beer. Nearby, a table of inebriated Africans watched him, looking bored, but vaguely curious, as if they had never seen a white man before. Their staring made him nervous, so nervous that he began to think they might not be drunks at all, but undercover agents sent by Paisley to watch him. What if his release was a trick, a ridiculous cops-and-robbers stunt to prove he was a spy? What if these men had been sent to follow him, to see if he tried to signal a secret contact, or to devise some fresh act of sabotage? John took a deep breath, telling himself to stop, that he was free, that these men were simple drunkards. The fear, however, remained.

The sweltering cabin was dark. He lit a candle. It was late, which meant the electricity had been shut down for the night. But sleep was hopeless. Maybe he had forgotten how, after so many nights lying awake in Paisley's cell, listening for their footsteps. The match was wet with humidity. He had to strike it several times before it flared.

The wick sizzled as it took the flame. It grew slowly, illuminating the room with a faint, yellow light casting dirty shadows, gloomy and malarial.

He could see the flame reflected in the mirror on the opposite wall, above the sink, stained gray by oily water that dripped in fits and starts out of faucets rimmed with rust. Beside the sink were a desk, a dresser, and a wardrobe, once elegant pieces constructed out of heavy wood. But dampness and neglect had turned them gray, into bloated husks, like driftwood.

Ah yes, how many nights had it been since he had slept? It was over, he kept telling himself. He was safe now. All he needed was a decent night's sleep, to cleanse his mind, to heal him. He needed to melt into this bunk, to dissolve into the pulse of the freighter's motion. *Ah yes*, she sounded like a weary lover, an old woman moaning, making love for the last time.

That was it, he thought: Become absorbed in the ship, the movement, the deep moan of the engines, the rush of the water.

It nearly worked. John was drifting off, slowly, deliciously, when the ship abruptly stopped. The engines cut off and the wash of water ceased. John listened hard to the silence where the heartbeat of the ship had been. He fought off an urge to panic, wiping his wet face with the back of his hand, staring at the candle. It was still burning, a beacon against the stillness, though something inside him whispered "Paisley" and his paranoia surged again. "Stop it," he said out loud, reminding himself of what the captain had told him, that the engines were in bad need of repair, that they frequently overheated and had to be shut down.

The heat was rising in the cabin. The small air vents above his head, driven by the movement of the freighter, had ceased to deliver their small relief. He considered opening a shutter, having sealed himself tightly in the cabin. But he didn't want to get up. He stared at the candle, the flame poised in a small puddle of dirty wax. He observed the flame closely for what seemed like hours, curious about the way it shrank, but in a groggy sort of way. Soon, the flame was bobbing just above the pool of wax, about to go out, though there still was plenty of candle left. John knew he should get up, that the air was getting thick. His lungs were aching, slowly being starved of oxygen, but he didn't care. He had dissolved into his bunk, into the low moan of the ship, content in the pools of sweat, the sour smell, the pallor of the dying flame.

The candle's flame finally rose in a short, spirited flutter and then blinked out. John Breslow's cabin became a black void as he waited for the dizziness to come. He did not relish the idea of suffocation, but it seemed pointless to get up, to expend any more energy on anything. The room was like a mold he was pressed into, wet, hot, almost solid. He closed his eyes, waiting, almost anxious to feel himself slip away. It would be like sleep, he thought, and the pain would go away, and he would dream, of his girlfriend, of home, of all the things he once had known, but now were finished, and then he felt himself drifting off, finally, after all these weeks, sleeping, sleeping.

He was awakened moments later by a sudden jolt and a sound of metal grinding, a cacophony of industrial mayhem, coming up from deep within the freighter's hull. Then there was a second jolt, and the ship was moving. Somehow, the old woman had been revived, brought back from the dead. And then he heard it: the deep, comforting pulse, *ah yes, ah yes.*

John opened his eyes, feeling the first, faint traces of fresh air blow across his face, tickling his beard, pure air mixing with the deadly soup in his cabin. He took a first, tentative breath, feeling dopey, his senses uncomprehending. He took a second breath and felt a sharp stab in his lungs. The intensity of the pain brought him back, and he remembered everything in a surge of recognition, his cell, the beatings, Paisley, his life before Africa. All was abruptly crisp and clear, his life illuminated in his mind like a series of markers, lined up as if they belonged to someone else. It was as if he were being allowed an opportunity to step away, to peruse his deepest impulses, to keep what he wanted, to reject the rest.

There wasn't a great deal he wished to keep. His had been a rather shallow life, comfortable, with most of the usual ambitions, though none of that seemed to matter now. The past few weeks had driven it all away. It no longer belonged to him. He listened to the engines, sounding strong again, as if the breakdown had revived some latent vigor in this ancient vessel. She seemed to be surging as she picked up speed and confidence, the ship cutting cleanly through the water.

John Breslow sat up, inadvertently bumping his head on the ceiling, forgetting he was on the top bunk. "Ouch," he said out loud. Then he laughed, aching all over, but feeling giddy, as if he wanted to sing. Then he was climbing off the bunk, laughing and hurting as he dropped down to the floor. He unlocked the padlock on his door and flung it open. The fresh, wet, cool air blew into his face, chilling his wet skin, making him shiver. He never had felt so refreshed, so stimulated. He began walking up the promenade. Everything was silent on the ship, except for the rush of air and water. He stepped down the ladder to the cargo deck and made his way toward the bow and the forecastle deck, standing high and regal above the lake.

He leaned against the railing, where it met in the V of the prow, feeling the power of the ship, relishing the dark waters, the sweet smell of the lake, the peace of the sky, filled with stars so bright that the decks of the freighter shined silver, a light that erased the old woman's scars, making her seem almost beautiful.

John took a deep breath, beginning to feel something of his old self, though he never would be the same person. He wasn't sure what this meant, what he would do differently, if he radically would change his life. But in the wind blowing hard against his face, in the steady motion of the ship, he could feel his vitality returning. The emptiness inside him was filling up and the fear was receding, though he knew it always would be with him. It would remain a scar, a source of secret strength, a reminder of what it took to break him, and what it took to make him whole.

FOR SALE:
THE *JÄGER*

BY RON RAU

Sitka, Alaska

Dear David:

So here it is late May already and my deadline to have a story in for *Boats* has come and gone (you only gave me two years), and I still don't have a thing to send you. But don't think I didn't try.

The truth is, these last couple of years I've been on boats too much to write about them. Do you know what I mean? Hell, for the last month I crewed out for our hectic black cod opening and was literally up to my ass in them. I just got off that boat two days ago. The fleet finally caught the quota and everyone was glad. For seventeen days and nights it was nonstop running, baiting, coiling, heading, gutting, icing. Make a delivery, get ice, bait up, and head out again. All the fisheries are like this now: hurry, hurry, hurry. Fishing used to be a laid-back life-style in Alaska. There used to be lengthy openings and no real pressure or stress. Now you're forever hurrying because openings are much shorter. You bust your ass to fill quotas so you can be solvent enough to bust your ass for the next quota. That's the way of it these days—just when you finally get your boat and machinery and crew working smoothly for one opening it's time to quit and regroup for the next.

We fished for the black cod (their market name is sablefish, and they all go to Japan) in over four hundred fathoms of water, on the edge of the Continental Shelf twenty to thirty miles off the coast. Nothing much lives down there with them, which is a good thing. They come up through half a mile of water completely intact. We got $1.65 a pound for them this year (down from $2.00 last year), and we caught 35,000 pounds in those seventeen days. The weather was great, too, and I only got seasick two or three times. Hell, I even *enjoyed* being seasick. It made me recall all those times I've been really seasick.

Maybe I should write something about being seasick? I've become something of an expert on the subject during these past twelve years. It does have a lot to do with boats, you know. I could start with the various stages of seasickness:

1. Denial: The symptoms of burping, hiccuping, nausea, and the smell of diesel hit you but you say, "No, I'm not going to be seasick. It must be a fuel leak."
2. Acceptance: Okay, it really is the curse. But in these seas it's not going to be so bad.
3. Contemplation of positive action: Maybe I should just throw up and get it over with.
4. Bravado: I don't want to throw up, and I still want the fish.
5. Involuntary response: Raaaaalph! Earrrrrl! You're at the rail and on your knees calling for your two buddies.
6. Apathy: I don't want the fish.
7. Fear: Oh, God, please don't let me die.
8. Despair: Oh, God, please let me die.
9. Healing: That wasn't so bad. I'm feeling better already.
10. Resurrection: I WANT THE FISH!

I could also write about how I discovered that adrenaline is an instant cure for seasickness. I was taking a shortcut through some rocks to calm water and I was deathly ill, in a prolonged bout of Stage Eight. It was a tricky passage and I was pointing the boat to where I thought we should be while trying to hold my head up and navigate and not really giving a shit (apathy is a very dangerous part of seasickness) about anything. I was barely watching the fathometer because I knew the channel so well. If I hit it correctly, I'd have twenty feet of water, more than enough. Then I remembered that sometimes even in calm water I missed the channel and went over rocks that were only ten feet below the boat. And then it suddenly occurred to me that I still had my stabilizers out and hanging down fifteen feet. If they snagged a reef in these seas, I might get my wish for Stage Eight. That's when my adrenaline kicked in and I was immediately cured of seasickness. I was suddenly alert and caring and tending to business. But half an hour later, after the danger had passed and I still had three hours to calm water, I was back at Stage Eight and wishing there was a way to call my adrenaline back into service.

Knowing that fiction is acceptable for *Boats,* I started something five weeks ago, a week before the black cod war, and was determined to get it off before the deadline. The story I started but never finished is about two commercial fishermen buddies who are in their thirties. Their names are Tom and Arnold and they live in a small Alaskan fishing village where they do everything together—fish, hunt, drink, fight. They even screw the same women.

A lot of the story is (or was going to be) about boats and winter fishing in southeast Alaska. I wanted to write about how it is when you're hiding from storms that can knock you and your boat on your ass. And I wanted to tell how it is to truly savor a calm, blue-sky winter day when a dozen one-hundred-dollar kings jump on the lines. Oh, Tom and Arnold were going to find some fish, all right. Tom was going to catch a lot of fish in his boat and Arnold was going to make a bonanza haul in his. I had it figured so that Arnold would stay out longer than Tom and then take off for town, trying to run ahead of a wildass storm that had been forecast for two days. But the storm catches up with him just after dark, when he's close enough to see the town's lights go on and the silhouettes of certain buildings. He grins. Then it happens. The sea pulls Arnold and his boat and his bonanza haul down into her irretrievable darkness. He puts out a Mayday but is never seen again.

I really was going to write this short story about boats and those who earn their living in them. But I didn't. A lot of why I didn't has to do with how it is when a boat truly does go down . . . for keeps.

The first thing you think of when you hear on the marine radio that a close friend's boat has gone down is: *Oh, no, not John's boat. He cared for it so much and so well.* And then you realize that John was on his boat and that you'll never see him again. Nor his boat.

I'm writing this from my lovely thirty-six-foot wooden troller. Its name is *Jäger,* and he was built in Prince Rupert in 1946, which makes him three years younger than me. I refer to *Jäger* as a "he" instead of the customary "she" because he reminds me of a strapping teenage boy. He's a good sea boat with a reliable Jimmy diesel in his belly, and he beats down waves that used to toss me around in my other boat, a twenty-eight-footer. Some of the best moments of my life have been spent on *Jäger.*

But now I have a 4-Sale sign hanging in the starboard window. The *Jäger's* truly for sale, and I'm getting out of this business. It finally dawned on me last November, after I had quit fishing for a month, that I had gone broke. I still owed on the previous year's taxes, hadn't made either the boat or permit payments, was maxed out on my only credit card, and had to take the Cincinnati Bengals in the Super Bowl *without* the seven-point spread. And then they told us that the Green House, a wonderful old two-story, four-bedroom house in town that four of us rented, had been sold and was being turned into a Fishermen's Wax Museum. A fishermen's wax museum? You don't know how many times last winter I said that to myself. It was that kind of year.

Anyway, the day after we were told about the Green House being turned into a place for tourists to gawk at wax images of me and my kind, I bought the 4-Sale sign. Hell, you would too! Even *I* couldn't ignore the irony and symbolism in this last slap in the face. It's clearly time to take the hint and heed the message. Right? Right!

For now, though, I'm still up to my ass in boats and fishing. I will be until the *Jäger* sells, which I hope is real soon because I'm planning on being in Michigan this summer. You see, I've spent the last twelve summers on the Pacific Ocean and I miss hearing crickets and tree frogs and bullfrogs. I miss hearing nighthawks in the darkness of a warm and dank summer night. And I miss sweet corn and *real* tomatoes.

I'm going back to Michigan, where I plan to have one hundred tomato plants growing in a dusty garden very soon. I want to shuffle out to my tomato patch wearing nothing but shorts and thongs and feel the hot sun on my back. I'll carry one of those new magnum Bic lighters that you can probably solder copper plumbing with and I'll be looking for tomato worm shit—little black droppings underneath the vines. I'll spend long minutes looking into the greenery for the creature and suddenly POW! there it is right where I've been looking all the time. Then I'll flick my Bic and torch the little bastard off the vine.

But, hey, make no mistake, all the time I'm staring into the vines for creatures to torch I'll be thinking about the *Jäger* and fishing and friends in Alaska. My eyes will be staring into the greenery but my mind will be wondering if there are many cohos or if anyone has done anything at Coronation Island.

Maybe after I'm settled into my new life in Michigan and not thinking about boats and fishing I'll be able to write a story about boats for you.

Yours,
Ron Rau

CANOE REPAIR

BY JOSEPH McELROY

IT WAS SUNSET and the boy was angry and wanted to be somewhere else. His father listened to him breathing. What did the boy expect? That's the difference between you and I, Zanes's fifteen-year-old son concluded cuttingly. And all Zanes had wanted to know was what was the use in soaring hundreds of feet above the granite hills and lakes in an expensive thing called a hang glider that might get you killed. Naturally Zanes would want to take a look at the contraption to see how it was made. What was so terrible about a father wanting to do that? The boy wanted to be somewhere else at this moment and at the same time he didn't. Zanes saw dark lake water cooling the airs above so rapidly that, venturing into lake space, an airborne figure loses altitude and tilts steeply downward. They stood side by side staring at the lake. Zanes was glad of the lake and the long alien canoe passing along the far shore.

It came out of a cove as quiet as deer swimming. The canoe was moving and it was still. Of that Zanes was certain. He and his son watched it and were absorbed in what had passed between them. What in hell is that thing? Zanes said. Remote were the glowing forms of two men paddling upright in unison and a woman amidships leaning back. Where were they bound? They were taking a spin. The man in a flowered shirt paddling stern was a black man. That's no fiberglass, said Zanes, unless—it's not a fake birch bark, is it? That's an Indian canoe, said Zanes's son, who knew everything, and Zanes breathed easier. Well, that's no Indian paddling stern, said the father. His son laughed and punched him on the arm. *Dad*, he complained. His son was trying.

I bet that boat can fly, the boy said. It looks, Zanes said—*alive* was what he nearly said—it looks like deer swimming. Deer? his son said. It would run rings around that old tub of ours.

Against pale poplar and dark pine along the far shore the canoe moved slick and straight, its motion simple as the lake, hidden and obvious and still. Two houses back in that cove had been built by a contractor for summer rental. One of them materialized at sunset, towels draped on the rail of the deck; at sunset a window beamed blindingly like one long flash.

I knew I would be called to give it up before I was ready. I think now that I have removed it in slow parts one after the other. Many a good canoe will have its thieves, though with the newer type canoes it is harder to get the parts loose. Some don't even seem to *have* parts. This was an old style, though quite new-made, one part bound to another.

Once when I lived in the city I took a trip into the country. I entered a village and saw a laundromat. An elderly lady with blackest-dyed hair watched through the plate glass window. She was not, somehow, doing her laundry. She was watching for someone. Her hands came to her hips, a panel truck pulled in at the curb. It was the dryer repair service. It had the same name as mine—Zanes. There was a barber shop next to the bakery, and I thought, I like this town, this village, and I will visit the lake. But first I will have a trim.

It was a drab mid-summer afternoon and Zanes and his son came out of the barn, where they had been making a space in which Zanes was determined to start from scratch and try to build a kitchen counter and sink unit. They were getting along. They had come out apparently to feel the faint rain swept across the lake by a southeast breeze. The unusual canoe was out there along the far shore, and the black man and the blonde woman were paddling not quite at the same pace. They worked together with an uncertain sedateness. You felt they were talking. The canoe's animal flanks and low length absorbed the two paddlers, who seemed to be sitting on seats below the level of the gunwales. The two Zaneses watched with pleasure as an outboard, with a man in the stern and a small child facing him, passed the canoe close and the canoe took the wake.

The woman shipped her paddle across the bowstem and twisted around to look at her companion. Her hand on the gunwale, she spoke until she was through. Something was happening. Hair to her waist, she had on a dark two-piece bathing suit. Her hair seemed too long. Hands on the gunwales, she raised herself and, her elbows shaky, lifted a knee. This stabbed into the gunwales an unwatery force, the woman shrieked, the near gunwale dipped, and the black man muscled his paddle in over the blade to jump them forward as the woman's paddle slid into the lake. His voice came across the water laughing or groaning. He snatched her paddle as it passed. They're kneeling, the boy said, that's how you paddle that canoe. Lower center of gravity, said his father. That's a fast canoe, said Zanes's son. Depends who's in it, said his father. Still, that thing can move, said the boy. Side to side, said his father. I'd like to see it sink, said Zanes's son. His father laughed and clapped him on the back. It belongs to somebody, he said. You probably *couldn't* sink ours, said the boy. Zanes followed his son's eyes. The black man two hundred yards away had swung his canoe around and could see them.

My time device would not take me back to the early settlers fighting off the Mohawks and Malecites or up into the dazzling, state-of-the-art patents of the next century necessarily. It would be different. One

early morning in our apartment whose days were numbered, I dis-
tinguished below me the sounds of small truck, taxi, large truck,
sports car, motorcycle, and the peep of bicycle brakes; I was cleaning
myself—as my father used to say—rinsing razor, answering the
questions of the night. I was measuring the haircut I had bought from
the proprietor of that village laundromat. And it came to me that we
would go and settle there.

You could say that Zanes's canoe was a good-enough canoe. A
fourteen-foot light fiberglass molded with thwarts that would take
your weight and with a bottom, according to the in-all-probability-
lying original owner, equal to any late-spring whitewater you would
run, or any swift summer shallows. Such a trip outside the lake to
begin with would require a car or pickup truck to get you *to* the river
if that was what you felt it necessary to do with a canoe—to make a
canoe *trip*. Or you could just use your canoe on the lake waters. At
dawn when your wife and son are asleep. In the heat of the afternoon when you want to cool your feet over the side—swim off your
canoe—capsize your canoe and that's O.K., too.

Rowing *looks* like work. Like exercise. A canoe on the other hand
was to take out. To feel it greet you, hold you again and you it. To let
the power of the water give against the blade like swimming. The
lake was part of the canoe, it occurred to Zanes. A canoe was to look
at as it passes. You don't need one, unless you think you do.

Unemployed youths from the next town, or from Christian settle-
ments in the hills, had found it useful to privately commandeer the
orthopedist's old green canvas and wood canoe a hundred yards
down the shore from Zanes's small dock once when the owner and
his wife and seven or eight children were not around, though they
did not damage it. An expenditure of energy is what you would call
that. Or wait for the right night to borrow the lawyer's glass-
bottomed rowboat that belonged in the Caribbean, not up north.
Again, an expenditure of effort, a response to stimuli. Or if experiment calls, wham some absent owner's kayak with a two-by-four,
imagining its highly resistant polyethylene to be fuselage.

Watch this man-made lake some weekday afternoon with no viable
river exit, and one day you see them—two, three, four of them, in
black in the hot sun with freeze-dyed hair. A shirt slashed down the
back and over the shoulder, an oversized suit jacket with rips safety-

pinned. Jammed-sounding music on a ghetto blaster the size of a small suitcase. A skull pendant, an iron cross from the war. Not fishing, not talking—what are they doing? The sleepy, lean one named Lung sits with the bird-hunting boomerang across his knees, he coughs hard, his face turned to the sky. They're in a rowboat that looks familiar. Have we seen that skiff before, moored to the blue buoy in the south cove, or did they haul that from someplace with a hookup behind their car and launch it at the public beach at the north end?

Alternative sportsmen, they will whack the soda dispenser at the laundromat even after the can drops. Will hang out on the sidewalk outside, chuckling at each other, will sit on their bikes, will lean against somebody's car, rolling it an inch or two against the brakes. There is Lung, with at least one slanted eye and a huge suit over his T-shirt; for he will talk to you. The little, portly, shaved-headed one is called the Mayor. Outside on the hood of a great old automobile that belongs to someone are spread the fortune cards of the girl with all the lipstick. Why do they hang out here, and why do they leave in an instant as if they all suddenly know something? Again, an expenditure of effort. They will empty warm soda on the pavement. Zanes the owner said to Lung, Why don't I mind you people? You're not *here* most of the time, Lung said. Where am I then? Zanes said. Living the lakeside life, said Lung.

Your vehicles are uninspected, the wheels of that enormous vehicle are way out of line, you don't work at anything, you smoke too much, you go in for fortune-telling when you could control your future, you don't trouble the laundromat but what are you doing here?, look at how my son organizes *his* life, you let time which you think you've plenty of escape you, and I would like to catch the waste of your way with time or use you in the working out of my time device: These things I would have said to Lung as the representative of that punk crew if I had found the words, for I think he would have listened. In any event he came back to my premises regularly; and, though he was scarcely older than my knowledgeable son, I felt that through some fellow feeling he would answer me sometime.

Zanes got his ideas shaving. He was looking at the stretch of upper jaw and cheek across which he drew his razor. He took care not to invade his goatee and mustache, but the mirror images of his eyes went their unseen way. Silent cars that generated power out of water was one of his ideas; underground energy-saving dwellings was another; that no idea was absolutely new but built on existing ideas was still another. When he took his canoe out, Zanes also thought.

The ideas knew how to get away sometimes. Opening a whole wheat pizza operation in the space vacated by a Lebanese bakery between the laundromat and the yarn shop was another idea. But Zanes's wife, who loved him, pointed out that his reason for coming here had been to have time, because the laundromat, already surprisingly profitable in a rural community, would practically run itself. As it had for the elderly couple who had died in each other's company of natural causes one afternoon during a visit by the dryer repairman to inspect malfunctioning pilots. She was right: Zanes had a restless mind, that was all. His father had always said, Retire early, look ahead, go into something else. Zanes thought of expanding to a second laundromat in a town nine miles away where there was a small college. He thought of a bookstore. But was it true what she said, that he was looking for work? She did not find him lazy, only unconscious. He woke in the night and looked at her and smelled her.

Fire flared in the far cove one summer night when Zanes and his wife were waiting for their son to return from the hang gliding at Glyph Cliffs. The flames were above the beach and must be on the porch of the black man's rented house. Zanes and his wife stood on the slope above their little dock. Figures leapt to the mutter and slide of music and in the light seemed to open and close, and a blank window was a dark, inchoate part. Voices were succeeded by the silent fire. They went at it again. A light bulb shot on and off in the house with an afterglow in the mind. Three or was it four people were dancing or wrestling or arguing, the tones distinct yet not the words. Something was going on. Look, the fire's calmed down, Zanes heard his wife say softly. They were squirting lighter fluid on their steaks probably, Zanes said. His wife elbowed him. He imagined her, and knew her words had reached some reservoir in his brain, where she was swimming at night, the luminous things like tiny muscular wakes lit up her thighs and the curve of her back. The sky's upper air by contrast was so full of gravity.

Headlights flung into the woods behind them. High beams wobbled and swung in past the barn, and the boy was dropped off. That's a relief, his mother said. He had said he was not ready for his first cliff launch, he was doing ground runs with borrowed gear but it wasn't so great yet. He was fifteen. A girl had driven him home. He told his parents what he had learned about the people across the lake. He always knew everything.

Zanes said they should install an anemometer next to the weathervane on the roof. His son put his hand on his father's shoulder. His son asked less. Had he learned his winds yet? The boy said there was only one way to do that. Let me know when you want me to come to the cliffs, his father said with unwieldy affection. Angry voices rose across the lake, and someone was singing at the rented house.

I entered the village never thinking I would have a haircut today. The elderly man who kept the barbershop informed me that he and his wife ran the laundromat but that even with twenty washers it practically ran itself. I saw a used, heavier-than-average fiberglass canoe and bought it before I left town. I asked the former owner to look after it for me. I breathed deeply and felt the air filling the space of my chest to be measured by another lifetime. I learned the following week that the barber had died hours after he had cut my hair, and I began to look at my haircut. I thought of the work that the man had done on me. I grew a goatee.

Zanes's son approached. The moon moved from behind a cloud, which was also moving. His hair was sticking up as if he had been asleep. He said that the black man who had the house across the lake and the canoe was the brother of a jazz musician from Boston named Conrad Clear and was a banker in Revere. The black man? his father said—where do you suppose he picked up that canoe? The blonde woman was from New York. Her teenaged son had his own house in the mountains north of here. Where does a teenager get off having his own house in the mountains? said Zanes's wife. But he was in China for the summer, said her son. Who was in China? asked Zanes. Her son was. And he has his own house? Zanes's wife asked. Where do you get all this? said Zanes. It's his canoe, said his son, he gave it to his mother to use. Doing other people's business, thoughts get diluted by the days, the days empty out into the night—and some leisure was gone. The boy did not wish to talk hang gliding. Zanes asked what was the best put together of the hang gliding rigs. The boy said LITE DREAM was a good one. His mother wondered if many people came out. A few just parked and watched, was the reply.

My son approached and the moon came out and blanched the lake waters. He told us who we were looking at across the lake. He went into the house. My wife reported that she had emptied the coin receptacles at the laundromat, been to the bank, and returned to pay the part-time girl her wages, when the black man and the extremely long-haired blonde had driven up in that silver car of theirs. They were really quite nice, my wife said, but they came in with three loads, and the only two machines not in use were being occupied by two of those punk kids. You know, the stocky, broad one, and the tall, skinny, Asiatic-looking boy with the tiny blue star on his cheekbone. Well, they were leaning up against these two machines by the window and Lung was communicating by sign language with their friends loafing on the sidewalk outside. The black man asked if they were using the machines and the Mayor asked what did he think they were doing. The black man had an unpleasant worried look on his round face, and he spoke again and was ignored by the two kids who might as well have been outside instead of blocking the machines, one of which was later found to have a puddle extending from under it. They're not exactly kids, I said. They're kids, said my wife. Well, they don't have enough to do, I said, and why am I hearing this *now?* I said. The shaved-headed pug they called the Mayor was talking with his hands to the girl outside with all the lipstick who had her cards laid out on the hood of that enormous old car, she's Lung's girl, my wife said. How do you know that? I asked, and where was everybody else? "Asiatic" didn't describe Lung, I was thinking—though having thought this I saw my wife might be right, though my son had told me the father was German-Irish. That's what I was getting to, said my wife. The black man had that awful worried look, and just then who do you think got up but Seemyon who was reading and came over and in that English of his told the boys to move it. Seemyon? said Zanes; it's his second home. Well, he said he was the best friend of yours, said Zanes's wife, which surprised me, and the Mayor said, Luck-y guy (like that), and on the way out the door the Mayor said, Black mother, but the woman said over her shoulder emptying one load, What's your problem, Sonny? and the Mayor looked in the door again and said, You're the one with the problem, Blondie, and the black guy almost made a move but didn't. But where was everyone else? I asked. I heard Lung outside say something, said my wife; then all the kids got into the car and left, said my wife. But I've spoken with Lung, I said. Aren't you listening to me? my wife said.

Seemyon Stytchkin frequented the laundromat by day. He kept his bulging military pack neat and he read his book and talked to those using the machines. He welcomed those entering. Once he mopped up a woman's emergency overflow while she was taking a long-distance call. A spring immigrant from Byelorussia and a trained marathon runner, Seemyon had been unwilling to take the exam for a taxi license in New York upon finding that the three hundred dollars he would have to raise to pay the taxi commission before he could take the exam was unrefundable should he fail. But at that moment in time, as these Americans said, he happened to see the motto "Live Free or Die" on the license plate of a car being towed away from a No Standing zone one late winter day in Greenwich Village and noted that the state was New Hampshire. Having determined to go there, he purchased a small, single-burner camping stove.

On the final leg of his foot journey north he was within running distance of the state capital and he began to jog. He entered a hilly town with arrows in all directions giving the mileage to lakes and ponds as yet unseen. He pulled up in front of a laundromat. He looked at his watch. He decided to end his two-month trip. A man with a goatee was grinning at him through the plate glass window. I was that man.

A silver sports car driven by a blonde, not un-Russian-looking woman had backed away from the laundromat and turned to accelerate down a steep hill, disappearing at speed into the dark one-car entrance of a narrow, shingle-roofed shelter built over the river, only to reappear on the far side. Seemyon had learned from his late father, the carpenter Vladimir, that one must have *two* good reasons for a major decision. As he was to tell me weeks later during the summer, arriving here, passing through New York, Connecticut, and Vermont, day turning to night, night to day, he had discerned in laundromats a closeness yet privacy between machine users, also a feedback here between machine and human occasioning acquaintanceships and time to read and think, a powerful collective motion within humming immobility. I said that to tell the truth our customers generally just sat and stared into space. Had I considered adding a dry cleaning operation to the laundromat, not to mention offering customers the option of leaving their laundry to be machined by the management? No, I liked the semiautomated, coin-operated integrity of our place. The second reason for Seemyon Vladimirovich's decision had been the silver car, for this car with its unforgettable license plate motto was the car Seemyon had seen being towed away in New York a few weeks before.

Zanes, what did you expect when you put your hard-earned cash into this place? Seemyon said one day, indicating the laundromat and the machine users. That it would work *for* me, said I. Money has a leakage factor, Seemyon went on, holding his book against his chest. It must keep moving, he said. Take this laundromat, he said. Water flows into the machine and stops. It is useful only while it is in the machine. It is moved and it stops. It is used and becomes then used water. It must move on—just as the water that replaces it must move into the machine from someplace else. The machine must hold the water, as I have proved when a machine has overflowed; but it is necessary for the machine also to let the water go. It is all motion and the prevention of leakage. When you left your job last year you were taking what you had and making it flow into a new system rather than holding on to what had been used. It would have leaked away if you had not made it move into a new system. You want to rid sometimes the system of water for a certain cycle and not bring in new waters. I found that I had gotten hungry listening to Seemyon Vladimirovich. Come to think of it, I was thirsty.

Zanes had been unmindful of the recipe collection his wife had compiled. She had begun, it seemed, years ago. Now it was going to be printed as a book. She said it was arranged like a story and she said—he had heard her say it like a promise—that she was sure they wouldn't make a dime on it. But now an astounding offer had come her way from New Hampshire TV.

Some days I liked Lung more than my own son. Sometimes I was unconscious of this. I told Lung of my wife's TV pilot. *Expo*sure, Lung said. That'll fix her, I said. *Cov*erage, he said. Tall in his huge-shouldered, otherwise unemployed suit, he joked, Do we get to come for a meal on camera? I said they were not even asking *me* until my wife established herself enough to make viewers curious about her private life. Lung coughed and coughed, as if this was how laughing came out of him. We'll look for you, he said. I said, Dawn is the time to see me. He coughed again and made some signs through the plate glass to the girl with the cards on the car hood, and she signed back. Lung said, She says you like the canoe, stick with the canoe. The Mayor arrived on his dirt bike and surveyed the scene. He didn't miss much. The black man and the blonde had recently eaten peaches while doing their laundry.

One airless morning the eve of Labor Day weekend, when Zanes's wife was awaiting a visit from the New Hampshire television people to iron out details for the pilot cooking series she would host at home, Zanes found his plate glass window smashed in two places that now looked target-like. A pink swastika had appeared on the glass door of the laundromat and someone's face also in pink with a grin.

The town cop agreed the perpetrators were a nuisance, but you could monitor just so many Yamahas and dual-exhaust wrecks passing through town. Zanes said he would talk to the visiting Russian to see what he knew. The son of the hardware store proprietor had done a hurry-up replacement on the window and by mid-afternoon the jeweler-girl who worked for Zanes part-time had razor-bladed and Windexed the swastika and the face off the door. Zanes had been unable to persuade the unpredictable repair man to stop in on his way home to check an old and possibly failing Speed Queen dryer. Zanes thought of Glyph Cliffs, but his son had gone to the state capital to visit a sporting goods store with a college girl in the hang gliding group. Zanes went home himself, found a second car in the driveway, assumed it was the TV people, put on a pair of trunks he found in the barn, and took his canoe out. He bent to his work. But he wondered what that long bark canoe felt like. Its length and strong delicacy. Its secret speed. Its time.

They were extremely lean, my son and Lung. Never having seen them together, I had not compared their faces. A narrowing and angle of the eyes in Lung and perhaps in my son gave a hint of the steppes. My son was younger than he looked, and Lung, I thought, older, though in sleep an alien age crept over his forehead and mouth, some pinch of pained concentration. I had long since thought through the utility of my time device. I had only to assemble it—but of what materials? People had a right to it. Like water-driven cars. Like the surprise union of two thoughts. I named a river town in Connecticut where there was a well-known laundromat and asked Seemyon on what day he had arrived there. He knew that laundromat. Had he seen the silver sports car pause there that day traveling at far greater speed than he? Seemyon was a runner and a reader, a Russian and would-be American; he ran everywhere, ran out to Glyph Cliffs, reported back. A talker and a listener, he would make sense of the Zanes life story and tell back even what I did not want to remember. You have made up three thousand greeting cards and twice sold your apartment in the city, he reminded me. When did all this happen? I said.

Zanes bent to his work. He paddled on the right side and kept on course by turning the blade inward as he was finishing his stroke. But he needed no course, he aimed at a brown duck with a white circle around her eye, then at jazz music coming from the south cove, a thump and groan, a wail and persistent intimacy which would have drawn him and his leakless yellow fiberglass onward had not Zanes shipped his paddle on the floor in front of him. Straddling his gunwales he let the water cool his feet. An outboard passed containing the Mayor and a blond, very tanned, glowering fellow.

Seemyon Vladimirovich was pulling beans for a market gardener who permitted him to camp on her land. He had "a thing" about firm ground, he was respectful of boats and saw their use value but had no use for them himself. Zanes scanned the shore. His wife was shaking hands at great length with a man.

Zanes stood up and the bow of his canoe jutted out of the water. Why should that happen when his weight remained the same? He crouched and made his way forward. He heard the drone of an outboard; it did not seem to be closing on him. He stood up and put a foot on a gunwale and rocked his canoe. Equilibrium stubborn as a gyro seemed built into the seamless molded material, and he applied himself and rocked the gunwale lower. Now with both feet he brought the gunwale down into the water but, meaning to jump, he lost his footing. His heels slipped out from under him, and as the other gunwale rolled up behind him and the canoe went over, Zanes sat down hard on the capsized bottom and, his arms circling for balance, he slid backwards into the lake. To the north, he heard a voice laughing.

Treading water, my hand upon the overturned canoe, I heard laughter to the north and recalled my paddle. Despairing very generally of my life, I went under and came up in the familiar darkness of the boat. It is as if the day has capsized and not you. A canoe is one boat you can find privacy under. You could adapt a boat for just this purpose. The fiberglass bottom sealed out the light of the sun but not the music from the cove—had it risen in volume? Was the sun graining its way through the fibers of my roof? Why should I not stay here? I could always work on my time device. A wind was coming up, and I heard a breathing sound of paddling.

He treaded water and in his mind smelled fish scales. A wind came up. Zanes felt a wash against his dome. A regular plash and churn approached, and, on a distressing day of smashed plate glass and the invasion of the TV people, he felt in the presence of some second reason he had come to be here—not habit, not comfort, not escape— a future voice that needed no words and was a return.

One bright mid-September afternoon, alerted to what he saw entering his woods, Zanes was not ignorant of the black man and what he brought. The canoe visibly shifting upon the diminutive roof of the silver sports car and overshadowing it, the black man had no right to drive in through the woods like that on a September afternoon. How do you drive with the front end of a canoe over your windshield? The bow like a beak closing down over the hood overslung it a good three feet. The single length of clothesline securing the bow to the middle of the front bumper went taut and slack as one tire hit a pothole, and the back end of the canoe was raked by a dangling, half-split pine bough. If the red blanket protecting the car roof wasn't actually slipping, a corner of it hung unevenly half over a window, and the clothesline around the broad belly of the canoe that passed through the windows was working loose so he was going to lose that canoe. The black man had no right even to *ask* to leave it "for the time being"—getting out of his car, its weird long load between them, and sauntering around the bow so he and Zanes could see each other. Not a tall man, he had a round African face. The bow had two yellow-green leaves stuck to it.

Mr. Zanes? the man asked, as if the name wasn't on the mailbox out on the road; I believe you operate the laundromat in the village? What a lovely spot, how much frontage do you have? He was getting around to what he really had in mind, which was incredible coming from summer people who were practically complete strangers.

He treaded water. He heard the wind far away. Zanes felt a wash against his dome. A regular plash and churn approached, and, on a distressing day of smashed plate glass and the invasion of the TV people, he felt in the presence of some second voice.

Did he hear it?

The voice said, Is anybody home? Alive inside the power of his pantings, he laughed out loud and felt his long dome bumped and a scratching as of sandpaper.

The Zaneses' fiberglass canoe had been rammed more than once. By a slow-moving outboard Chris Craft piloted by a priest and carrying a group of elderly Catholic ladies, and again by an inboard Chris Craft when its operator had become fascinated by the two girls he was pulling each on one water ski and had seen Zanes in time to steer off, just shaving Zanes's bow though putting Zanes himself in the path of the tow rope. Sideswiped also by an aluminum canoe swinging around on a tow rope behind an outboard; attacked twice by visiting freshwater wind surfers yelling commands at him right up to impact; and once, during an eclipse of the moon, rammed by his own dock. Almost imperceptibly nicked, the fiberglass hull kept its finish.

I knew the voice after all and ducked under the gunwale to come up and show myself to Conrad Clear's brother. Oh, you're all right, the black man said peering down as if my identity had not been at issue. I thought you might be—the black man did not finish. Balanced large-scale and old above me, the bark canoe up close seemed to touch my eyes.

He treaded water and felt the rusty drip-stain and snake mottle over the hull. Along the gunwale every few inches were bindings of some woody material. The birch had aged, it was interesting to examine, a mottled pale brown. Which side of the bark was the outside of the tree? On the outside a flap of bark the length of the canoe came down below the gunwale. The word "outwale" came to him. The out-wale's come loose in a couple of places, he said, and the black man said, The outwale? That's not good. He leaned over to look and the canoe tipped with him.

You know these powerboats, they start polluting the environment around this time on a Friday, Clear said. Aren't boats crazy? Swinging about, he backpaddled to say, Well, back to work. It was a joke. My capsized canoe was drifting homeward, its paddle safely inside. Work, I thought. What if my time device already exists? It might still need to be repaired from time to time.

Store a canoe complete with paddles and cushions "for the time being"? Now how would that be possible when at this point in time the Zaneses' garage was out of the question?—and as for the barn . . .
    At least have a look at it, the black man said. He worked on his knots at the back bumper. He ran the clothesline out from stern to stem, where the slender bow thwart it was lashed to could have snapped considering how the bow had been bucking. You could feel his duty, he almost loved the canoe; it did not seem to be his. At last

he and Zanes raised the canoe off the top of the silver car, gripping the gunwales at each tapering end of the canoe, feeling it try to turn over. Grass brushed against the bottom like a drum when they laid it down. The canoe creaked somewhere in the length and give of its gunwales, its ribs and grain and pegs. The men stood near each other, looking into the canoe. Its grand lines flared to a beam so wide it seemed low and was. Which end was which? Ribs curved with a beautiful singleness up to the gunwales, and, out of the bent tension in which they seemed to grip and bow the ribs, as you ran your eyes over it and felt it the canoe developed a force of tightness and actual lift, as if the noble forcing of the ribs into this oval narrow form turned the weight inward into lightness. Zanes ran his fingers along a carved rib that tapered just below the gunwale. I think the ribs are cedar, the black man said. He breathed and Zanes knew he was watching him. Yes, the man said. I suppose the thwarts are, too. Zanes knelt and drew his palm along the outside of the canoe, the weather-rusted, raw but not raw bark. The outwale, did you say? the man said. I guess I did, Zanes said. Seams, evidently covering vertical splits in the bark every couple of feet, were sealed or reinforced (if they were seams) with ridges of some hardened, pitchy-looking gum. Zanes went inside and ran his fingers down a rib to the floor where a damp green leaf was stuck. He stood up and the black man lowered his eyes to the canoe and nodded. You could take a trip in it, he said.

This long boat that was interesting as hell asked too much, it was a present to be shared and left you stupid on your home ground, outwitted but maybe not. Zanes could hear himself think as if his thought slipped out of him. Please use it, the black man said. It would be better if it were used. You probably know more about this thing than I do, the black man said. He looked at the lake. The Zaneses' yellow fiberglass canoe was beached and overturned near the little dock. A paddle leaned across it. This one is a lot of fun, the man said. I almost didn't make it here. It's eighteen feet long. It's tippy, but it'll take four people if you're not going far.

The paddles were on the small side as if for short strokes, and a moose carved in a burned-looking brown appeared on each narrow blade, a jaw behind the muzzle and no horns. I saw you out in it, said Zanes. Yes, said the black man. He glanced at his watch. Zanes looked at his. They had been standing here with the canoe for a good half hour. Have you ever tried paddling amidships when you're alone in that long canoe? Zanes asked, you might get better control in windy conditions. Too late, said the black man. Where's the blonde lady? Zanes asked. She's long gone, said Conrad Clear's brother; she didn't even stay through Labor Day. This belongs to her son. But who knows where he is—or cares. Zanes said, Not me, and, saying it, changed his mind. Why don't you care, he asked the black man, if you love his mother? His father spoiled him, and now he's eighteen, was the calm reply.

Cluttered as the barn was, the canoe could conceivably be slung from the rafters. Does it leak? Zanes asked, when he had meant to say no to the whole proposition, especially the fifty dollars. Not much—you splash a little, said Clear; I've heard a canoe like this will last about ten years. He looked at the lake. We have the house another ten days, but I have to go. This is one pretty man-made lake, he said. Zanes said, Come back, and the man laughed. It was interesting to see a black man out in this boat, said Zanes, and Clear laughed sharply in an erupting way so Zanes felt uncomfortable and then didn't. How'd he get hold of it? Zanes asked. Oh his father presented him with it, but he could care less, Clear said. Who could? asked Zanes. The man laughed. My canoe's going to last fifty to a hundred years, Zanes said, yours you can recycle. The man laughed. Zanes remembered once seeing him come close inshore shortly after dawn.

One early morning in August before I drove in to the village to open the laundromat I checked our meteorological station for temperature and humidity, and for precipitation during the preceding twenty-four hours. At eye level upon a four-legged stand, this white-shingled box on the slope above our modest beach had come with the house. It had belonged to a veteran of the Coast Guard who had retired inland from Cape Cod.

I smelled the difference between grass and pine, between kerosene from the barn and the relatively new paint on the old shutters of our house, smelled the difference between a dewy asbestos shingle fallen from the barn roof which needed repair and some moldy residue close by, possibly the field mouse not quite left for dead by the cat watching at the foot of the sugar maple. I will smell at a distance. I will get down on my knees to prove to myself that this was what I smelled.

I looked down the shore. The herons feeding on the reflections in the lake shallows when I coasted near in my canoe were nowhere to be seen this morning. The early sky was like the lake; brisk ripples set by a northeast breeze came at me like sound. One day I would look up and see my son in the sky "boating" from one thermal updraft to the next, hung in his tapered cocoon sack like an insect's body below its red, green, and yellow LITE DREAM hang glider wings purchased for him probably quite soon by his father. Then the dark waters cooled the air above it as my winged son who in this noble new useless sport wished to invest his all, ventured into lake space, lost lift, tilted steeply downward as if to attack the lake, and dived at a bright trajectory only his father might intercept in his admittedly heavier-than-air fiberglass canoe.

I raised the door of the weather box to fasten it shut, and I heard the soft dive and gulp of a paddle and the following churn. Turning, I found the black man and his unusual canoe close inshore, and felt he was not yet a father. Why does somebody in a boat passing your trees, the windows of your house, your modest dock trespass seemingly more than a person walking in your woods? I smelled coffee richly dripping and poppy seed blue corn muffins being lifted from the kitchen oven. The black man nodded at me and swept his paddle wide to bring his bow around. Was it a green boulder I had never seen? The boat answered instantly, its always surprising length unwieldy spun from the stern. The man flipped his paddle over to the other side and steadied his bow for the far cove. "Boat" is what you call a canoe if you are a serious canoeist. He had quite a considerable bald spot coming. He was taking his canoe out first thing before anyone was awake. That was a canoe. I smelled a shallot, a yellow pepper, a tablespoon of sweet butter frying. I thought, My wife's cookbook, my time machine. All these words she was using!

The TV fellow was really extremely brown in his blue jeans and black crocodile T-shirt. He was saying goodbye in the driveway. His name was Guy. He told me I must be mistaken, there were no herons on a lake like this. You sure they weren't flamingoes? the man joked. I must be imagining them, I said, maybe that's why they're so tame when I approach them at dawn in my bark canoe, have you ever *eaten* heron? I asked him. He said, Oh, you have a bark canoe. We're boarding it for someone, my wife said. When he was gone, my wife acted embarrassed. We rolled the canoe over. She was admiring the canoe and I was standing right behind her.

You didn't have to, you should have taken the fifty dollars just for the responsibility. It's a very valuable canoe, she said. It's strong, I said, and went and gave it a killer kick with my workshoe. One of those boys, the Oriental-looking one, told me it was a wild canoe. It was a trip, she said. It may be here forever, I said, you know these well-off city types, next year they're island-hopping in Greece. Sounds like *you'd* like to go, she said. Yes I would, I said; but she shook her head, No you wouldn't, she said. *You* might, I said, thoughtlessly, and she laughed. She realized I was right. Maybe you'll tell me when the time comes, I said. Maybe I will, maybe I won't, she said undecided. He said it belonged here, I said. Now why did he say that?

The man had left a New Hampshire number that was not local.

I want to work on it, I said without thinking. You what? she softly demanded. How did those kids hear about it? I said. They've seen it, my wife said, *I* heard that nasty little punk the Mayor that the police wouldn't arrest say to the fortune-telling girl with all the lipstick and one or two others standing there, *Yeah, yeah,* he said, they better take *care* of that weird canoe. I don't think he's dangerous, I said, just a learner. Nasty, she said, shitty-looking little resentful unemployed loafing big-talking window-smashing sex-retarded potbellied bully racist—she ran out of words—Mayor, I said, helping her out, and she nodded seriously, Yes, Mayor, she said. She put her hand on my shoulder. Guy said they will give us a new counter and sink unit.

He got his son to help sling it from two beams. But then Zanes had to examine the inside again, and they lifted it out of the slings and laid it down out on the grass. The boy had to meet his friends. A college girl from the hang gliders came and picked him up, it was her last day.

Zanes knelt and smelled the bark strips that bound each end of the tapered bow thwart to a gunwale. Five thwarts—shorter at bow and stern, longer amidships. How did you tell bow from stern? He sniffed the stitches, the lashings. What did cedar smell like? A cedar closet. But cedar? He didn't think he had a cedar tree. One fraying, hairy lashing had loosened. He pulled at the loose binding and found he could unwrap and unthread it. Would the mid-gunwales spring if a short thwart at bow or stern gave way? He tried to understand how the bark flap along the outside of the canoe was attached. All this sort of at the same time. He turned the canoe over on the grass. It was clouding up. The canoe could be left where it was. It was a boat that liked cool weather. Not a living thing at all, so why *was* it alive? A red squirrel appeared on the overturned bottom and was sitting upright, looking like it was getting ready to chew on the canoe.

The hoodlum window-smashing energy-spenders who according to me had gotten the date of Halloween wrong, had been traced to the college town nine miles away through the license plate of a girl's now unregistered but recently spottily repainted Toyota sedan in the trunk of which was found a paint brush wrapped in plastic wrap that smelled of thinner and betrayed specks of pink on the metal casing in which the bristles were fixed. The plot thickens, Seemyon Vladimirovich said. Why didn't I care?

These youths were regular spectators at Glyph Cliffs, and had been pointed out to the police there by Seemyon as having hassled the black man and the blonde woman at the laundromat. The evidence remained inconclusive. When I came to unlock the coin boxes that evening, Seemyon pointed out the Mayor, Lung, and a California-looking fellow in the group on the pavement outside as if I had not seen them. Something in me had not. It was the canoe. It was racism pure and simple against the black man who had come in with the white woman, Seemyon said, pure and simple. He reached for his military pack, he was leaving. I believed he might one day soon break into a run and depart for the state capital. I said if they knew the black man was the brother of a well-known jazz player, they would feel different. They do know that, said Seemyon to my surprise. Who is this California-looking fellow? I said. They come and go—and the swastika? said Seemyon staring into my face. I think they just don't have enough to do, I said. Then hire them, said Seemyon, glancing at his watch. This place pretty much runs itself, I said. Tomorrow is another day, said Seemyon, you should visit Glyph Cliffs and check out the hang gliding technology, he said. The lumberyard owner who was also a contractor had obtained for me a four-foot cedar board. It had a soft, less sweet hue, a wood tinctured with a rose or purple shadow compared to the simpler brown of varnished plywood; and it was rippled with creamy, narrow white lengthways shapes of grain knotted with ovals tilted like galaxies. The canoe spent the night outside, and like a sleepwalker I went out once to touch it and saw a split of light in the cove across the lake. The next morning I noticed a thwart-lashing loose at one end.

His son paddled stern and they took the bark canoe over to the south cove. Zanes did not tell him where to go. The two summer houses were boarded up. We ought to take that overnight trip we always talked about, said Zanes. He didn't know what his son was thinking. They swung around and in the October woods Zanes saw someone move. Yet this need not be unusual. He turned to speak to his son and got a look at someone whose head had a fleeting Indian look to it. He glanced back not quite far enough to meet his son's eyes. You want to get your own hang gliding equipment, I want you to have it, he said. I have to pay for it, his son said. Well, I think you should pay for some of it, but it's going to cost a few hundred dollars before you're done.

His son held his paddle steering and Zanes scarcely looked again at the fellow watching them from the shore. He thought the head had been shaved, it caught the forest light. I'm going to pay for all of it, Zanes's son said, if you can loan me the money. I was thinking that you might need someone to help run the other laundromat if you decide you want it. A twinkle of water appeared between the planks in front of Zanes's knee—had he dripped the water in with his paddle? It came to him like common sense remembered that you patched a leak on the outside, and you would have to find it first. He would buy a chunk of roofing tar. His shoulder ached and he lifted his paddle blade over the bowstem to the left side. He dug in hard and the bow moved its knowing focus. Maybe his son had not even wanted to paddle stern. I'm not going to acquire a new operation just to give you a part-time job, Zanes said. The shaved Indian head in the south cove had not been the Mayor's, at large and trespassing where nothing much was at risk, it hadn't even been shaved but it had given off a light. Is there somebody over there? Zanes said. Probably, his son said.

All but one of the machines were in use that evening. A half-gallon milk container was on fire on the sidewalk and three youths watched it burn down. I adjusted the station band of my transistor to get the President's eight o'clock message to the nation. I had been looking forward to listening to it with Seemyon. Seemyon had already told me what the President would say. Seemyon was ruddy and thoughtful. He had heard the press release broadcast on the 4:00 P.M. news while taking a break with his employer. A woman came and I gave her two dollars in quarters, the change machine had broken down.

No one among the machine users seemed to be waiting for the President's speech.

Seemyon glanced at his large, complex wristwatch. Zanes wanted to get home to the canoe. Zanes was both here and at the lake. What if space was time? Your ideas are ringing a bell, he told Seemyon, shall we listen to the President even though we know what he is going to say? Zanes turned up the volume. Yet he had had an idea that he really wished to broach with the Russian and now it was gone, and in its place was a split of light between the green boards upon a window of the rental house, Zanes had seen it when he had slipped out in the middle of the night to touch the bark canoe. How did the maker get the cedar strips to bend into ribs? He soaked them.

I had known since the city that the source of a leak is often not at the point where the leak is experienced. Used for his own purposes, the laundromat and village and I would soon be left by Seemyon, who was moving on.

But to conclude my point, said Seemyon: Your laundromat—these look-alike, top-loading, electrically linked machines—is engaging actually in automated *thought,* I believe. *And*—Seemyon glanced at his watch—you will be glad to know that I saw a jalopy with a pink swastika at the Glyph Cliffs an hour ago. I recognized the hooligans and I have their license plate by heart. You have helped me; I try to help you now.

The bark was turning darker; what happens to a tree with its bark peeled off, does it grow new skin? But of course!—the maker had cut *down* the birch tree first. I saw the rings, I felt the decades and felt for them.

The gunwales had been lashed to the bark hull through threading holes. These had evidently been made with an awl, they had widened and you could see daylight through them. So in the unlikely event that you were that low in the water you would have almost a natural leak. Zanes looked for marks of birds' beaks. The ribs held the bark, and the gunwales held the ribs—almost forty ribs. A body was what it was. Zanes got himself under the thwarts and lay down in the canoe. His wife called from no doubt the kitchen.

She did not call again. Her hair awake like a perfume over my cheeks, unconsciously I savored the fresh herbs in her hair, the scent of baking in the material of her dress and the moisture along her collarbone; and though she must raise herself a little to bring her knees forward rib by rib along the floor planks where the cradling gunwales were widest apart, with my hands like a gentle massaging shoehorn I made sure the small of her back and her strong, flaring behind did not exert pressure on the thwart and so she rubbed it only in passing.

If a thwart broke, then the other four would be under increased tension, and if another broke, the gunwales could begin to spring and the canoe would begin to open, undoing the maker's work. Flat on his back but not quite flat, Zanes smelled the sharper, gamier cedar and the sweeter birch, he gripped a thwart like a ladder rung. Who made this boat? Who really owned it?

Inside the canoe his arms imagined themselves reaching out. Lengthways bark flaps along the inside of the gunwales as well as the outside were sewn in with bark and you had to believe with a tool made by the maker. Parts became distinct; the beautiful canoe could loosen in your mind. Zanes thought how you would begin, once you had skinned a great tree. Stake it out.

* * *

He had forgotten the cushions. He could see that her knees hurt as she drew her paddle blade through its stroke and lifted it to bring it forward, she sat back on her behind and leaned her back a little against the bow thwart. Can you lean against these? she said, showing him her profile. I guess so, he said. She paddled once and held her paddle across the bow for a moment having earned what came next. Zanes, what are you going to do about the hang glider question? she inquired. She started paddling bravely, so Zanes had to bring them back on the blue buoy they were supposed to be making for. It was October time, a lovely bond of early chill, leaves small and preciously sharp among the pines. I want him to have the equipment, Zanes said. I can feel the water under me, his wife said, I can just feel it. You know, Zanes said, you better not lean back too hard on that thwart. She said, It feels like it's vibrating right up my legs, you know?

She did not care what we did, we were there, she did not need to look around.

Zanes worked the slings toward each other along the beam. Now they could cradle the seventy-pound canoe upside down—so he could get in under it and raise it out himself. The beam he and his son had chosen put the canoe directly under a small leak in the roof. Zanes didn't hesitate to leave the canoe outside on the grass if he would need it later, but he sensed that the bark hull didn't like direct sun. He could go and look at it, the seam pitch softening on a warm October noon, and he would tuck for the time being a lashing that had come loose back into the awl hole.

   They had an accident off Glyph Cliffs. The California-looking fellow had borrowed a rig and, launched, it had simply fallen as if there were big holes in the wings.

You have a canoe there, the voice said over the phone late at night. Which one are you talking about? I said, not thinking where I was. The good one, the young voice said cuttingly. I hung up on the insult, guessing it was the absent owner, it didn't sound as nasal as the Mayor. It was certainly the middle of the night, I was in my time device probably and thought nothing of the interruptions to my sleep. I would speak to Lung in case the Mayor had some mischief in mind. I had perhaps not actually been asleep. I was taking the canoe apart. Opening it. I went back to bed. Would I put it back together?

Clear apologized for calling so late the following night. I was asleep. The blonde woman had asked Clear to phone me, but *she*, then, would not get off the phone with him. Her son was coming to collect his canoe the day after tomorrow. He said you didn't want to give it to him, Clear said, and I told her you were right. It's his turn, I said, and Clear laughed.

He woke to the window, a darkly single, ghastly or friendly, occupied light lifting the maple from below, but it faded and moonlight from the lake came down, as he came awake. He listened to his hair rub and pull between the pillow and his scalp and he laid his fingers upon his wife's hunched shoulder. He listened with hearing as sharp as his mother's the day she died. What was she listening for?

Along the cedar gunwale of the bark canoe, feeling the flaps of the inwale and the outwale and the bound stitchings which, he now believed, were of slit spruce root, somebody was running a hand. Running ahead all along the edge of the canoe fore and aft, both sides, foreseeing use, recollecting the method part by part of the maker. But who was the thief? And was it thievery? A night engine soft as an electric car would not have been able to mask tires mashing driveway gravel and dirt: and he had heard nothing, he had seen on the great canoe only hands. The canoe attracted others to it, they were in its future. It was not the Mayor making off with the bark canoe or taking a two-by-four to it in the middle of the night. Zanes felt only the silence of four in the morning near him on his way to the bathroom with his clothes. He would risk his wife's waking, because he and the thief were going to take the canoe out.

Some forgetfulness softened the piney night air—was it humidity?— and the descending clarity of late October waited moonlit in the sky. In balance the bark canoe held by its gunwales above your shoulders might have lifted off above your head if you had given it the exact path it asked. You know your ground and where the spongy bank gives way toward the dim beach, the active little wash at the edge and the summer detergent froth. Water at the shins, and the long frame balanced is flipped over into the water, the paddles loosed from their coupled lashing at two thwarts amidships.

It's light above but the canoe is dark, is it that the light of night at whatever distance needs extra speed to catch our canoe, or is it a clandestine humidity we turn upward in as the paddle lifts forward? There's no one else in the canoe, it quivers slightly on the dark water feeling you with a sideways quickness that is a promise of forward speed. The paddle stroke gives heart to the boat. As if an hour has passed and you're meeting yourself coming back, a cough comes from the north or from the shore. Pulling hard on the paddle with the hand just above the blade, you lean joyfully back against the thwart and it gives way and tears free.

Upright, you go on, you control it all with your torso and you find the water in its powerful give nearer than the skin of your knees, or is it water on the floor planks and if so where has *it* come from, China?

We have a serious leak. Is the leak like worry, no more than worry? Like a brief time, the split of light visible in the cove is between the boards of a window belonging to that house and you have already seen it, yet this may be the actual first time, and if you got right up next to it the lighted space inside would open to you.

Light rose to the surface of the lake and how long had this trip gone on? It's a measure of its own leak—this canoe—but the inch of water around your knees, does it come from one leak?, and at what rate?, there's no wristwatch, it's on the bed table near your wife, and this canoe needs to be repaired on home ground.

At a hundred yards your trees and the brick end of your house and the person standing on your bare, barely visible dock are beginning to take shape though it won't be day yet. Is water itself pressing against the leak now, and is this another part of the bark canoe, this leak? The person dwarfing the dock second by second is certainly Lung, and it must be five-thirty. Why is there not much time?

Zanes beached the bark canoe and told Lung where to find the saw-horses. He told him to keep his voice down. Lung came from the barn

with a sawhorse in each hand, his elbows back. There was actual
work to be done. Why was Lung here? Zanes turned.

I saw through the sifting darkness of the shore across the lake, but I
could not see the split of light in the summerhouse. The moon had
gone on. If there was a car over there it would be silver.

They carried the canoe up the bank, an inch of water shifting fore and
aft, and they set it on the sawhorses. The bottom was wet and they
might need more water inside to show the leak. Zanes went to the
barn and found the shiny rock of roofing tar inside a bucket. Would
tar work? Every minute things showed more. Lung had on a jean
jacket and green chinos. Then Zanes saw the bicycle. Find some dry
wood, he said, I think I've got a pot in the garage, keep your voice
down. He filled the bucket at the lake. Lung hadn't said a word.

Over there the sky filled the trees out like growth and darkened them
with a dawning darkness. I found the silver car, part hidden by house
or trees or distance. Like the canoe, it had been used by others for the
summer. The bark canoe waited above the ground. I poured in my
water, a drip had appeared only near the stern between the seventh
and eighth ribs.

Only one awl hole was broken, but the stitches were loose or ragged or out. Zanes pointed out the loose stern thwart. Lung moved it
gently on the hinge of its one good binding at the other gunwale.

I took my sheath knife and I split, not too well, two slender lengths
and we put them between the gunwales to check the span. Length of
thwart is width of gunwale.

The whittling took time, the tapering and the shortening. I had no
awl. It got light. A narrow bit did it even better. But the patch—the
tar to tar the leak! I said we should have started the tar before cutting

the wood because the patch would take time to dry. Lung said what
was my rush. I went to the bank and looked at the cove and the silver
car. Some tree gum had been used for one already existing patch, you
could smell it. The patch takes time to dry. Like putting a potato in to
bake long before the hamburger gets into the frying pan, we needed
to do the patch.

Or one person can do one job and one can do the other. But Lung
wants to be in on the patch.

That's it for that pot, I said quietly. Turn it into your tar pot from now
on, said Lung. He poked the fire in the barbecue. What were you
doing here? I said. I was here before *you,* said Lung. I was here when
you came down and got the canoe and took it out, he said. I didn't
have much time left, I said, unconsciously putting things together
now. You busted that piece, Lung said. Better go back to the lashing,
I said. How did I know that the owner of the canoe was coming
soon? Was it my time device operating again?

A canoe is what it makes you do. In the dewy cool the patch was soft
still. He had used a fraction of the tar he had broken off to heat, and it
was receding now to glassy bituminous hardness. He had wiped the
putty knife on the grass.

I felt my wife awake, but not my son. Have you seen my son at Glyph
Cliffs? I asked. Lung drew a thong of bark taut from the thread hole
and, holding the bottom of it, knotted the rough lashing as tightly as
he could. He checks everything out, Lung said, he helps them get off.

I'd like to do this again, Lung said thoughtfully. I mean I didn't get to
go out in it. Maybe you'll have to bust it again for us to repair it. Then
again we could make one from scratch now that you see how it's put
together, it's a very cool thing. I used to like to shoot birds you know
but I was never that crazy about boats, I'd like to take a spin in this
one, but I got to go to work now.

Why didn't you speak up when I came out here in the dark in the first place? Zanes asked. Felt stupid, said Lung. I guess I did say catch me early, Zanes said.

Across the lake the silver car moved and its length seemed to collapse. We had a smell of road work from the tar. We went and ran our hands over the tough skin of the hull and lost track for a minute. Lung got under it and looked at his handiwork. I thanked him. He didn't look at me. We stared at the hull for a while.

This has to go back to the owner, Zanes said. You always have the other one, Lung said and laughed. Why are you called Lung? Zanes asked. It's whatever you want, Lung said. Answer me, Zanes said, laughing.

What's going on here? my wife occupying the moment in her blue robe said through the screen door that shone in the sun. I said, Lung, I don't know where the time went. I'll bet you didn't even know I was here, my wife said. You weren't, I said. My wife asked Lung if he would like some breakfast. He said he never ate in the morning.

Lung's bike seat was too low and I offered to raise it, but Lung was on his way. So long, Lung, said my wife humorously. Let's have dinner on camera, Lung called back. The patch was of course not dry, but the canoe could be moved. The alarm clock in my son's room started distantly ringing. The patch was soft and the hull of the canoe was damp. The alarm got turned off. I think Lung likes you, my wife said, but he certainly picks an early hour for his visits. We had to work on the canoe before the owner came, I said. The owner? my wife said. Is he going to take it?, thank goodness. Well, what do you know, she said—for, just as Lung had pedaled out of sight onto the town road, the silver car had entered the woods. This particular canoe trip was over.

Low and slow it made its way among the potholes and ruts. The driver was a blond fellow. The clothesline was in the barn.

Who's that driving? said Zanes's wife.
Don't you remember? said her husband.

Above me, I felt the presence of my son at his window. If I didn't take down the screens, it would soon be summer again.

321

ABOUT THE EDITOR

David Seybold is the editor of three previous collections, *Waters Swift and Still* (with Craig Woods), *Seasons of the Hunter* (with Robert Elman), and *Seasons of the Angler*. He lives in New London, New Hampshire.